INTERNATIONAL ASPECTS OF GERMAN RACIAL POLICIES

THE SUBSTANCE OF THIS BOOK
WAS SUBMITTED IN SUPPORT
OF A PETITION PRESENTED
TO THE ASSEMBLY OF
THE LEAGUE OF NATIONS
ON SEPTEMBER 30, 1936
BY THE
ORGANIZATIONS LISTED
ON PAGES 233–4

INTERNATIONAL ASPECTS OF GERMAN RACIAL POLICIES

BY

OSCAR I. JANOWSKY

Assistant Professor of History

The College of the City of New York

AND

MELVIN M. FAGEN

Executive Secretary

Conference on Jewish Relations

WITH A PREFACE BY

JAMES BROWN SCOTT

AND POSTSCRIPT BY

JOSIAH C. WEDGWOOD, M.P.

NEW YORK

OXFORD UNIVERSITY PRESS

1937

Printed in the United States of America

PREFACE

WITH its thought-provoking Introduction, its excellent and careful study of a problem of universal interest, and with Appendices which include the admirable statements of Mr. James G. McDonald, former High Commissioner for Refugees Coming from Germany, the monograph, *International Aspects of German Racial Policies*, raises certain questions of the first importance in the field of international law. Before referring to these, however, it may be well to emphasize the once disputed but now admitted fact that there *is* an international law, a law between nations so generally recognized and accepted that it is applied not only by international tribunals but, on occasion, by national tribunals the world over. In its older terminology, the "law of nations," it is specifically mentioned in the Constitution of the United States, and it is referred to in the German Constitution of 1919 [1] and in the constitutions of many other countries. It is cited, too, in innumerable documents, in the foreign offices of every nation. However, it is not necessary to labor the point, for the evidence is overwhelming that international law is a recognized and living law.

Now this law has to do with the rights and duties of states. But states are made up of human beings, of men, women and children; and the primary purpose of the state is to protect the fundamental human rights of its inhabitants. Therefore international law should, and indeed must, take cognizance of such rights. We in the United States are particularly fortunate in our familiarity with the rights in question, for they have entered into the very warp and woof of our national life. The signers of the Declaration of Independence, on the ever

1. In Article 4: "Die allgemein anerkannten Regeln des Völkerrechts gelten als bindende Bestandteile des deutschen Reichsrechts."

memorable Fourth of July, 1776, declared that they held certain "truths to be self-evident." What are these truths? "That all men are created equal, that they are endowed by their Creator with certain unalienable Rights, that among these are Life, Liberty and the pursuit of Happiness." Moreover, they held, and so declared, that the aim and purpose of government was to protect these "unalienable rights." And therefore "That to secure these rights, Governments are instituted among Men, deriving their just powers from the consent of the governed."

This conception of human rights, subsequently embodied in the Constitution of the United States, became, in the course of time, the conception of all of the Republics of the American Continent. The truth of this statement is evidenced not only by their constitutions but by a Declaration of the Rights and Duties of Nations which was adopted on January 6th, 1916, by the American Institute of International Law, a scientific body whose members comprise leading authorities on international law in the Western World. This declaration contains a preamble from which quotations of some length must be made. In it the members of the Institute affirmed that "the municipal law of civilized nations recognizes and protects the right to life, the right to liberty, the right to the pursuit of happiness as added by the Declaration of Independence of the United States of America, the right to legal equality, the right to property, and the right to the enjoyment of the aforesaid rights." They further declared that "these fundamental rights, thus universally recognized, create a duty on the part of the peoples of all nations to observe them." With respect to the nature and purpose of government they added that "according to the political philosophy of the Declaration of Independence of the United States, and the universal practice of the American Republics, nations or governments are regarded as created by the people, deriving their just powers from the consent of the governed, and are instituted among men to promote their safety and happiness and to secure to the people the enjoyment of their fundamental rights." But these rights were not, in their conception, matters only of national law and government. They could be stated and applied as well in the international field: "we deem that these fundamental rights can be stated in terms of international law and applied to the relations of the citizens or subjects of the states forming the Society of Nations."

Following the preamble the American Institute adopted six articles on the rights and duties of nations, of which, for present purposes, we quote only the sixth:

> VI. International law is at one and the same time both national and international: national in the sense that it is the law of the land and applicable as such to the decision of all questions involving its principles; international in the sense that it is the law of the society of nations and applicable as such to all questions between and among the members of the society of nations involving its principles.

We have thus not only the national recognition of fundamental human rights, but a continental recognition of those rights and their adoption as the very foundation of international law.

Some thirteen years later the *Institut de Droit International*, the foremost unofficial organization of international jurists in the world, met for the first time in the United States. On Columbus Day, October 12th, 1929, it adopted a "Declaration of the International Rights of Man," a document which marks an epoch in that it constitutes a long step toward the universal recognition of fundamental human rights. In a preamble so important that it must be reproduced in its entirety, the *Institut* declared:

That the juridical conscience of the civilized world demands the recognition for the individual of rights preserved from all infringement on the part of the State;

That the declarations of rights, written into a large number of constitutions and especially into the American and French Constitutions of the end of the 18th century, are ordained not only for the citizen, but for man;

That the 14th Amendment of the Constitution of the United States prescribes as follows: ". . . nor shall any State deprive any person of life, liberty, or property, without due process of law, nor deny to any person within its jurisdiction the equal protection of the laws";

That the Supreme Court of the United States has unanimously decided that by the terms of this amendment it is applicable within the jurisdiction of the United States "to every person without distinction of race, color, nationality, and that the equal protection of the laws is a guarantee of the protection of equal laws";

That it is important to extend to the entire world international recognition of the rights of man;

Having thus laid the foundations, as it were, the *Institut* proceeded to adopt six articles specifically enumerating the duties of states with respect to the rights of human beings: Their meaning is so clear, the doctrines which they embody so enlightened, that they speak for themselves and may therefore be quoted without a word of comment:

Article 1

It is the duty of every State to recognize the equal right of every individual to life, liberty and property, and to accord to all within its territory the full and entire protection of this right, without distinction as to nationality, sex, race, language, or religion.

Article 2

It is the duty of every State to recognize the right of every individual to the free practice, both public and private, of every faith, religion, or belief, provided that the said practice shall not be incompatible with public order and good morals.

Article 3

It is the duty of every State to recognize the right of every individual both to the free use of the language of his choice and to the teaching of such language.

Article 4

No motive based, directly or indirectly, on distinctions of sex, race, language, or religion empowers States to refuse to any of their nationals private and public rights, especially admission to establishments of public instruction, and the exercise of the different economic activities and of professions and industries.

Article 5

The equality herein contemplated is not to be nominal, but effective. It excludes all discrimination, direct or indirect.

Article 6

Except for motives based upon its general legislation, no State shall have the right to withdraw its nationality from those whom, for reasons of sex, race, language, or religion, it should not deprive of the guarantees contemplated in the preceding articles.

From these three fundamental documents may be drawn what seems to be an unanswerable conclusion, that the primary purpose of the national government with its laws, and of the international community with its laws, is to insure for the individual, irrespective of nationality, sex, race, language, or religion, the full enjoyment of his or her rights as a human being. So-called laws, whether they be national or international, are not worthy of the name of law if they fail of this purpose. If law is to justify itself in our world it must eschew injustice, inequity and inequality. In a word, law to be law, to be accepted and applied as such, must be reasonable and just, moral as well as social; it must also be applicable alike to man and woman, and everywhere and at all times consistent with the nature and dignity of the human being.

JAMES BROWN SCOTT

President of the American Society of International Law
President of the American Institute of International Law
Member and former President of the *Institut de Droit International*

CONTENTS

PREFACE by James Brown Scott v
INTRODUCTION
by James N. Rosenberg and Morris R. Cohen xv

I. PRECEDENTS FOR INTERNATIONAL ACTION TO SAFEGUARD HUMAN RIGHTS 1
The Right of Humanitarian Intercession 3
The Practice of Humanitarian Intercession 6
The Minorities Treaties and the League Guarantee 27
Germany, the Rights of Minorities and Humanitarian Intercession 32

II. INTERNATIONAL LEGAL ASPECTS OF GERMAN NATIONAL SOCIALIST POLICIES 44
A. Violations of the Rights of Other States 49
1. Forced Emigration 49
2. Denationalization and Withdrawal of State Protection 60
a. The Burden Imposed upon Neighboring States 68
b. The Breach of Undertaking 72
3. Violations of the Territorial Sovereignty of Neighboring States 78
B. Germany's International Obligation to Protect Minorities in Its Territory—The 1919 Exchange of Notes 94

III. THE TASK OF THE LEAGUE OF NATIONS 110
The Bernheim Petition: Action of the Council in 1933 110
Action of the Assembly in 1933 116
The Need for Further Action 121

APPENDICES

I. A. The Letter of Resignation of James G. McDonald, former High Commissioner for Refugees (Jewish and Other) Coming from Germany 131

B. Annex to McDonald Letter Containing an Analysis of the Measures in Germany against Non-Aryans 142

INTRODUCTION 142

§ I. *Discriminatory Legislation: The "Aryan" Decrees* 146

The Government Service 153

The Professions 155

Educational and Cultural Fields 158

"Exceptions" from Discrimination 161

Extension to Industry, Agriculture and Commerce 163

Notes 168

§ II. *Administrative Measures and Party Activity* 171

Law and the Judiciary 172

Medicine 174

Education 175

Artisanship 177

Commerce and Industry 178

The Boycott of "Non-Aryans" 181

Notes 187

§ III. *Application of Racial Law by the Courts* 191

1. The Doctrine of Racial Inequality before the Law 192
2. Judges as Agents of the National Socialist Party 193

3. Latitude Given to Judges through the Abolition of the Guarantees of a Fair Trial 194
Marriage and Divorce 196
Children 199
Lawyers, Judges, Arbitrators, etc. 201
Business and Commerce 204

Notes 210

§ IV. *"Unwelcome Guests"* 217
Deprivation of Citizenship and Denationalization 217
The Intent of the Government 222
The Refugee Problem 223

Notes 227

APPENDIX II
Petition in Support of the Letter of Resignation of Mr. McDonald, Addressed to the XVIIth Assembly of the League of Nations 229

APPENDIX III
The Persecution of "Non-Aryans" in Germany—A Selection of Expressions of Opinion 238

POSTSCRIPT by Josiah C. Wedgwood, M.P. 259

INDEX 261

INTRODUCTION

Is national sovereignty so absolute that a government may without limit oppress or even destroy whole groups of its citizens? Have other states no right or duty to protest or intercede, even when such oppression casts burdens upon them? What is the civilized world to do when a nation makes the persecution of its minorities a matter of declared official governmental policy? These are the basic issues which this book examines in the light of international practice during the past three centuries.

In 1933, the National Socialist Party came into power in Germany and immediately embarked upon a deliberate policy of depriving "non-Aryans" (i.e. Jews and Christians of Jewish ancestry) of their civil and political rights. The civilized world at first hesitated to believe that hundreds of thousands of innocent men, women and children would be immolated merely because of their ancestry. But when legislation and extra-legal measures, including a relentless boycott, humiliated and segregated the "non-Aryans" and began gradually to deprive them of the means of earning a livelihood, when violence and terror drove tens of thousands of German citizens to seek refuge in neighboring lands, protests arose in every part of the world calling for action by the League of Nations.[1]

Twice during 1933 the League of Nations responded to these protests. In the spring of that year the League Council demanded that Germany, then still a League member, perform its international obligations with respect to minorities in Upper Silesia. Germany yielded, to the extent of promising to comply with her covenants. In the following September, Nazi persecution was again condemned by the leading statesmen

1. See Appendix III.

of the world in a memorable discussion before the Sixth Committee of the League Assembly; and every one of the fifty-six states members of the League endorsed the principle of equal treatment for all minorities and nationals irrespective of race, religion or language. Even the present German Government, concerned for the fate of its own German minorities in foreign lands, joined in this resolution. It contended, however, that "non-Aryans" within Germany were not minorities and therefore not entitled to protection; but Foreign Minister Beneš (now President) of Czechoslovakia, the present British Colonial Secretary, Ormsby-Gore, Senator Bérenger of France and other notable statesmen answered for the League that a group becomes a minority whenever it is set apart by discriminatory legislation. To these declarations Germany made no reply.

Despite these forthright discussions and resolutions, the League limited its positive action to the appointment of Mr. James G. McDonald as High Commissioner for German Refugees with an Advisory Committee of representatives of thirteen governments. The High Commission, though not made an official body of the League, was to seek places of refuge and to organize assistance for the exiled victims of Nazi policies.

Germany withdrew from the League in October, 1933. At no time did it manifest the slightest concern with the problems of the High Commission: either with the sufferings of the refugees, or with the burdens imposed upon neighboring states which were called upon to harbor the exiles. Relentlessly the turn of the thumbscrew continued to crush the "non-Aryans" who were thus in increasing numbers forced to seek refuge abroad. By the close of 1935, almost one hundred thousand refugees had left Germany. The promulgation in September of that year of the Nuremberg Decrees, which withdrew citizenship from all Germans who were deemed to have as much as one quarter "non-German blood," turned additional hundreds of thousands into potential refugees.

The task of settling the unfortunate exiles with but a pittance at his disposal from the League,[1] was insuperable. Mr. McDonald after two years of heroic effort and of accomplishment far greater than could in the circumstances have been expected filed his Letter of Resignation.[2] In that historic document, he marshalled the undisputed facts and showed that the problem could not be solved by philanthropic action but "must be tackled at its source if disaster is to be avoided." This, he declared, "is the function of the League which is essentially an association of states for the consideration of matters of common concern;" and the League, he said, was particularly authorized to act because "the protection of the individual from racial and religious intolerance is a vital condition of international peace and security." The League and its members, concluded Mr. McDonald, must make "a determined appeal to the German Government in the name of humanity and of the principles of the public law of Europe. They must ask for a "modification of policies which constitute a source of unrest and perplexity in the world, a challenge to the conscience of mankind, and a menace to the legitimate interests of the States affected by the immigration of German refugees."

Mr. McDonald's plea was based upon sound principles of international law. Similar views have been enunciated and reiterated by scholars, statesmen and enlightened governments ever since the seventeenth century. In 1795, with the French Revolution and the consequent European War before

1. The League contributed only $15,000 per year to the High Commission, not even enough for the Commission's administrative expense.
2. See Appendix I for the text of McDonald's Letter and Annex.

him, Immanuel Kant, the greatest of German philosophers, published his inspiring essay on Universal Peace. His classical thesis derived from Greek philosophers and Roman jurists was that peace among nations will be possible only through a federation of republics, that is, by states governed by laws that safeguard human rights. There can be no world peace if nations are lawless in their domestic affairs.

To the people of the United States these ideals have become a cherished tradition which has found expression in numerous instances of intercession on behalf of oppressed minorities in foreign lands.[1] For a century, the denial of human rights by tyrannical governments has repeatedly evoked intercessions and protests by the government of the United States, expressed in the notes and messages of Presidents, Secretaries of State and diplomatic officers abroad. The faith which actuated these protests has recently been reaffirmed by President Roosevelt who, in addressing the Inter-American Conference for the Maintenance of Peace at Buenos Aires, warned that "lack of social or political justice within the borders of any nation is always cause for concern."

The oppression of minorities has thus repeatedly been condemned not only because it violates elementary justice and decency but also because of the recognition that the persecution of any one minority strikes at the very foundations of all human rights and is a menace to all peoples everywhere. Thus in Germany today the attacks on "non-Aryans" have served as the spearhead of a progressively widening drive against the civil, political and religious rights of all German citizens. The jailing of Protestant ministers and Catholic priests, the suppression of liberal and democratic thought and free scientific inquiry, as well as the utter dis-

1. See pp. 13 to 27 for a detailed account of these intercessions.

regard of the rights and sensibilities of other nations, are the natural correlatives of the dogma of racial superiority.

Policies of hatred or violence cannot be confined within any frontier and will not stop with Jews. They inevitably lead to international bitterness and strife, and block efforts at international coöperation. This is a truth long recognized by contemporary statesmen who have warned the League on numerous occasions that internal persecutions bear the seeds of international conflict and that the very system of minority guaranties under the League is founded upon this principle.

The League has since 1933 taken no action to remind the German Government of the wrongs inherent in its oppressive policies. It has not heeded Mr. McDonald's warning that the refugee problem "must be tackled at its source." It did not discuss a Petition filed with it in September, 1936, by a number of organizations in Europe and the United States.[1] But these profound issues will not down. They cannot be solved by temporizing or evasion. They will arise again and again to challenge the League of Nations and the conscience of mankind.

The emigration of Jews and "non-Aryan" Christians from Germany continues. It will increase as discriminatory decrees are re-enforced by economic dispossession and by the further inevitable destruction of the liberties of all who oppose the will of the Nazi government. The recent formation in the United States of a committee of leading Christians to aid non-Jewish refugees from Germany shows how well justified were the warnings of Mr. McDonald that the problem would continue to increase in gravity.

The term of office of the present High Commissioner for Refugees will expire in 1938. At that time the Assembly of the

1. See Appendix II for text of this Petition and list of signatories.

League, according to its own resolution, will be called upon to "determine the general principles which, after that year, should govern the attitude of the League toward the refugee problem as a whole." Will the League then face the fact that this is not merely a "Jewish" or a "German" problem? Will it recognize that the mailed fist which has struck down helpless Jews and "non-Aryans" and has destroyed all political and civil liberties is also hostile to all religious freedom?

These ancient yet pressing issues are raised anew in this book, written and published under the sponsorship of the American Jewish Committee and the Conference on Jewish Relations, two American societies which seek not only to defend the rights of Jews but also to point out why persecution of any minority is but the entering-wedge for an assault upon all human liberties.

Starting with the body of fact contained in the Letter of Resignation of Mr. McDonald, this book shows in amply documented fashion, why the persecution of "non-Aryans" in Germany is a matter of international concern. Evidence is adduced demonstrating that ever since the seventeenth century the states of the world have recognized their responsibility for the maintenance of human rights in countries where such rights were denied to those who differed from the majority in religion, race or language. The burdens which the refugee problem has imposed upon other states, and the violations of international law inherent in the Nazi policies are analyzed. The efforts which the League of Nations has made to remind Germany of her obligations as well as the urgent need for further action are clearly indicated and, it is shown, in conclusion, that the League Covenant provides ample authority for peaceful intercession, not only to relieve the sufferings of the persecuted, but also to ensure world peace. It is hoped that this book, setting forth the humane precedents established by civilized nations during more than two hundred years may help toward the restoration of international sanity.

James N. Rosenberg Morris R. Cohen

CHAPTER ONE

PRECEDENTS FOR INTERNATIONAL ACTION TO SAFEGUARD HUMAN RIGHTS

SINCE its establishment in 1933, the German National Socialist Government has systematically persecuted a large body of its citizens and subjects.[1] Hundreds of thousands of law-abiding and loyal individuals have been deprived of citizenship, of civil and political equality and of the means of earning a livelihood. Fully one hundred thousand persons have already sought relief in flight, and the increasing rigors of persecution must inevitably drive more and more victims to leave their homeland and seek refuge abroad.

Such persecution is not without precedent, although the pretended cause of persecution, difference of "racial" origin, appears novel. In former times, intolerance and oppression were visited upon those who differed in religious belief from the dominant element in the country, whereas today the fiction of religious equality is maintained in Germany. The effect, however, is the same. Men, women and children have been deprived of elementary human rights, humiliated and impoverished. Distinctions between racial and religious persecution are meaningless; for, as the American Government became aware in its controversy with Tsarist Russia, the two questions are inseparable.[2] It is immaterial whether religious belief or racial origin is advanced as the excuse for making

1. For a description of the methods and results of the National Socialist program, see the Letter of Resignation of James G.McDonald, High Commissioner for Refugees (Jewish and Other) Coming from Germany, addressed to the Secretary General of the League of Nations (London, December 27th, 1935), especially the Annex, Chapters 1–4.
2. *Papers Relating to the Foreign Relations of the United States* (hereafter referred to as *Foreign Relations*), 1895, pp.1058ff.

life unbearable for a large body of human beings. Fundamental is the fact that innocent persons are deprived of essential and primary human rights.

However, are not the policies of the German Government a matter of purely "domestic concern"? Since the "Aryan" decrees are directed primarily against German subjects, does not national sovereignty preclude any interference by third parties in the internal affairs of the Reich? This question has been asked before and the answer is found both in long established custom arising out of the relations between states and in the opinions expressed by distinguished jurists. It is clear and emphatic to the effect that governments are justified in insisting that the "principles of decency and humanity" be maintained in the international community.

That the international community has been increasingly concerned with the recognition and defense of human rights is the theme of this chapter. First, authorities will be cited to establish the right of intercession on behalf of the victims of persecution. Secondly, the practice of governments during the past three centuries will be analyzed in order to establish the fact that ample precedent exists for peaceful humanitarian intercession by the civilized states of the world when minorities are denied elementary human rights. International concern for human rights will be shown to have originated in the desire to assure religious toleration to co-religionists in foreign lands—this international concern evolving gradually into the principle of religious equality, i.e. that civil and political equality must not be denied to those differing from the majority of the population in religious belief or practice. It will also be noted that the method of humanitarian intercession has undergone modification: diplomatic representations were, until the close of the World War, the favorite means of approach to a foreign government; but along with the diplomatic appeal to humanity, the practice developed, especially during the nineteenth century, of embodying guarantees for religious equality in treaties involving the cession of territory or the recognition of new states. Considerable attention will be devoted to the Minorities Treaties which were adopted at the close of the World War because they constitute the most notable attempt yet made to assure equality of rights to persons differing from the majority of the population. Finally, evidence will be adduced to prove that, until the rise of National Socialism to power, the German Government had itself recognized the right of humanitarian intercession and championed the rights of minorities. The conclusion is obvious. In resorting to a policy of persecution, the National Socialist Government has violated a long-established principle of international morality, and the international community is justified in interceding on behalf of the victims of oppression.

The Right of Humanitarian Intercession

Many eminent authorities from Grotius to those of our own day have recognized the right of intercession to protect the victims of persecution and oppression. Grotius, writing early in the seventeenth century, qualified the general rule of non-intervention by pointing out that

> "the case is different if the wrong be manifest. If a tyrant . . . practices atrocities towards his subjects, which no just man can approve, the right of human social connection is not cut off in such a case." [3]

In more recent times numerous writers on international law have likewise insisted that the denial of human rights is a

3. Grotius,H., *De Jure Belli et Pacis*, Whewell transl., Cambridge, 1853, II, pp.308, 440.

matter of international concern. They maintain that members of the international community are authorized to intervene when a state flagrantly disregards the rights of its own subjects. Paul Fauchille, director and founder of the *Revue Générale de Droit International Public*, wrote:

> "This conclusion follows: intervention is legitimate *vis-à-vis* a State which is in a condition of anarchy or whose institutions are actually inhumane; if a State cannot impose upon others the form of its government it can at least demand that they submit to a rule of law, in conformity with the principles of civilization. The interdependence and solidarity between States as well as the rights of humanity demand this." [4]

Martens, an outstanding authority on international law, maintained that the guarantees of religious liberty which were incorporated in the Treaty of Berlin, proved

> "sufficiently that modern civilized states have in no manner waived the right to impose, if necessary, on Christian governments certain strict obligations in favour of tolerance and of the civil equality of all denominations."

Public opinion, Martens continued,

> "irresistibly compels governments to pronounce their judgments and to take steps, as soon as such truly deplorable phenomena as religious persecutions or denials of the civil rights of . . . subjects of this or that denomination make their appearance." [5]

4. Fauchille,P., *Traité de Droit International Public*, 8th Edition, Paris, 1922, I, part I, pp.570–2.
5. Martens,F., *Völkerrecht: Das Internationale Recht der Nationen*, Berlin, 1883, II, pp.109, 111. Professor Borchard also speaks of the ". . . fact that where a state under exceptional circumstances disregards certain rights of its own citizens, over whom presumably it has absolute sovereignty, the other states of the family of nations are authorized by international law to intervene on grounds of humanity. . . ." Borchard,E.M., *The Diplomatic Protection of Citizens Abroad*, N.Y., 1915, p.14.

Bluntschli, who was professor of law at Heidelberg, wrote:

> "If . . . a violation occurs of the universally recognized rights of man or of international law, an intervention for their protection is justified by the same reasons as the interference of civilized states in the case of violations of law which amount to a public danger." [6]

The meaning of the term "intervention" is generally left undefined, but most jurists who sustain this right subscribe to the view of Sir Robert Phillimore, a member of the British Privy Council and Judge of the High Court of Admiralty, who approved of intercession to uphold religious equality by "remonstrance, by stipulation, by a condition in a Treaty concluding a war waged upon other grounds." Thus Heffter, a German jurist whose work on international law has exerted great influence beyond as well as within the borders of his country, favored intercession. He said:

> ". . . Moral duty, however, ordains and justifies the attempt at peaceful intercession with a view to averting injustice, and, if nevertheless, there is a perseverance in injustice, particularly if a despotic government tramples down every law, the entire breaking off of all relations. . . ." [7]

6. Bluntschli,J.K., *Das moderne Völkerrecht der civilisierten Staaten*, 3rd Edition, 1878, p.270.
7. Phillimore, Sir Robert, *Commentaries upon International Law*, 3rd Edition, London, 1879, I, p.622; Heffter,A.W., *Das Europäische Völkerrecht der Gegenwart*, 1888, p.114. For other opinions recognizing the right of intervention or intercession on humanitarian grounds see Wheaton,H., *Elements of International Law*, 6th Edition, Boston, 1855, p.100; Oppenheim,L., *International Law*, 3rd Edition, 1920, I, p.462; Stowell,E.C., *Intervention in International Law*, Washington, 1921, pp.51–8; Lingelbach,W.E., "The Doctrine and Practice of Intervention in Europe," *Annals of American Academy of Political and Social Science*, July, 1900, pp.28–9; Mandelstam,A., "La Protection Internationale des Droits de l'Homme," Académie de Droit International, *Recueil des Cours*, 1931, IV, pp.194–7.

The Practice of Humanitarian Intercession

Citations from classical and more recent authorities might be multiplied, but more important is the consideration of what the Hague Conference defined as one of the sources of international law, namely, the "usages established between civilized nations." [8] We are concerned not with abstract principles, but with positive facts: States have interceded to uphold human rights for more than three hundred years and the results of such efforts are embodied in important treaties.

In modern times the first instances of such international action date from the rise and growth of Protestantism during the sixteenth and seventeenth centuries. The disruption of religious uniformity divided Germany into Catholic and Protestant principalities, and the ensuing bitterness found release in cruel and bloody wars. The desire for self-preservation led the Protestant princes to aid one another against the superior forces of Catholicism, and religious sympathies moved men of all faiths to insist, when in a position to do so, that freedom of worship be not denied to co-religionists in foreign lands. The principle of religious liberty had not yet dawned upon the minds of the contending parties, but since no decisive victory could be won by either side, a compromise became necessary; and compromise resulted in a measure of toleration as an unavoidable expedient.

After years of sanguinary conflict, the Peace of Augsburg (1555) authorized each prince to decide whether Catholicism or Lutheranism should be the faith professed in his territories. The Lutheran faction did demand that co-religionists in Catholic lands be guaranteed freedom of worship, but this

8. See Scott, J.B., *The Hague Peace Conferences of* 1899 *and* 1907, II, p.113.

was refused, and subjects were obliged to conform to the faith dictated by the governor of the state, or else to emigrate. In fact, so limited was the concession to Protestantism, that none but Lutherans, not even Calvinist princes, were tolerated. It required more wars and more bloodshed to win equal recognition for Calvinist rulers in Germany. This was achieved by the Treaty of Westphalia (1648) which also afforded some relief to subjects, i.e. to religious minorities resident in the German states. Catholic and Protestant (Lutheran or Calvinist) minorities living under rulers of the opposite faith were assured freedom of worship, provided that privilege had already been granted to them by their sovereigns. Moreover, the Lutheran and Calvinist princes agreed not to interfere with the religious observance of their subjects in new territories which might be annexed subsequently.

However, it must be reiterated that even in 1648, and for more than a century thereafter, religious liberty in the modern sense did not exist: when European Governments intervened to prevent persecution in Christian lands, it was only on behalf of members of certain religious denominations. During the seventeenth century, for example, Cromwell succeeded in mitigating the persecution of the Waldenses by the Duke of Savoy, and Holland interceded in favor of the French Calvinists. Similarly when states were obliged to cede territory, they sought by means of treaty stipulations to protect from religious persecution some of the subjects handed over to alien rule. Thus when Sweden was awarded Livonia, when, somewhat later, Holland annexed the city of Maestrecht and when Poland was partitioned in 1773, provisions were incorporated in the respective treaties to assure freedom of religion to Roman Catholics.[9]

9. An example of this type of enactment is the Treaty of Paris of 1763,

By the close of the eighteenth century it had become an established practice for European States to intervene on humanitarian grounds in order to further the welfare of one or another (Christian) religious minority resident in another state. Moreover, in attempting to safeguard co-religionists in the non-Christian Orient against persecution, it was difficult to single out for favored treatment only one type of Christian. The doctrine of religious toleration, therefore, tended to become generalized so as to include *all* Christians. Thus in the Treaty of Kutchuk-Kainardji (1774) between Russia and the Ottoman Empire we find the following guarantee:

> "Article VII. The Sublime Porte promises constantly to protect the Christian Religion in all its Churches. . . ." [10]

What is more, we find in the eighteenth century a precedent for humanitarian intercession on behalf of *non-Christians*. When in December, 1744, Jews were banished from the Kingdom of Bohemia, the sympathies of Great Britain and Holland were enlisted to make representations to Empress Maria Theresa. Lord Harrington instructed the British Ambassador in Vienna to exert himself "with all possible zeal and Diligence" in the endeavor

> "to dissuade the Court of Vienna from putting the said Sentence in Execution, hinting to Them in the tenderest

which surrendered Canada to Great Britain. Article IV of that Treaty reads: ". . . His Britannic Majesty agrees to accord to the inhabitants of Canada liberty of the Catholic religion." de Martens, G.F., *Recueil de Traités*, I, p.109. See also pp.481f; *The Cambridge Modern History*, N.Y., 1934, II, pp.276–7; IV, pp.410–3; von Balogh, A., *Der Internationale Schutz der Minderheiten*, Munich, 1928, pp.7–9.

10. For the text see Foreign Handbooks, *History of the Eastern Question*, London, 1920, p.67.

> and most friendly Manner, the Prejudice that the World might conceive against the Queen's proceedings in that Affair, if such Numbers of innocent People were made to suffer. . . ." [11]

The appeal to humanity proved effective and the edict was revoked.

Thus international concern with the maintenance of human rights originated, in modern times, with the desire to aid co-religionists in foreign lands. It evolved into the effort to assure freedom of religion to all Christians in the Orient, and on occasion extended to the protection of non-Christians. But it was not until the nineteenth century, after the humanitarian impulses of the *Aufklärung* and of the French and the American Revolutions had exerted their influence,[12] that the doctrine of religious *equality*, and international responsibility for its observance, was clearly formulated. When on July 21st, 1814, the union of Belgium and Holland was effected by treaty, the Powers guaranteed the inhabitants of the territory not merely religious *toleration*, not merely the privilege on sufferance to practice and preach a certain faith, but full *equality*—civil and political equality without which religious freedom is incomplete. Article II of that treaty reads:

> "No innovation shall be made in the Articles of this Constitution, which assure equal protection and favour to every sect, and guarantee the admission of all citizens, whatever their religious belief may be, to public employments and offices." [13]

11. Wolf,L., *Notes on the Diplomatic History of the Jewish Question*, London, 1919, p.11.
12. In November, 1791, the first ten amendments to the Constitution of the United States were declared in force. The first amendment included a guarantee against federal interference with religious liberty. At approximately the same time religious liberty was proclaimed in France.
13. Hertslett,E., *The Map of Europe by Treaty*, I, London, 1875, p.38.

It should be noted that in extending the meaning of religious freedom to include civil and political equality, the article just quoted does not single out any religious confession or faith for favored treatment. It treats equally "*every sect*" and guarantees equality of status to "*all citizens, whatever their religious belief may be.*" In this instance, therefore, religious freedom ceases to be a special privilege and becomes a *human right*—the right to equality of opportunity regardless of religious affiliation. Discrimination in civil and political rights thus stands condemned along with the intolerance which denies a human being the right to worship God in his own way.

Having set a precedent for international responsibility in upholding religious, civil and political equality, it was inevitable that the Powers should continue to intercede on behalf of minorities who suffered or were likely to suffer discrimination at the hands of backward and intolerant majorities. Hence the diplomatic history of the nineteenth century furnishes numerous instances of international action to prevent the denial of such rights. Even during the period of reaction which was ushered in by the return and final overthrow of Napoleon in 1815, the doctrine of the French Revolution that "all men are born and remain free and equal in rights" was not without effect. The Congress of Vienna, anxious as it was to undo the liberal and humanitarian work of the revolutionaries, nevertheless wrote into the constitution of the newly-formed Germanic Confederation the following article:

"The different Christian sects in the countries and territories of the Germanic Confederation shall not experience any difference in the enjoyment of civil and political rights.

"The Diet shall consider of the means of effecting, in

> the most uniform manner, an amelioration in the civil state of those who profess the Jewish religion in Germany, and shall pay particular attention to the measures by which the enjoyment of civil rights shall be secured and guaranteed to them in the Confederated States, upon condition, however, of their submitting to all the obligations imposed upon other citizens. In the meantime, the privileges already granted to this sect by any particular State, shall be secured to them."[14]

The representatives of the Powers at the Congress of Aix-la-Chapelle (1818) likewise declared that the problem of civil and political equality for the Jews should "equally occupy the statesman and the friend of humanity."[15]

In the above pronouncements the Powers were content to reaffirm a worthy ideal, but when the Balkan peoples suffered oppression, positive action was taken to put an end to persecution and to establish religious liberty and human rights. Greece was liberated by the intervention of Great Britain, France and Russia, and when the new State was recognized in 1830, care was taken that the new masters should not deny equal human rights to their minorities—Christian, Jewish or Moslem. The Conference of London declared as follows in the Protocol of February 3rd, 1830:

> "The Plenipotentiaries of the three Allied Courts . . . agreed that all the subjects of the new State, whatever may be their religion, shall be admissible to all public employments, functions, and honours, and be treated on the footing of a perfect equality, without regard to difference of creed in all their relations, religious, civil or political."

14. Article XVI of Annex IX to the Vienna Congress, Treaty of June 9th, 1815, in Hertslett, *op. cit.*, I, p.205.
15. Wolf, *op. cit.*, p.16.

When subsequently additional territories were awarded to the new Kingdom, the Great Powers stipulated as a condition that "entire civil and political equality" should reign in the new, as well as the old provinces.[16]

Since the middle of the nineteenth century the Great Powers have repeatedly been called upon to prevent persecution in the Balkans. Time and again we find either the Concert of Europe or individual states taking action to maintain religious, civil and political equality. When, after the Crimean War, Moldavia and Wallachia were set up as an autonomous Roumanian principality, an attempt was made in the preliminary conference of Constantinople (1856) to assure equality to all by means of the following articles:

> "Article XIII. All religions and those who profess them shall enjoy equal liberty and equal protection in the two principalities.
>
> "Article XVI. All Moldavians and all Wallachians will without exception be admissible to public employment.
>
> "Article XVIII. All classes of the population without any distinction of birth or religion shall enjoy equality of civil rights, and in particular the right of property in all its forms. . . ."[17]

However, when assured that the emancipation of the Jews would be achieved gradually, the Powers consented to in-

16. The Treaty of 1863, by which Great Britain, Austria, France, Prussia and Russia recognized the cession of the Ionian Islands to Greece, provided that "the principle of entire civil and political equality between subjects belonging to different creeds, established in Greece by the same Protocol [that of February 3rd, 1830], shall be likewise in force in the Ionian Islands." Holland, T.E., *The European Concert in the Eastern Question*, Oxford, 1885, pp.33, 49. See also pp.55, 64–5.
17. See Temperley, H.W.V. (ed.), *A History of the Peace Conference of Paris*, V, 1921, p.114.

clude a less drastic provision in the final Convention of Paris of August 10th, 1858. They guaranteed political and civil equality to Moldavians and Wallachians "of all Christian rites" and added that "the enjoyment of these rights can be extended to other religions by legislative enactment." [18]

When it became evident that the assurances with respect to the Jews were not being fulfilled, the Powers intervened again. The Roumanian principality protested that this constituted interference in its internal affairs, but the reply of Great Britain was categorical. A despatch of 1867 to Bucharest declared that "the peculiar position of the Jews places them under the protection of the civilized world." [19] In 1872, the protection of the civilized world was again invoked, and the foreign consuls at Bucharest addressed a collective protest to the government of the Prince against the acts of "violence, quite unworthy of a civilized country." The participation of Peixotto, the representative of the United States, in this protest, was approved by the Secretary of State, Hamilton Fish, who wrote,

> "Whatever caution and reserve may usually characterize the policy of the Government in such matters, may be regarded as inexpedient when every guarantee and consideration of justice appear to have been set at defiance in the course pursued with reference to the unfortunate people referred to."

And the American Consul was instructed not to be "backward in joining any similar protest, or other measure which the foreign representatives there may deem advisable." The Secretary of State went so far as to instruct the American

18. *Ibid.*, V, pp.114–5.
19. *British and Foreign State Papers*, Vol. 62, p.705. See also pp.679–711.

Ministers at the Courts of the Great Powers to make known to the Governments to which they were accredited the sympathy of the United States for "the inhumanly persecuted Hebrews" in the hope that such action "might quicken and encourage" efforts to redress wrongs which the note characterized as "so enormous, as to impart to it, as it were, a cosmopolitan character, in the redress of which all countries, governments, and creeds are alike interested." [20] Such was the position taken by Great Britain and the United States more than half a century ago when Roumania sought to deny the right of humanitarian intercession by pretending that the persecution of its Jewish subjects was a matter of domestic concern.

The most notable instance prior to the twentieth century of international action to maintain human rights occurred in 1878, when the Congress of Berlin met and recognized the independence of three new states and the autonomy of a fourth. Not for a long time had such an occasion presented itself, as Waddington, the French Plenipotentiary, put it, "to affirm anew the principles which constitute the honour and the security of civilized nations." Waddington, who appears to have taken the initiative in this matter, urged the Congress not to admit a new state into the family of nations unless it first agreed to "acknowledge the principles which are the foundation of the social organization in all the States of Europe, and to accept them as a necessary condition for the favour which it seeks." [21]

The proposals which Waddington introduced were strongly

20. *Foreign Relations*, 1872, pp.690–1. See also pp.55, 183, 193. It is significant that the *German representative*, Thielan, heads the list of Consuls who protested in the collective note referred to. The spokesman of Tsarist Russia alone refused to participate in this humanitarian intercession.

21. *British and Foreign State Papers*, Vol. 69, pp.960, 983.

supported by Lord Beaconsfield and Lord Salisbury for Great Britain, by Prince Bismarck for Germany, by Count de Launay for Italy and by Count Andrassy for Austria-Hungary. The representative of Tsarist Russia, Prince Gortschakoff, alone raised objections to the international guarantee of human rights, and significantly enough the position taken by Tsarist Russia resembled closely that maintained to-day by National Socialist Germany. Gortschakoff wished to reduce the meaning of religious liberty, which had come to embrace civil and political as well as religious equality, to the primitive and narrow concept of religious toleration to inferiors. His views, however, found no support among the statesmen of the civilized "West" in 1878, and when he spoke disparagingly of the Russian Jews, Prince Bismarck, the Iron Chancellor, took occasion to remark that

> "It is perhaps to the purpose to attribute the regrettable condition of the Israelites [of Russia, Serbia, Roumania, etc.] to the restrictions placed upon their civil and political rights." [22]

The spokesman for the Tsar had to give way; and articles were incorporated in the Treaty of Berlin binding Roumania, Serbia, Montenegro and Bulgaria to assure religious, civil and political equality to all, irrespective of creed or confession. Article XLIV, relating to Roumania, reads:

22. *Ibid.*, Vol. 69, pp.959–61. The Protocol of the Congress summarizes Gortschakoff's views as follows: ". . . If it be a question solely of religious liberty, Prince Gortschakoff declares that it has always been applied in Russia. . . . But if it be a question of civil and political rights, his Most Serene Highness asks that the Israelites of Berlin, Paris, London or Vienna, to whom assuredly there could be no question of refusing any political or civil right, should not be confused with the Jews of Serbia, of Roumania, and of certain Russian provinces, who are, in his opinion, a veritable scourge to the native populations."

"In Roumania the difference of religious creeds and confessions shall not be alleged against any person as a ground for exclusion or incapacity in matters relating to the enjoyment of civil and political rights, admission to public employments, functions, and honours, or the exercise of the various professions and industries in any locality whatsoever.

"The freedom and outward exercise of all forms of worship shall be assured to all persons belonging to the Roumanian State, as well as to foreigners, and no hindrance shall be offered either to the hierarchical organization of the different communions, or to their relations with their spiritual chiefs." [23]

The decisions of the Congress of Berlin, as well as the action taken previously to assure religious, civil and political equality in Holland and Belgium, in Greece, and in the Roumanian Provinces, established the principle of international responsibility for the maintenance of human rights, at least in new and enlarged states. When, therefore, Roumania evaded Article XLIV of the Treaty of Berlin by declaring its Jews "aliens not subject to foreign protection," and by requiring them to apply *individually* for naturalization, Great Britain and, particularly, the United States did not hesitate to intercede and to voice their disapproval.[24]

The American Government had expressed concern for the welfare of the Roumanian Jews before the independence of Roumania had been recognized,[25] but it is in John Hay's celebrated "Roumanian Note" of 1902, that we find the boldest assertion of the rights of a foreign power to intervene

23. See Articles V, XXVII, XXXV and XLIV of the Treaty of Berlin in Hertslett, *op. cit.*, IV, London, 1891, pp.2769–70, 2781, 2785–6, 2790.

24. Great Britain recognized the independence of Roumania only when assurances were given that the Jews would be emancipated gradually. *British and Foreign State Papers*, Vol. 71, p.1187.

25. See above, pp.13–14.

on humanitarian grounds. This Note is deserving of careful consideration because its argument has pertinent bearing upon the present German situation. After referring to the "... arbitrary and controvertible premises that the native Jews of Roumania domiciled there for centuries are 'aliens not subject to foreign protection,'" the Secretary of State proceeded to enumerate the disabilities under which the Jews were laboring in the following significant words:

> "The political disabilities of the Jews in Roumania, their exclusion from the public service and the learned professions, the limitations of their civil rights, and the imposition upon them of exceptional taxes, involving as they do wrongs repugnant to the moral sense of liberal modern peoples, are not so directly in point for my present purpose as the public acts which attack the inherent right of man as a breadwinner in the ways of agriculture and trade. The Jews are prohibited from owning land, or even from cultivating it as common laborers. They are debarred from residing in the rural districts. Many branches of petty trade and manual production are closed to them in the overcrowded cities, where they are forced to dwell and engage, against fearful odds, in the desperate struggle for existence. . . ."

The ways of oppressors change but little! Even a cursory glance at the Annex to the Letter of Resignation of James G. McDonald, High Commissioner for German refugees, will reveal that the words of Hay, with but slight modifications, describe accurately the plight of Jews and "non-Aryans" in Nazi Germany. And the effects of oppression, too, are the same. The victims of Roumanian persecution, like those of National Socialism, sought relief in flight. Hay was outraged by governmental policies which threw upon "the long suffering generosity of a more-favored community" a mass of destitute and despairing "outcasts, made doubly paupers by physical and moral oppression in their native land. . . ." Such policies, declared the American Secretary of State, the Government of the United States could not tolerate.

> ". . . This Government can not be a tacit party to such an international wrong. It is constrained to protest against the treatment to which the Jews of Roumania are subjected, not alone because it has unimpeachable ground to remonstrate against the resultant injury to itself,[26] but in the name of humanity."

Hay could not invoke the Treaty of Berlin because the United States was not a signatory thereto. But he did intercede in the name of the principles of religious liberty and civil and political equality because, said he, "they are the principles of international law and eternal justice. . . ."[27]

This note was communicated to the Powers parties to the Treaty of Berlin in the hope that measures would be taken to persuade the Government of Roumania to abandon its policy of discrimination. The British Government joined the United States "in deploring the depressed condition of the Roumanian Jews," and proposed to the Great Powers that combined representations be made at Bucharest. The threat was sufficient to induce the Roumanian authorities to annul an act passed by their Parliament which would have made it impossible for Jewish artisans to practice their trade. However, the primary aim of intercession—equal rights—remained unrealized. The American Government was instrumental in raising the question again at the Conference of Bucharest, in 1913, but no more than assurances were secured—assurances which remained unfulfilled when the World War broke out in 1914.[28]

26. See below, pp.56–7.
27. *Foreign Relations*, 1902, pp.910–4.
28. *Ibid.*, pp.42ff., 442, 549–50, 684, 915, 1048; 1903, pp.702, 704; Wolf, *op. cit.*, pp.37–8, 47.

The new states of the Balkans figured so prominently in the interventions of the nineteenth century to uphold human rights that the impression is created that only *new* states might be cautioned against persecuting minorities. Such, however, is by no means the case. When the notorious ritual murder charge was brought against the Jews of Damascus in 1840,[29] several Powers intervened, and the American Consul at Alexandria was informed that President Van Buren was "anxious that the active sympathy and generous interposition of the Government of the United States should not be withheld from so benevolent an object. . . ." He was therefore instructed by Secretary of State John Forsyth to employ his good offices and efforts "to the end that justice and humanity may be extended to those persecuted people, whose cry of distress has reached our shores." [30] The same spirit characterized the attitude of the Government of the United States when outrages were committed against the Jews of Teheran in 1897. The American representative appealed to the Persian authorities " . . . from motives of humanity and of sympathy with those who are called upon to suffer" to put an end to the interference with the liberties "of this loyal, intelligent and industrious section of His Majesty's subjects," and John Sherman, then Secretary of State, approved of this action "in the interest of common humanity and in accordance with the precepts of civilization." [31]

In Morocco, too, the denial of human rights occasioned repeated intercession by foreign Powers. In 1864, Sir Moses Montefiore went to Morocco and, with the support of the

29. Damascus was then ruled by Mehemet Ali, the unruly vassal of the Sultan of Turkey.
30. Adler, C., *Jews in the Diplomatic Correspondence of the United States*, Baltimore, 1906, pp.4–5.
31. *Foreign Relations*, 1897, pp.429–31.

British Government, appealed for just treatment of non-Moslems. The Madrid Conference of 1880 took similar action. When, despite assurances by the Sultan of Morocco, the natives continued to harass the Jews, the representatives of the Powers were "unflagging in their efforts to lessen the burdens of the oppressed. . . ." Most persistent, however, were the efforts of the American Government. During the 1870's and 1880's, the American representatives at Tangier and Madrid, with the cordial sympathy and support of the State Department, interceded "in the interests of humanity and civilization"; and, at the Algeciras Conference (1906), the American representative, Henry White, was instrumental in having adopted a resolution which called upon the Sultan to see "that the Jews of his Empire and all his subjects, without distinction of religious belief are treated with justice and equity." [32]

Nor must it be assumed that intercession on behalf of humanity affected only out of the way or insignificant states. The concern of the Powers obliged the Sultan of Turkey to give assurances in the form of a decree (Firman) "emanating spontaneously from the sovereign will." This was the *Hatti-Humayoun* of February 18th, 1856, in which the Sultan assured full freedom of religion to all of his subjects and annulled "every distinction or designation tending to make any class whatever of the subjects of my Empire inferior to another class, on account of their Religion, Language, or Race. . . ." [33] In taking note of these assurances, Article IX of the Treaty of Paris (1856) clearly provided that the Powers had not thereby acquired the right to interfere in Turkish internal affairs,[34] but when in 1860, the Druses attacked the

32. *Ibid.*, 1878, p.691; 1881, pp.1054–6; Wolf, *op. cit.*, pp.92–9.
33. Hertslett, *op. cit.*, II, pp.1243–9.
34. *Ibid.*, p.246.

Syrian Christians, French troops were landed in order to put an end to the outrages.[35]

At the Congress of Berlin, too, when the question of religious liberty in the new principalities was under consideration, Lord Salisbury submitted provisions to assure equality to the inhabitants of the Turkish provinces. The Turkish representative at the Congress thought it wise not to object, but he proposed the addition of an introductory phrase to the effect that Salisbury's proposition would constitute no innovation but would merely reaffirm former assurances of the Sultan. The British statesman remarked laconically that assurances had indeed been given but that they "had not always been observed in practice." However, he did not oppose the insertion of the face-saving formula desired by the Turks, and Article LXII of the Treaty of Berlin declared as follows:

> "The Sublime Porte having expressed the intention to maintain the principle of religious liberty, and give it the widest scope, the Contracting Parties take note of this spontaneous declaration.
>
> "In no part of the Ottoman Empire shall difference of religion be alleged against any person as a ground for exclusion or incapacity as regards the discharge of civil and political rights, admission to the public employments, functions and honours, or the exercise of the various professions and industries.
>
> "All persons shall be admitted without distinction of religion, to give evidence before the tribunals.
>
> "The freedom and outward exercise of all forms of worship are assured all, and no hindrance shall be offered either to the hierarchical organization of the various communions or their relations with their spiritual chiefs." [36]

35. Stowell, *op. cit.*, pp.63ff.
36. *British and Foreign State Papers*, Vol. 69, pp.935, 942–3, 1009–10; Hertslett, *op. cit.*, IV, pp.2796–7.

The most significant precedent involving foreign intercession on behalf of the victims of persecution was that affecting Tsarist Russia. Like Germany of to-day the Russian Empire maintained that the disabilities imposed upon the Jews constituted *racial* rather than *religious* discrimination. Moreover, as a Great Power, the Tsar's Government was in a position to deny to any foreign Power the right to interfere in what it considered its internal affairs. But these claims did not deter the United States Government from protesting energetically against the denial of human rights.

The immediate concern of the American Government was with the fact that the right to travel and reside in Russia was denied to American citizens of the Jewish "race," but every opportunity was utilized to make it clear that the American protest was directed also against the persecution of the Russian Jews. At the close of 1880, in the course of conversations relative to the rights of American Jews in Russia, the American Minister at St. Petersburg took occasion to point out that his Government "took a deep interest in the amelioration of the conditions of the Jewish race in other nations. . . ." When informed by the Russian authorities that the native Jews would not be granted civil and political equality, John W. Foster, the American Minister, expressed regret because, he said, the United States Government desired to see the restrictions upon native, as well as foreign Jews, removed.[37]

The American Government attempted at times to limit its intercession to the immediate problem of protecting American citizens, but it became increasingly clear that civilized intercourse with Russia would be impossible for American Jews so long as discrimination and oppression was the lot of Russia's native Jews. This was expressed emphatically by Secretary

37. *Foreign Relations*, 1881, pp.996–1000ff.

of State James G. Blaine in the dispatch of November 22nd, 1881, to James Russell Lowell, United States Minister to London. Blaine wrote:

> "It was perfectly clear to the mind of the late President that an amelioration of the treatment of American Israelites in Russia could only result from a very decided betterment of the condition of the native Hebrews—that any steps taken toward the relief of one would necessarily react in favor of the other—and that, under the peculiar and abnormal aspects of the case, it is competent and proper to urge upon Russia action in consonance with the spirit of the age. To his successor in the Chief Magistracy, these conclusions are no less evident."

Blaine stigmatized the illiberal policies of the Russian Government in words which may well be applied to the present German situation. He said:

> "It cannot but be inexpressibly painful to the enlightened Statesmen of Great Britain, as well as of America, to see a discarded prejudice of the dark ages gravely revived at this day. . . . No student of history need be reminded of the lessons taught by the persecutions of the Jews in Central Europe, and on the Spanish Peninsula. Then, as now in Russia, the Hebrew fared better in business than his neighbor; then, as now, his economy and patient industry bred capital, and capital bred envy, and envy persecution, and persecution disaffection and social separation. The old tradition moves in its unvarying circle,—the Jews are made a people apart from other peoples, not of their volition, but because they have been repressed and ostracised by the communities in which they mixed. The *ghetto* of mediaeval times still preaches its eloquent lesson, which the nations have done well to heed. In Great Britain and in the United States, the Israelite is not segregated from his fellow men, a social Esau, alike

repellent and repelled. His equal part in our social framework is unchallenged; his thrift and industry add to the wealth of the state; and his loyalty and patriotism are unquestionable. So, likewise, in the great states of Europe, until we reach the Russian frontier. . . ."

Nor was Blaine content with mere denunciation. He was anxious to put an end to the deplorable state of affairs and instructed the American Minister to urge upon the British Government the desirability of common action. He was even hopeful of enlisting the aid of other Powers, at least in the cause of protecting the rights of their Jewish citizens who visited Russia.[38]

Tsarist Russia remained impervious to all humanitarian appeals and the problem continued to occupy the attention of the American Government. When reports reached the United States in 1882, that the Russian Jews had been the victims of rioting and attacks, Secretary Frelinghuysen informed the American Minister in St. Petersburg that the prejudice of race and creed had aroused considerable feeling in the country, and, while cautioning the Minister that it was not the right of the United States "officiously and offensively to intermeddle," he did authorize him to

> ". . . state, with all proper deference, that the feeling of friendship which the United States entertains for Russia prompts this Government to express the hope that the Imperial Government will find means to cause the persecution of these unfortunate fellow beings to cease." [39]

In the 1890's the problem once more became acute and Blaine, again Secretary of State, in referring to new repressions raised the issue of enforced emigration [40] which John

38. See Kohler, M.J., *The United States and German Jewish Persecutions*, Cincinnati, 1934, pp.41–2.
39. *Foreign Relations*, 1882, p.451.
40. See below, pp.56–7.

Hay was to make famous. He declared that some 200,000 Russian Jews had within ten years established themselves in the United States and formed a worthy element of the population. But he feared that an increase in the number of refugees "in need of immediate, and in many cases of long continued, assistance and care" might create an insoluble problem. He therefore instructed the American Minister to inform the Russian authorities that the Government and people of the United States deprecated the enforcement of measures which threatened to disturb the economic and social stability of other states and wounded "the universal and innate sentiment of humanity." [41] Blaine's instructions to the American Minister, and the other communications of the State Department to which reference has been made, were confidential and practically unknown to the public. But the persecution of the Russian Jews disturbed the people of the United States to such an extent that President Harrison felt obliged to declare in his annual message (December 9th, 1891) that the refugee problem created by Russia, "as well as the suggestions of humanity," furnished ample ground for the protests which had been lodged with the Russian Government.[42]

To these representations and appeals Tsarist Russia turned a deaf ear. Not only did the oppression of native Jews persist, but American citizens of the Jewish faith continued to be discriminated against when visiting Russia. On these grounds the House of Representatives of the United States, by a vote of 301 to 1, passed a resolution calling upon the President to terminate the commercial treaty of 1832 with Russia. So strong indeed, was the determination of the American people to demonstrate their opposition to Russia's policies that Pres-

41. *Foreign Relations*, 1891, pp.737–9ff.
42. *Ibid.*, 1891, p.xiii.

ident Taft immediately took action and on December 15th, 1911, notified the Russian Government of the denunciation of the Treaty. He asked the Senate to confirm his action, and that body without a single dissenting vote sanctioned the abrogation of the Treaty. The American Ambassador took especial pains to inform Sazonov, the Tsarist Minister of Foreign Affairs, that the action of the House of Representatives had been

> "unquestionably influenced by a sincere conviction that such action might have far-reaching results in inducing Russia to abandon not only restriction of foreign Jews, but restriction of her own Jews, . . ." [43]

The American protest against the denial of human rights in Tsarist Russia, and the positive provisions for equality which were stipulated in the Treaty of Berlin, bore witness to the growing consciousness of international responsibility for the maintenance of religious, civil and political equality. Commencing in the sixteenth and seventeenth centuries with tentative efforts to relieve members of a particular denomination from religious persecution, humanitarian intercession had broadened from precedent to precedent until it came to include the defense of religious toleration as a principle, regardless of the particular faith to which a person or group belonged. During the nineteenth century the principle of toleration and sufferance was extended to embrace equality; and the denial by a state of civil and political equality to any of its subjects on account of religious belief or confession became a basis for international protest and warning.

By the beginning of the twentieth century, it had become common international practice to demand from new states, before according them recognition, assurances with respect

43. *Ibid.*, 1911, pp.696–7.

to religious, civil and political equality, and to intervene when an illiberal and backward government, like the Porte, maltreated its minorities. Even a Great Power, like Tsarist Russia, could not prevent foreign intercession on behalf of humanity. But the international efforts to protect oppressed groups often proved inadequate, largely because no provision had been made for the enforcement of obligations. The persecuted peoples could hope to find relief only through the occasional intercession of one or another of the Great Powers. These Powers, because of diplomatic complications, frequently could take no action at all; or, if representations were made, it was only after persecution had become so cruel as to arouse universal condemnation.

Nor were these the only reasons for the failure to afford full protection to oppressed minority groups prior to the World War. The guarantee of human rights was generally expressed in terms of *religious* freedom, and a number of states, notably Prussia and Roumania, while making constitutional provision for religious equality, discriminated against Poles or Jews on linguistic, national or racial grounds. That oppression was an evil, even if the justification was difference of language or race rather than of religion, was quite obvious, but only on rare occasions did the Powers venture to demand equality for minorities regardless of *birth* [44] or of *race, language or religion.*[45]

The Minorities Treaties and the League Guarantee

The first opportunity to further and solidify the rights of minorities presented itself in 1919, when the statesmen of the victorious Allies assembled at Paris to establish peace, and when people throughout the world demanded, in President

44. As at the Conference of Constantinople, see p. 12.
45. As in the *Hatti-Humayoun*, see p. 20.

Wilson's words, "justice to all peoples and nationalities, and their right to live on equal terms of liberty and safety with one another, whether they be strong or weak." [46] The Paris Peace Settlement produced the Minorities Treaties, the most comprehensive plan yet evolved to afford protection to groups which suffered or were likely to suffer oppression.

The guarantees which the Allied statesmen thought necessary for the protection of minorities were not prescribed indiscriminately for all states. The representatives of the victorious Great Powers thought too highly of their free institutions and liberal intentions to require special assurances from their own governments. Even Germany and Italy, at that time not yet darkened by the shadow of intolerance, were considered sufficiently homogeneous or adequately civilized to be exempted from definite engagements. It was the lesser states, of limited experience in democratic government, which were compelled to contract international obligations not to maltreat their numerous minorities. Thus provisions for the protection of minorities were incorporated in the peace treaties of the smaller defeated states, namely, Austria, Hungary, Bulgaria and Turkey. More important were the special Minorities Treaties which the Allied and Associated Powers imposed upon the new and enlarged states of Poland, Czechoslovakia, Jugoslavia, Roumania and Greece.

The foundation of the new structure of minority protection is *equality in rights*. All inhabitants "without distinction of birth, nationality, language, race or religion" are assured "full and complete protection of life and liberty" and religious freedom. Most careful safeguards are provided that persons differing from the majority of the population in race, language or religion should not be denied citizenship and treated as

46. See House,E.M., and Seymour, C., *What Really Happened at Paris*, N.Y., 1921, p.204.

aliens. And all nationals, or citizens, of the states affected, the treaties stipulate, "shall be equal before the law and shall enjoy the same civil and political rights without distinction as to race, language or religion." [47]

The Minorities Treaties thus seek to prevent discrimination not only on grounds of *religion* but also of *race* or *language*. What is more, the enforcement of the obligations has not been left to the haphazard intercession of individual states but is entrusted to the League of Nations, as a factor in the new scheme of collective responsibility and collective security. The states bound by the Minorities Treaties have agreed that the stipulations for the protection of racial, religious and linguistic minorities constitute "obligations of international concern" which may not be modified without the assent of a majority of the Council of the League of Nations. The individual members of the Council are empowered to bring to its attention "any infraction, or any danger of infraction" of the provisions, and the Council is authorized to "take such action and give such direction as it may deem proper and effective in the circumstances." Finally, differences of opinion "as to questions of law or fact" arising under the Minorities Treaties must, if a member of the Council or one of the Principal Allied and Associated Powers so demands, be submitted for final settlement to the Permanent Court of International Justice.

As soon as the League of Nations began to function, the Council of the League, and particularly the Assembly and its Committees, began to devote much attention to the perfection and extension of the collective responsibility for the protection of minorities. At the very first Assembly, in December, 1920, Lord Robert Cecil proposed that new states seeking

47. See texts in League of Nations, *Protection of Linguistic, Racial and Religious Minorities by the League of Nations*, Geneva, 1927.

admission into the League of Nations be required to give assurances guaranteeing the rights of minorities. The proposal was adopted in a modified form, and a number of states, including Lithuanian, Latvia, Estonia and Albania were refused admission into the League of Nations until each had expressly committed itself in a Declaration, made before the Council of the League, to respect the rights of minorities.[48]

The precedent set in 1920 has been followed consistently during the past fifteen years. At practically every session of the Council and Assembly various questions affecting minorities have arisen and at all times it has been reiterated that the protection of persons differing from the majority in race, language or religion constitutes one of the major functions of the League of Nations. This thought was expressed by Professor Gilbert Murray before the Second Assembly (1921) in the following words:

> ". . . The question of minorities is one of absolutely primary importance for this League. The old Europe as it stood before the war had many elements of instability, and one of the most marked, one of the most universally recognized, was the existence in many of the great States of Europe of minorities which were discontented and disaffected towards the existing *régime*. . . . this particular duty of seeing that there does not grow up in Europe a mass of discontented people under governments by which they feel they are not quite fairly treated . . . is one of the obvious duties of the League of Nations." [49]

Professor Murray and other distinguished advocates of justice and world peace thought that *all* states, even those which

48. See League of Nations, *The Records of the First Assembly* (1920), *Plenary Meetings*, pp.406–7, 568–9; *Minutes of the Fifth Committee*, pp.201–10.
49. League of Nations, *The Records of the Second Assembly* (1921), *Plenary Meetings*, p.836.

were not bound by contractual obligations to protect minorities, should assure full equality to those of their subjects who differed from the majority of the population in race, language or religion. In urging the adoption of such a resolution, Motta, the Rapporteur to the Third Assembly (1922) on the question, said:

> ". . . I feel that I speak for . . . all the delegations when I express my extreme gratification that the Assembly should be intervening in the minorities question . . . and that the League of Nations, by giving expression forthwith to the noble aims and spirit of the Covenant,[50] should become, as it were, the guardian of minorities throughout the world."

The Assembly expressed its approval of these words by voting (on September 21st, 1922), without a dissenting voice, in favor of the following resolution:

> "The Assembly expresses the hope that the States which are not bound by any legal obligations to the League with respect to Minorities will nevertheless observe, in the treatment of their own racial, religious or linquistic minorities, at least as high a standard of justice and toleration as is required by any of the treaties and by the regular action of the Council."

50. The aims of the Covenant of the League of Nations are expressed thus in the Preamble:
The High Contracting Parties,
In order to promote international co-operation and to achieve international peace and security
by the acceptance of obligations not to resort to war,
by the prescription of open, just and honourable relations between nations,
by the firm establishment of the understandings of international law as the actual rule of conduct among Governments, and
by the maintenance of justice and a scrupulous respect for all treaty obligations in the dealings of organized peoples with one another,
Agree to this Covenant of the League of Nations.

It was hoped that the era of persecution because of differences in race, language or religion was drawing to a close. States containing numerous minorities had been expressly bound by treaty not to maltreat them, and every member of the League in voting for this resolution became morally obligated to assure justice and toleration to its minorities.[51] Little did anyone suspect that the "yoke of oppression" would reappear in Germany.

Germany, the Rights of Minorities and Humanitarian Intercession

Germany as a defeated Power had no share in the writing of the Minorities Treaties, nor was it permitted to participate in the work of the League of Nations during the formative years. But it would be a mistake to assume that the new German Republic had undertaken no obligations whatever to protect minorities, or was unfavorably disposed toward such a *régime*.

It is true that Germany, alone among the defeated Powers, was not required to sign a minorities treaty. But that was due to the general belief that no minorities would remain in Germany. The Jews, it was assumed, would constitute the only group differing from the majority in race or religion, and the German Jews, enjoying full equality, were imbued with a spirit of patriotism and national solidarity and did not, therefore, desire special international guarantees. Thus when Paderewski, the Polish spokesman, complained that no provision had been made to protect Poles resident in Germany, the Committee on New States which drafted the Minorities Treaties informed the Supreme Council of the Peace Conference as follows:

51. For this discussion see League of Nations, *The Records of the Third Assembly* (1922), *Plenary Meetings*, pp.171–4ff., 185–6.

"With regard to the absence of reciprocity of the guarantees given to the Germans and the Poles, the Committee must point out that there will remain very few groups of Poles in Germany. . . ."

Had it known, the Committee on New States went on to say, that a plebiscite would be arranged in Upper Silesia, it "would have asked for the insertion in the Treaty with Germany of a clause protecting Polish minorities." At all events, if a Polish minority remained in Germany, "it would be the obvious interest of Germany to grant them the indispensable guarantees, and the Powers would certainly be able to get an understanding when the time came." [52] The plebiscite in Upper Silesia did result in the retention by Germany of a considerable Polish population and the Allied Powers, acting through the Conference of Ambassadors, obliged Germany to accept "at least for the transitional period of fifteen years" stipulations for German Upper Silesia similar to the provisions of the Polish Minorities Treaty. When the need arose, therefore, Germany was required to assume obligations which were placed under the guarantee of the League of Nations.[53] Now that a new and unforeseen necessity has arisen, the League of Nations can hardly fail to intercede in order to prevent the oppression of a large body of people who differ in "race" from the majority of the population.

There were other reasons why a specific treaty binding Germany not to maltreat its minorities was considered unnecessary. At the time of the Peace Conference (1919), the German Government was greatly disturbed at the prospect of having millions of Germans torn from the Fatherland and placed under alien rule. There was every likelihood that

52. Miller, D.H., *My Diary at the Peace Conference*, privately printed, XIII, pp.178, 192.
53. See League of Nations, *Protection of Linguistic, Racial and Religious Minorities by the League of Nations*, *op. cit.*, pp.65ff.

some would suffer oppression at the hands of the new masters, but the Reich, defeated and exhausted, was in no position to assure protection to its lost children. It therefore proposed to the victors that minorities be protected *on a reciprocal basis:* Germany undertook to assure equality and cultural autonomy to the minorities resident within its frontiers and demanded that the League of Nations guarantee similar treatment to the Germans of the ceded territories. The *pledge* was given in the "Observations on the Conditions of Peace" which the German delegation submitted to the Peace Conference on May 29th, 1919. It read:

> "Germany advocates in principle the protection of national minorities. This protection may be settled to the best purpose within the scope of the League of Nations. Germany on her part, however, must demand such assurances as are already fixed by the Peace Treaty for those German minorities which, by cession, will pass over into alien sovereignty. . . . *Germany on her part is resolved to treat minorities of alien origin in her territories according to the same principles.*" [Italics ours.] [54]

The resolve of the German Government to assure equality to all citizens who differed from the majority of the population was not a statement of policy which might be repudiated at will. It was a commitment to the Allied and Associated Powers who *took note* of the guarantee in the following words:

> "The Allied and Associated Powers are prepared to accord guarantees, under the protection of the League of Nations, for the educational, religious and cultural rights of German minorities in territories transferred from the German Empire to the new states created by the Treaty. They take note of the statement of the German Delegates

54. *International Conciliation*, 1919, II, p.1228.

> that Germany is determined to treat foreign minorities within her territory according to the same principles."[55]

The fact that the Powers did no more than "*take note*" of the German pledge does not absolve the Reich from fulfilling the obligations which it assumed, nor does it free the Powers from the duty of protesting against German repudiation. The Treaty of Berlin employed the identical term in Article LXII which bound the Ottoman Empire to assure religious, civil and political equality to its minorities. Then, too, the Powers did no more than "take note of this spontaneous declaration,"[56] but the Sultan was no longer free to disavow his plighted word.

Moreover, the demand of Germany that obligations be imposed upon Poland to respect the rights of minorities, and consequently the pledge to assure equality to its own minorities, was meant to include the Jews. In the very same document in which the pledge was given, the German delegation warned that the Poles might persecute the German population of the ceded territories, and added:

> "What dangers threaten the national minorities in Poland is shown most clearly by the massacres practised on the Jewish population since November 11th. . . . Should the new Poland be formed according to the provisions of the peace draft, without the necessary guarantees for the minority peoples being accurately established at the same time, it would mean the advancement of the pogrom limit far towards the west."[57]

The treatment meted out by the Nazi Government to Jews and "non-Aryans" furnishes a sad commentary on Germany's anxiety in 1919 lest the Polish Jews suffer pogroms.

55. *Ibid.*, p.1359.
56. See above, p.21. See below, p.102.
57. *International Conciliation*, 1919, II, pp.1246–7.

The pledge to treat its minorities in accordance with the principles of justice and humanity was fulfilled loyally by the German Government until the advent to power of the National Socialists. The Weimar Constitution guaranteed to all Germans *without exception* full equality before the law and equal civil and constitutional rights; and a special article assured the minorities freedom in the "development of their national peculiarities." The State of Prussia, too, reversed its pre-war policy of intolerance and accorded generous treatment to its minorities.[58]

It was the determination to deal justly with its own minorities that enabled the German Government to insist on every occasion that Germans living abroad be protected against discrimination. Thus in 1923, when the Permanent Court of International Justice was considering the question of German colonists in Poland, the Reich Government in a note to the Court asserted " . . . its right and its interest in the carrying out of the protection of minorities guaranteed to Germany by Article 93, paragraph 1, of the Treaty of Versailles."[59] Surely the right to intervene on behalf of the German minorities in Poland or other states must be conditional on the fulfillment of the German pledge. This elementary principle of justice and fair play was recognized by many leaders of the German Republic, for, time and again, at the sessions of the Reichstag and in public addresses, these men emphasized the reciprocal relationship between the protection of German minorities abroad and the treatment accorded within Germany to persons differing from the

58. See especially Articles 109, 110, 113, 119, 128, 136 of the Weimar Constitution in Kraus,H., *Das Recht der Minderheiten*, Berlin, 1927, pp.260–4. See also pp.269ff. and Rathenau,F., "Prussia's New Polish Policy," *Berliner Tageblatt*, November 20th, 1928.

59. Quoted in League of Nations, *Official Journal, Minutes of the Council*, 1923, p.1291.

majority in race, language or religion. When, in June, 1925, Schiele, the Conservative ("German National") Minister of the Interior who had the full confidence of President von Hindenburg, said in the Reichstag that no German Government would fail to demand just treatment for the German minorities of adjacent lands, he coupled that declaration with this significant remark:

> "We must expect that the German, wherever he finds himself in a national minority, will be treated in the same manner as others wish minorities to be treated in Germany." [60]

In 1926, Germany became a member of the League of Nations and willingly accepted [61] the Assembly resolution of September 21st, 1922, which called upon all states to observe a high standard of "justice and toleration" in the treatment of their minorities. The pledge was thus confirmed, and Germany felt free to champion the cause of minorities before the Council and Assembly of the League of Nations.[62]

The Council had evolved a procedure in minorities questions which called for intercession only when a state had been charged with the violation of its Minorities Treaty. To the German Government this appeared inadequate, and its representatives persistently and passionately pleaded for the broadening and deeping of the rights of minorities: for con-

60. Quoted in Wertheimer,F., *Deutschland, die Minderheiten und der Völkerbund*, Berlin, 1926, p.4. See also pp.3, 61, 64.

61. See League of Nations, *Official Journal, Records of Fourteenth Ordinary Session of Assembly (1933), Minutes of Sixth Committee*, p.42. In a discussion in the Sixth Committee of the Assembly in October, 1933, von Keller, the German representative, spoke of the Assembly resolution of September 21st, 1922, as ". . . a resolution which Germany has acknowledged in all respects." But in 1933 von Keller maintained that this resolution did not apply to the Jews.

62. For opinions expressed in the Reichstag, on the desirability of League membership in order to guard the rights of minorities, see Wertheimer, *op. cit.*, pp.60–2ff.

tinuous supervision by the League of Nations; for intervention in cases of infraction of the provisions of the treaties; and for a generous regard for the well-being of those who differed from the majorities of the various states in race, language or religion. Gustav Stresemann told the Council in 1928, that

> ". . . were the League . . . to cease dealing with the rights of minorities, it would be losing one of the reasons for its existence and would cease to represent for some States the ideal which induced them to join it." [63]

Julius Curtius who was German Minister for Foreign Affairs in 1930, insisted that "the protection of minorities must be . . . not a temporary but a permanent thing." And Hermann Müller, one-time Chancellor of the Reich, Carl von Schubert, a leading figure in the Foreign Office, Koch-Weser, a Minister of Justice and the Interior, von Rosenberg, an Envoy Extraordinary and Minister Plenipotentiary, even von Neurath, the present Reich Minister for Foreign Affairs, in fact all who were empowered to speak at any time in the name of Germany, urged that all states should deal with their minorities in a generous spirit so as to allay suspicion and promote mutual understanding between nations. The protection of the rights of minorities was not the ideal of one man or one party. It was the consistent policy of the German Government as it was a chief objective of the League of Nations.

This intercession on behalf of oppressed peoples was particularly potent because Germany had loyally fulfilled its pledge to assure justice and equality to its own minorities. Therefore, when demanding justice for Germans living abroad, the Reich delegates to the League made certain to

63. League of Nations, *Official Journal*, *Minutes of the Council*, 1929, p.70.

call attention to the generous minorities policy pursued by their own country. At a Council meeting in 1931, Curtius, the Reich delegate, coupled the condemnation of the violence which was reported to have taken place in Poland with the declaration that the German Government had "always been inspired by the spirit and letter of the procedure for the protection of minorities. . . ." And when the Polish representative asserted that the hostility to Germans in Polish Upper Silesia was due to the maltreatment of Poles in Germany, particularly along the frontier of the "Corridor," Curtius said,

> "I should be quite right in refusing to examine allegations referring to districts in which Germany has no *legal* obligations. As, however, Germany has always laid special stress on the general *moral* idea of minority rights, irrespective of treaties, I willingly waive my rights to plead the Council's lack of competence in this matter. . . ." [Italics ours.]

And he challenged the Polish Government to contrast the treatment of minorities in Germany and Poland.[64] Germany's hands were then clean and its spokesmen could well afford to demand equal justice from others.

As late as 1932, when von Neurath, the present director of German foreign policy, was already in power, the "moral idea" of justice and equality for all, irrespective of treaties, still prevailed. In that year the German Government was called upon to refute charges of discrimination brought before the Council by the Polish minority in Germany. The German Foreign Office thereupon included in its observations to the

64. See League of Nations, *Official Journal, Minutes of the Council*, 1931, pp.169–70, 177. Germany was even prepared to discuss seriously and along "positive lines" the proposal to extend the minorities system to all states. See *Ibid., Eleventh Ordinary Session of the Assembly, Minutes of Sixth Committee*, p.42; *Records of Thirteenth Ordinary Session of Assembly, Minutes of Sixth Committee*, p.42.

Council a statement which had been written by an official of the German Government and which strikingly portrays the statesmanship and humanity that animated Germany only a few years ago. It read in part:

> "If we demand that the culture of our fellow-countrymen, separated from us by force, should be recognized, and that they should be free to foster and develop it, we cannot deny the same rights to other races. . . .
>
> "But what will happen if in a spirit of pusillanimity and timidity, we place fetters on the foreign element in our country? . . . Will not the pressure by which we hold down the Polish element produce a counter-pressure under which the German element in Poland would suffer far more seriously than at present? And who would be better entitled and authorized to take a leading position in the world, not only as regards her own minorities outside the country, but also minorities in general, than Germany, whose greatest federal State has now afforded such extensive rights to its strongest minority? Thus the greatest measure of liberality will be the best protection for German culture. . . . Prussia has learned a lesson from history. May the German school gain its victory by fair play." [65]

A year later the National Socialists were in power. They repudiated the humane and pacific policies which the previous German Governments had so diligently pursued. Germany, unfortunately, had learned no lesson from history.

* * *

65. The "Observations" were submitted on March 30th, 1932, and signed by von Bülow, the Permanent Secretary of the German Foreign Office. Von Neurath did not become Foreign Minister until June, 1932, but he was Germany's first delegate to the Council when it considered, in December, 1932, the petition of the Poles and the German "Observations" of which the above statement forms a part. See League of Nations, *Official Journal*, *Minutes of the Council*, 1932, pp.1939, 2146–52, 2167–8.

In disavowing the principles of civil, political and religious equality, and in denying international responsibility for their maintenance, the National Socialist Government is abandoning not only the ideals of post-war democrats like Stresemann, but also the best traditions of the German nation. When racial and religious intolerance flared up in Germany in the 1880's, a large number of the most distinguished representatives of the German people—men who have made German culture universally admired and respected—protested vigorously against the slanders and attacks upon the Jews. In Berlin, a manifesto was issued by seventy-three eminent "Aryans," including Anders, Droysen, Kirchhoff, Werner Siemens, Weber, Mommsen, Virchow and others. These men denounced the "shameful manner" in which "race hatred and fanaticism of the middle ages" were being revived and directed against "our Jewish fellow citizens," and called upon men and women of all parties to defend the principles of justice and equality. The Crown Prince, who later became Emperor Frederick, likewise condemned the anti-Semitic agitation as "a shame and a disgrace to Germany." [66]

Even more significant is the fact that the leaders of German nationalism have denounced racial and religious discrimination. During the early part of the nineteenth century, Prince Hardenberg exerted considerable pressure upon the Free Cities of Hamburg, Bremen and Lübeck to grant equality to the Jews. The fate of the Jews in the provinces and cities of Germany, he declared, was not "a matter of indifference to the Prussian State," which had just removed Jewish disabilities. In the name of humanity and prudent statecraft he called upon the Hanseatic Cities to renounce the policy of "oppression and abhorred exclusion from rights, to which they are entitled as men." In like manner, William von Humboldt,

66. See *The Times* (London), November 18th, 1888.

Hardenberg's friend and advisor, urged the abandonment of

> ". . . the unhuman and prejudiced manner of thinking which judges a man, not in accordance with his actual characteristics but according to his descent and religion, and considers him, not as an individual, but as one belonging to a race, and necessarily sharing alleged common attributes of the race. . . ." [67]

Prince Bismarck, a conservative and nationalist—the man who discounted the value of democratic parliaments and unified Germany by means of "blood and iron"—paid a tribute to the ideal of religious liberty and the civil and political equality that it entails. Reference has already been made [68] to his pointed remark at the Congress of Berlin that the deplorable condition of the Russian Jews might well be attributed to the disabilities under which they labored. As Chairman of the Congress and as German Plenipotentiary, he supported the effort to guarantee to all inhabitants of the new Balkan States religious, civil and political equality. "The support of Germany," he said, "is always accorded to every motion favourable to religious liberty." And in 1892, soon after his retirement from office, he said in answer to a question respecting the Jews,

> "The Jews bring into the mentality of the various German tribes a certain *mousseux* that should not be underrated. If I were still Minister the principle that I would recommend in regard to the Jews is: *La recherche de la confession est interdite.*" [69]

During the World War, too, when German arms were for the moment victorious and the Kaiser's Government was in a

67. See texts in Kohler,M.J., *Jewish Rights at the Congresses of Vienna and Aix-la-Chapelle*, N.Y., 1918, pp.11–2, 31–2, 71ff.
68. See above, p.15.
69. Jöhlinger,O., *Bismarck und die Juden*, Berlin, 1921, p.185; Wolf, *op. cit.*, pp.29, 30.

position to dictate terms of peace to Roumania, it did not fail to require of the latter assurances that religious, civil and political equality would prevail in the country. Article XXVIII of the Treaty of Bucharest of May 7th, 1918, provided:

> "The diversity of religious belief shall not exercise any influence on the legal position of the inhabitants and especially on their civil and political rights. The principle laid down in paragraph I is also to be applied to persons in Roumania having no nationality, including Jews hitherto regarded as foreigners. For this purpose, until the ratification of the Peace Treaty, a decree will be proclaimed whereby all persons having no nationality, who participated in the war or who were born in and reside in the country and descend from parents born there, are to be immediately regarded as Roumanian subjects with full rights." [70]

The racial policies of the National Socialist Government are not those of the founders of modern Germany; not even of those of most conservative tendencies. For, in matters relating to the preservation and extension of religious liberty, and its concomitant civil and political equality, there are no radicals or conservatives. The absolute Prussian monarchy of Hardenberg's day, Bismarck's united and triumphant Reich and the Germany of the Kaiser, which underwent the trials and tribulations of the World War, all intervened in the affairs of backward states in order to assure religious, civil and political equality to all, including the Jews. In defending the oppressed, Hardenberg, Bismarck and the Kaiser's Government championed the "laws of humanity." In the light of the "laws of humanity," the National Socialist policies stand condemned, and the international community is authorized to intercede in order to bring relief to the victims of oppression.

70. Temperley, *op. cit.*, III, p.48.

CHAPTER TWO

INTERNATIONAL LEGAL ASPECTS OF GERMAN NATIONAL SOCIALIST POLICIES

WE have seen that the persecution of minorities as a deliberate national policy has long been regarded by the states of the world as justifying and requiring peaceful intercession on grounds of humanity. Are there, in addition, any specific principles of international law which are being violated by the present German Government in its treatment of "non-Aryans"? Do these violations give states injured thereby a right to protest to the German Government?

The right of a state to legislate towards its own nationals or those within its jurisdiction is not an absolute power the illegal consequences of which other states, or the international community, are obliged to suffer in silence. Nor is it a right unlimited by the prescriptions of international law. On the contrary, it is a right which may be abridged either by obligations undertaken to another state that require the observance of a certain course of action or limited by the sovereign rights of other states that may be infringed thereby. As the Permanent Court of International Justice declared in sustaining the plea of the German State against Poland:

> "With regard to international law, and of the Court which is charged with its application, national laws are simple facts, manifestations of will and of state activity, on the same level as judicial decisions or administrative measures. The Court is certainly not bound to interpret the Polish law as such, but there is no obstacle to its pronouncing on the question whether, in applying this law, Poland is or is not acting in conformity with its obligations. . . ."[1]

1. Judgments 6 and 7 of the Court concerning certain rights and inter-

Even the German National Socialist Government has acknowledged the fact that its internal legislation cannot be allowed to hamper the fulfillment of its international obligations.[2]

"A State cannot," the Permanent Court has held, "adduce as against another State its own Constitution with a view to evading obligations incumbent upon it under international law or treaties in force."[3]

Therefore, the policies adopted and carried into effect by the German Government toward those within its jurisdiction are not according to the principles of international law by definition, unalterably, or exclusively a domestic question. To the extent that they constitute a violation by Germany of an international obligation incumbent upon her, or directly result in certain denials of right toward other states, they partake, so to speak, of an international character and are subject to the rules and principles of the law of nations. For, even in the absence of a formal obligation or undertaking, in so far as the action of the German Government directly results in the infringement of the sovereignty of other states, the rules of international law apply and the defense of do-

ests in Upper Silesia, *Publications of the Permanent Court of International Justice* (hereafter cited as *Publications*), Series A, p.19.

2. See statements of Herr von Keller before the 73rd Council, League of Nations, *Official Journal* (hereafter cited as *O.J.*), May 26th and June 6th, 1933. Also, in 1929, the German Government, replying to a questionnaire of the Preparatory Committee for the Conference for the Codification of International Law, declared: "Obviously, as international law is binding on all members of the community governed by international law, a state cannot disclaim responsibility by appealing to the provisions of its municipal law." (Conference for the Codification of International Law, *Bases of Discussion*, Vol. 3, *League Document*, C. 75, M. 69, 1929, V. p.167.) Article 14 of the Constitution of the German Republic, which is legally still in force, declares that the generally recognized rules of international law are binding in the German Reich.
3. Advisory Opinion on the Status of the Free City of Danzig, *Publications*, Series A/B No. 44, p.24.

mestic jurisdiction as an exclusive principle falls. No state may, the Permanent Court has held, successfully raise the defense of exclusive domestic jurisdiction as an absolute bar to the application of rules of international law, even in matters the jurisdiction over which in principle belongs to that state.[4]

It was in full recognition of this fact that the Committee of Jurists appointed by the Council of the League to determine whether the dispute between Finland and Sweden over the ethnic minority in the Åland Islands arose out of a "matter which by international law is solely within the jurisdiction of Finland" decided that, although Finland possessed sovereignty over the islands, the legal question involved was not one solely of domestic jurisdiction.[5] Despite the fact that there was no specific treaty limiting Finland's right to dispose of the islands as it pleased, the Committee agreed with the Swedish contention that "even though the question originated in a domestic state of affairs, it could have international consequences, and therefore take on an international character." [6] Subsequently, a Committee of Rapporteurs appointed by the Council to consider the merits of the question held that it was not the intrinsic nature of the issue which gave it an international character, but the "extension and international importance" which it had assumed and which took it out of the field of purely domestic jurisdiction.[7]

It is clear, then, that besides the existence of specific undertakings which may restrict its full freedom of action, international law imposes another limitation upon the right of a

4. Advisory Opinion No. 4, Tunis Morocco Nationality Decrees Case, *Publications*, Series B, No. 4, p.24.
5. *O.J.*, Sp. Supp. No. 3, October, 1920.
6. The legal question, in this particular instance, was whether Finland had a *de jure* right to the islands.
7. Committee of Rapporteurs on the Åland Islands Dispute, *Report*, published by the Ministry of Foreign Affairs, Stockholm, 1921, II, pp.76, 102.

state to legislate toward those within its jurisdiction. That is to say, even though the state may be acting in a sphere which international law leaves to it as a "reserved domain" of jurisdiction, the use of this right, recognized in principle, may degenerate into such an abuse of power that a violation of the rights of other states results.[8] In this eventuality, international law limits the subjective right of the legislating state and forbids an action which, because of its externally harmful social consequences, constitutes a denial of right to other states and to the international community. As Jackson H. Ralston, the Arbitrator in the Venezuelan cases, said:

> ". . . there may be a broad difference between the right to exercise a power and the rightful exercise of that power."[9]

The rule which imposes upon the possessor of a right the obligation *sic utere tuo ut alienum non laedas* (so use thine own as not to injure another) is well-established in international law.[10] Just as in any other society, the social peace and vital interests of the community of states may be violated by the unqualified freedom of action undertaken by one member without regard to the rights of others. The exercise of a power or competence which is in principle left to a state may, through arbitrary and indiscriminate use resulting in harmful social consequences, become an abuse of right, a violation of international law. Thus the *Institut de Droit International* has resolved that international law not only delimits "the domain of competence" left to states, but also applies to the manner and method of the exercise of that competence "in so

8. See Lauterpacht,H., *The Function of Law in the International Community* (Oxford, 1934).
9. The Boffolo Case, Ralston, Jackson,H., *Venezuelan Arbitrations of 1903*, p.70.
10. See Westlake,John, *International Law* (Cambridge, 1906), II, p.313.

far as it concerns other states or the international community."[11]

So firmly established is this rule of abuse of right that it was specifically mentioned as one of the "general principles of law recognized by civilized nations" which the Permanent Court of International Justice is obliged to apply to the cases brought before it. The Committee of Jurists which met at The Hague in 1920 to draft the Statute of the Court acknowledged it as a tacit rule in the judicial process.[12] M. Ricci-Busatti declared that if the action of a state was not contrary to any admitted rule of international law but within the sphere of its sovereign competence, it would still be necessary to apply the principle of "abuse of right" and other doctrines of equity and justice.[13] Lord Phillimore agreed that this principle was one of the general rules of law which the Court would be bound to use.

It is clear, then, that the actions and policies of the German Government in the exercise of her sovereign rights toward her nationals and those within her sphere of jurisdiction must nevertheless meet two tests imposed by the law of nations: they must be in conformity with her specifically accepted international undertakings; and they must observe the equally sovereign rights of other states and of the international community. For, as we have seen, if in the exercise of her rightful governing powers the German Government

11. In its meeting at Oslo in 1932 (*Annuaire de l'Institut de Droit International*, t.37). See also the Declaration of Rights and Duties of Nations adopted by the American Institute of International Law on January 16th, 1916 (20 *A.J.I.L.* Supp., 1926, p.311), and the Declaration approved by the Union Juridique Internationale on November 11th, 1919 (*Séances et travaux*, 2nd Session, 1929, p. 174).
12. *Procès Verbaux des Séances du Comité des Juristes* (The Hague, 1920), pp.314–5.
13. He gave as an example of the necessity of its application the conflict which may arise because of the exercise by a state of the right to define the limits of its territorial waters.

adopts policies and takes actions which are either maliciously designed to violate, or have the effect of infringing, the rights of other states, an abuse of power will have resulted, entailing the responsibility of the German State for a breach of international law.

In the light of these principles, therefore, the policies and methods employed by the National Socialist Government have raised certain serious questions of international law which justify the collective concern of the League of Nations and the community of states.

A. Violations of the Rights of Other States

There are three principal violations of the rights of other states for which the German National Socialist Government, by its deliberate abuse of power, is responsible under the rules of international law:

(1) The forced emigration of thousands of individuals from its jurisdiction and their imposition upon the territory of neighboring states;

(2) The denationalization of, and refusal to accord full diplomatic protection to, thousands of individuals who have thereby been cast stateless upon other countries; and

(3) The attempt to exercise extra-territorial criminal jurisdiction, which has taken the form of acts of violence and terrorism in the territory of neighboring states.

1. Forced Emigration

The avowed aim of the National Socialist Government is to force the emigration on a vast scale of the "non-Aryan" population of Germany.[14] This objective is being attained

14. For example the Reich Minister of Economics, Dr. Hjalmar Schacht, issued a decree in March, 1935, in consultation with the Reich Minister of Interior, Frick, which declared that "any measure which pro-

through a systematic program of discrimination and humiliation [15] which is calculated to induce the flight from their homes of hundreds of thousands of individuals. These refugees, both actual and potential, are, and will continue to be, forced to enter other lands where, largely penniless and without the protection of a state, they must exist as dependents, deprived of the most elementary human rights.[16]

The burden thus cast upon other states by this program of the National Socialist Government has already received the attention of the international community. The International Labour Conference in a resolution passed on June 29th, 1933, asked the Labour Office to study the economic and social effects of this large-scale emigration, for, as the resolution pointed out in justification of its concern:

> "Serious repercussions are to be expected in the adjacent countries to which these refugees have found their way. . . ." [17]

Likewise, the Fourteenth Assembly of the League of Nations in adopting the resolution establishing the Office of a High Commissioner for Refugees (Jewish and Other) Coming from Germany, based its action upon the fact that

motes the emigration of Jews must be welcomed." (*New York Times*, March 13th, 1935, p.13.) Thus "non-Aryans" have been allowed to carry on manual work only for the purpose of training for emigration. As for students the *Reichdevisenstelle*, in May, 1934, issued a circular encouraging the temporary emigration of "non-Aryan" students whose studies in foreign countries "may generally be considered as a desirable preparation for future emigration." Likewise, Minister of Education Rust has ordered that "non-Aryan" students may be granted permission to take examinations in the universities only if they are able to prove that they contemplate emigration (*Frankfurter Zeitung*, May 17th, 1934).

15. See *Letter of Resignation* of James G. McDonald, Annex.
16. See pp.60–1.
17. International Labour Conference, Seventeenth Session, Geneva, 1933, *Record of Proceedings*, p.687.

> ". . . their [the refugees'] presence in those countries constitutes an economic, financial and social problem which can be solved only by international collaboration."

Before the Second Committee of the Fourteenth Assembly, also, M. de Graeff, Delegate of the Netherlands, emphasized that

> ". . . in this period of unemployment it is out of the question that all these refugees could find means of existence in the countries bordering on Germany. As the result of the German Government's provisions for preventing the flight of capital, only very few of them have financial resources of their own." [18]

At the fourth meeting of the Governing Body of the High Commission for Refugees (Jewish and Other) Coming from Germany which was held on July 17th, 1935, Mr. James G. McDonald placed the total number of refugees and emigrants from Germany since the establishment of the National Socialist regime at approximately 80,000. Some 25,000 had emigrated to overseas countries, primarily Palestine and the United States of America; 17,000 more had emigrated overseas after residing in European countries; and over 25,000 were still living in European countries, principally France, The Netherlands, Great Britain, Czechoslovakia and Spain. Since then, however, thousands more, especially after the announcement of the Nuremberg laws in September, 1936, have been forced to take refuge in other countries; and it is estimated that by January, 1937 over 100,000 refugees had left Germany. At least one-fifth of the refugees in European countries are either actually dependent upon or in need of relief. This number has tended to increase as the restrictions on emigration with property have increased, forcing the

18. October 4th, 1933. *O.J.*, Sp. Supp. No. 117, pp.22–4.

refugees to become almost immediately dependent upon outside assistance. Furthermore, because the German government has taken drastic measures against those returning, not only preventing them from taking employment, but confining them in so-called "re-education camps," the High Commissioner reported that it was impossible to recommend in any case that persons who had left Germany should return.[19]

However well founded the right of a state to exercise jurisdiction over its territory, or to legislate with regard to its own nationals, it is a fundamental rule of international law that no state may with impunity violate the territorial sovereignty of other states. When the exercise of such a power casts a heavy burden upon other states, international law holds the legislating state guilty of an abuse of right and permits international concern with the cause of such an unwarranted imposition. As President Harrison of the United States said in his annual message on December 9th, 1891, speaking of the policies then pursued by Russia towards her Jewish subjects:

> "The banishment, whether by direct decree or by no less certain indirect methods, of so large a number of men and women is not a local question. A decree to leave one country is, in the nature of things, an order to enter another—some other. This consideration as well as the suggestions of humanity furnishes ample ground for the remonstrances which we have presented to Russia." [20]

19. High Commissioner to the Governing Body of the High Commission for Refugees (Jewish and Other) Coming from Germany, *Report*, July 17th, 1935, Fourth Meeting, London, p.18. See also the *Voelkischer Beobachter* of March 9th, 1935, which confessed that the purpose of this incarceration was to prevent non-Aryans and other refugees from returning to Germany.

20. *Foreign Relations*, 1891, p.xiii; Moore, J.B., *Digest of International Law* (Washington, 1906), VI, p.359.

In other words, even though a state expel—whether directly or by indirect compulsion—its own nationals, the violation of international law consists in the burden thus placed upon receiving states. So basic a principle of international justice is the rule forbidding the forced emigration of nationals of the expelling state that, as one authority has written, "it is taken for granted even when it is not expressed." [21] For, as has been recognized in numerous arbitral judgments, the unlimited right of a state to expel its own nationals or aliens from its territory involves a reciprocal relationship, and the consent of a second state to receive the individuals in question.[22] Since this right, therefore, is by its very nature an imposition upon some other state, it is subject to the most severe restriction to prevent its abuse and is always open to review by an international tribunal.[23] "The country exercising the power of expulsion must," decided Ralston in the Boffolo case,[24] "when occasion demands, state the reason of such expulsion before an international tribunal, and an insufficient reason, or none, being advanced, accept the consequences." [25] Indeed, the German Government itself

21. De Boeck, C., *Recueil des Cours*, 1927, III, Vol. 18, p.443.
22. Ralston,J.H., *Venezuelan Arbitrations of 1903:* The Oliva Case (p.771); the Paquet Case (p.265); the Boffolo Case (pp.696, 705). Moore,J.B., *A History and Digest of International Arbitrations*, Vol. V, pp.3347, 4936. La Pradelle and Politis, *Recueil des Arbitrages Internationaux* (1906), I, pp.512 et seq., 472, 552–6. Cf. also Report of Uribari, Arbitrator in the Arata Affair, September 30th, 1901, given in Descamps and Renault, *Recueil des Traitês du XXe Siècle*, I, p.709.
23. "La conscience juridique universelle proteste contre l'usage arbitraire du droit d'expulsion," von Bar, K.L., in *Journal de Droit International Privê*, XIII, p.6.
24. *Op. cit.*, p.696. Although the Boffolo case involved the expulsion of an alien, Ralston's decision emphasized the imposition upon the receiving state rather than the principle of diplomatic protection of nationals.
25. Furthermore, the abuse of power resulting from an exercise of the right of expulsion which infringes upon the sovereignty of other states has been declared to be a violation of international law by the

has declared that an abuse of the right of expulsion is "contrary to all prescriptions of international law."[26] When, following the peace settlement, large numbers of Germans living in the Rhine region of Alsace and Lorraine were expelled by the French Government, Germany invoked the principles of international law as well as "considerations of justice and humanity," and pointed out the exceptional severity of the measures taken which would not even allow the expelled persons to bring with them all of their property and violated a promise given some years previously that they would be allowed to remain in peace.[27]

Because a state permits refugees from Germany to enter upon its territory, it is not thereby estopped from claiming that the German Government has imposed this burden upon it without its consent. For, in order to prevent this burden from being cast upon them, receiving states would have to commit two violations of international law: they would have to forbid the access of all Germans to their territory, which would violate the terms of the treaties of friendship and commerce which they have signed with Germany and would give

Institut de Droit International, "Projet de Règlementation de l'Expulsion des Étrangers" (Article 11), September, 1891, in its meeting at Hamburg: "A state cannot, either by administrative or judicial procedure expel its own nationals whatever may be their differences of religion, race, or national origin. Such an act constitutes a grave violation of international law when its international result is to cast upon other territories individuals suffering from such a condemnation or even placed merely under the pressure of judicial proscription." *Annuaire*, t. XI, pp.278–9. See also the "Règles Internationales sur l'Admission et l'Expulsion des Étrangers," adopted by the *Institut* on September 12th, 1892, at Geneva. *Annuaire*, t. XII, p.219.

26. *Le Temps*, August 14th, 1922, p.2.

27. "Mass expulsion," the German Government wrote "which arbitrarily and suddenly deprives hundreds of nationals of a state of the means of existence is contrary to all prescriptions of international law and all considerations of justice and humanity. . . . The German Government submits the most energetic protest against the measures taken and against those which the French Government still envisages." *Ibid.*

the latter a right to retaliate in kind; and, they would have to renounce their sovereign right to grant asylum to victims of persecution.[28] No state can be required, in order to assert a right under international law, either to commit a violation of law or to forego its own sovereign rights. The fact that receiving states do not expel refugees from Germany back to the country which persecutes them, or that they do not bar their frontiers to individuals coming from Germany, does not spell out consent on their part to receive the burden imposed upon them by the policies of the National Socialist Government.

In three notable instances the violation of international law constituted by such large scale forced emigrations has been pointed out by states suffering from the abuse and has been made the grounds for international protest. In each case the international action was taken not on behalf of the nationals of the protesting state but rather on behalf of the nationals of the expelling state; and, in each case, denying the latter's unlimited right to treat its own nationals as it pleased without concern for the rights of other states. The three cases in question were parallel in many respects to the present forced emigration of individuals from Germany: the system of legislative discrimination toward its Jewish population which was adopted by the Roumanian Government after 1878; the policies of the Tsarist *régime* of Russia during

28. See p.71. The right of a state to grant asylum to individuals who are fleeing from persecution and discrimination is commonly recognized in international law. States can no more be required to refuse entry to refugees than they can be made to extradite a political offender. In the case of *U.S. ex rel Giletti* v. *Commissioner of Immigration* (35 F. 2d, 687, C.C.A. 2d, 1929) it was held that the deportation to Italy of an anti-Fascist would be equivalent to extradition for a political offense, and since it was the traditional policy and right of the United States not to assist in the prosecution of political offenders against foreign states, it would not bring about the same result even as an incident in the enforcement of its own laws.

the late nineteenth century; and the refusal by Turkey following the war to receive back its Armenian nationals. In each instance, the violation of international law was held to consist not in the breach of a treaty obligation, but in the abuse of the right of expulsion through the forcing of a mass emigration of nationals of the state in question.

Although the United States of America was not a party to the Treaty of Berlin, the burden of emigration which fell upon it as a result of the Roumanian persecution of the Jews gave Secretary of State John Hay the right to say, "The act of Roumania itself has effectively joined the United States to them [the signatories] as an interested party."[29] "Every Government welcomes," the Note ran, "the voluntary immigration of aliens under conditions fitting them to become merged in the body politic" of the country. But, nevertheless, "it behooves the state to scrutinize most jealously the character of the immigration from a foreign land and if it be obnoxious to objection, to examine the causes which render it so." The general principle governing this forced emigration in international law was expressed by the American Government in the following terms:

> "Should these causes [for emigration] originate in the act of another sovereign State to the detriment of its neighbours, it is the prerogative of an injured State to point out the evil and make remonstrance; for with nations, as with individuals, the social law holds good that the right of each is bounded by the right of the neighbour."

There was not, the Note acknowledged, an actual order of expulsion; but this result was being attained through "the cumulative effect of successive restrictions" which gave human beings in such circumstances "no alternative but

29. American Circular Note to the Great Powers, August 11th, 1902, *Foreign Relations* (1902), pp.910 et seq., 42 et seq. and 550.

submissive suffering or flight." The United States, therefore, considered that such emigration was "a burden to the community upon which the fugitives may be cast." And although the United States offered "asylum to the oppressed of all lands . . . its sympathy with them in no wise impairs its just liberty and right to weigh the acts of the oppressor in the light of their effects upon this country, and to judge accordingly." Its protest was for that reason based both on the grounds of humanity and upon the resultant "injury to itself." [30]

Likewise the United States established its right to protest against Russia's treatment of her Jewish population on the legal principle of abuse of power.[31] In Secretary of State Blaine's Instructions to the American Minister on February 18th, 1891 he pointed out that this policy on the part of Russia raised for other states "the difficult problem of affording an immediate asylum to the million or more of exiles without seriously deranging the conditions of labour and of social organization in other communities. . . ." This burden created the violation of international law and equity.

> "The government of the United States," Blaine wrote forcefully, "does not assume to dictate the internal policy of other nations, or to make suggestions as to what their municipal laws should be, or as to the manner in which they should be administered. Nevertheless, *the mutual duties of nations require that each should use its power with a due regard for the results which its exercise produces on the rest of the world.*" [italics ours.] [32]

The Conference of Lausanne in 1923 was also concerned with the right of a state to persecute its own nationals and to force them to take refuge in neighbouring lands. The Turkish

30. See above, p.18.
31. *Foreign Relations*, 1891, pp.737–9.
32. See also President Harrison's statement on this question, above, p.52.

Government had refused to allow the Armenians, who had left its territory during the war, to return and had later confiscated the property left behind by them. When the Conference turned to a discussion of this action, the Turkish Government raised the defense that her treatment of her own nationals was a domestic affair, not ruled by international law, and outside the scope of international concern.[33] All the states represented refused to accept this contention and turned to a consideration of the principles of humanity and the canons of international law which were thus being violated.

The American Delegation first drew the attention of the Conference to the fact that the amnesty granted by Turkey after the war did not include the Armenian refugees and pointed out that "the commonly accepted principles of humanity demand that disposition be taken on behalf of the Armenians and other refugees." [34]

But, as Mr. Richard Washburn Child, the representative of the United States, pointed out, in addition to the duty of defending the interests of humanity there was an obligation to preserve the principles of international law. "We believe," he said, "that recent precedents, appearing to establish the right of nations to expel large numbers of their citizens who consequently are destined to come under the protection of other nations, must be attentively examined before being favourably welcomed, so as to avoid the result that a new and reprehensible practice may be allowed to contradict international law and justice." [35]

33. Conference of Lausanne, *Sous-Comité des Minorités*, Procès-Verbal, No. 14, January 2nd, 1923, p.529.
34. *Ibid.*, Procès-Verbal, No. 11, December 29th, 1922, p.501.
35. Conference of Lausanne, *Recueil des Actes* (Paris, 1923), Première Série, I, Procès-Verbal de la Première Commission, No. 13, December 12th, 1922, p.167.

Toward the opening of the second part of the Conference, Sir Horace Rumbold of Great Britain spoke of the "serious denial of the rights of minorities" which this action represented and furthermore refused to grant that a state could without a violation of international law thus infringe upon the rights of other states. "It is also," he added, "the commission of an injustice toward the countries in which they [the refugees] have found temporary asylum, because no country has a right to leave its nationals indefinitely as charges of another state." [36] General Pellé of France, M. Montagna of Italy and M. Venizelos of Greece associated themselves with the words of Sir Horace Rumbold.

When, in the following meeting of the First Committee, the Turkish representative refused to allow its right "to take measures of security against elements of disorder" to be questioned,[37] Mr. Ryan of Great Britain reminded him that "the injustice committed would not only affect the individuals directly hurt by it, but also the countries adjacent to Turkey which had to shelter all these exiles." It would be, as General Pellé declared, a dangerous innovation in international public law.[38] For, he said, "one of the essential rules of international law demands that if these refugees committed no crime they must be allowed to return to their homes." [39] There was no right whatsoever according to which a state could "permanently exile hundreds of thousands of its own nationals who, if they were suitably treated, would contribute to its force and its prosperity." [40]

It is this same principle of international law which the

36. *Recueil*, 2e Série (Paris, 1923), Procès-Verbal, No. 9, May 19th, 1923, p.98.
37. *Ibid.*, Procès-Verbal, No. 11, p.130.
38. *Ibid.*, p.131.
39. *Ibid.*, Procès-Verbal, No. 12, p.157.
40. *Ibid.*, p.157.

German Government has defied in forcing thousands of its nationals to flee from its territory and to seek refuge in neighboring states of asylum. The defense of sovereignty and domestic jurisdiction can no more justify such expulsion and its effects in infringing upon the territorial sovereignty of other states than could the arguments of Turkey, of Russia or of Roumania silence the voices of protest from the international community or render inoperative the fundamental principles of international law. The international community has a legitimate and proper interest in the discontinuance of such an abuse of power and an obligation to safeguard the basic laws of the society of states.

2. *Denationalization and Withdrawal of State Protection*

Another serious violation by the German Government of the rights of other states has resulted from the withdrawal of German citizenship and nationality from "non-Aryans" who are consequently left either stateless or without diplomatic protection.

By the terms of the Reich Citizenship Law of September, 1935, all persons of "non-German or cognate blood" are deprived of German citizenship. This withdrawal of civil and political rights applies to individuals more than one of whose four grandparents were Jewish. It reduces almost one million of such persons to the status of guests or wards of the state and takes away from them all rights as against the state which thus disowns them. It is even questionable whether by this law persons of "non-German blood" are considered to be "nationals" of the German state, that is, entitled to the diplomatic protection of the Reich. For, German nationality is granted by this decree only to those who belong to the "protective association" of the German Reich. If, in fact, all those of "non-German blood," over a million persons, are deprived of nationality by this legislation, then serious questions of international law and widespread international difficulties inevitably arise.

This ambiguity has been resolved for thousands of individuals by the specific revocation by the Government of their German nationality on grounds of their "racial origin" or political views.

This punitive measure has been taken, in most instances, after the individual has been forced to leave his home as a refugee and seek shelter in another country. It has had the effect of creating a mass of stateless refugees in the countries immediately bordering upon Germany, and in depriving the preponderant number of refugees of state protection. For, even those refugees whose nationality or naturalization has not been withdrawn have been faced with the refusal on the part of the German consular authorities to grant them the full and complete protection which is accorded other German citizens. In effect, they too have been made virtually stateless. Those individuals naturalized between 1918 and 1933, whose nationality has been withdrawn and who still remain in Germany are regarded as aliens and may be expelled.[41]

The Law of July 14th, 1933, provides for the Withdrawal of Naturalization and the Loss of German Nationality in the following cases: [42]

> (1) Where a person has been naturalized during the period between November 9th, 1918, and January 30th, 1933, and where his naturalization is now regarded as "undesirable" (Article 1);
>
> (2) Where a German national, residing abroad, has "prejudiced German interests by an attitude contrary to

41. Law of March 23rd, 1934, regarding expulsion from the Reich, *Reichsgesetzblatt*, No. 32.
42. *Reichsgesetzblatt*, No. 81, 1933, I, p.480.

his duty of loyalty" towards the Reich; or has refused to return when ordered to do so by the Minister of the Interior (Article 2).

The manner in which the decisive question of Article 1 is to be decided, namely, whether the naturalization of a person is regarded as "desirable," has also been set forth by law. The Acting Reich Minister of the Interior, Pfundtner, issued a decree on July 26th, 1933,[43] which declared that it should be determined according to "national racial" principles, and that in this connection the following were especially undesirable as German nationals:

(1) Jews from East European countries (Austria, Poland, Czechoslovakia, etc.), and

(2) Criminals, or those who have acted detrimentally to the welfare of the Reich or nation.[44]

The law also provides that denationalization shall likewise cancel the national status of members of the victim's family. In the case of revocation of naturalization, the persons who would not have acquired nationality but for the act of the naturalized individual automatically lose their nationality together with him. For those whose nationality is withdrawn because of their alleged hostility towards the National Socialist Government, it is to be decided in each case to what an extent this denationalization will apply to the spouse and legitimate or adopted children. Furthermore, their goods and property in Germany may be confiscated.

By January 1st, 1937, a total of 4,545 withdrawals of nationality had been announced and officially published in the *Deutsche Reichsanzeiger*, the official gazette. Of this number, 4,409 were revocations of naturalizations (particularly of

43. *Ibid.*, No. 87, 1933.
44. I.e., those who oppose the National Socialist régime.

Jews of Eastern European origin and their families) on the basis of Article 1 of the Law of July 14th; and 136 were withdrawals of nationality from those who as refugees had written or spoken in opposition to the National Socialist Government. The following table illustrates the persistency with which this process is being carried out:

PERIOD	ARTICLE 1		ARTICLE 2	TOTAL
	Total individuals	*Wives and children*		
1933				
August 25th	—	—	33	33
1934				
Jan.–March	199	93	36	235
April–June	292	111	—	292
July–Sept......	233	82	—	233
Oct.–Dec	283	110	28	311
1935				
Jan.–March	1,322	659	—	1,322
April–June......	831	275	39	870
July–Sept......	841	257	—	841
Oct.–Dec	408	212	—	408
Totals....	4,409	1,799	136	4,545

Such denationalization results in statelessness for entire families, including even children born in Germany. For, the nationality laws of practically every state in the world provide that after naturalization the loss of the former nationality results and that no automatic resumption is possible.[45]

45. The Polish Law of Nationality of January 20th, 1920, declares that "Polish citizenship shall be lost by acquiring foreign citizenship" (Article 11). The Austrian Law of July 30th, 1925, as well as the Nationality Laws of the other East European States, contain the same provision. See Flournoy, Richard, and Hudson, Manley, *A Collection of Nationality Laws*, pp.18–9. This compilation is made from the official *Reich Government Journal*, and includes only those denationalizations which the Government has chosen to make public.

This dire penalty has been imposed upon those naturalized Jews of East European origin both retroactively and solely by reason of their descent. No fraudulent intent, no subsequent act of crime or of bad faith, no deed of commission or omission need be adduced to justify the denationalization. The extreme vagueness of the law, permitting the withdrawal of "undesirable" naturalizations, is sufficient to cover all cases. This arbitrary, retroactive denationalization applies, furthermore, to individuals who in order to become naturalized had to pass severe tests of character and morality. The German Law on Nationality [46] required that the applicant for naturalization show that he "has led a blameless life" and that he is "able . . . to support himself and his family."

Is Germany legally free to carry out this policy of wholesale denationalization? Although a state has the sovereign right, under international law, to accord, refuse or revoke nationality, this right is limited both by obligations undertaken restricting it and by the equally sovereign rights of other states. The latter are not bound to suffer in silence the harmful effects of such an exercise of power, nor are they obliged to permit the defense of sovereignty to condone violations of international law and equity.

That questions of nationality are not merely a matter of domestic concern, but ruled by international law, has been decided by the Permanent Court of International Justice in its Advisory Opinion on the French nationality decrees in Tunis and Morocco.[47] In defending its sovereign right to legislate without interference regarding the nationality of those within its jurisdiction, the French Government argued that

46. The German Law of July 22nd, 1913, may be found in Flournoy, R., and Hudson, M.O., *op. cit.*, p.307.
47. *Publications*, Series B, No. 4.

this was a fundamental prerogative the exercise of which was solely a domestic matter.[48] The British Government pointed out [49] that the right of a state to legislate with regard to nationality has its origin in and is strictly limited by the territorial sovereignty of a state. Those acts of a state whose immediate effects fell into the territorial sovereignty of another state could not be defended as solely within the legislating state's jurisdiction. That domestic jurisdiction, the "reserved domain," is limited only to "matters of ordinary domestic and internal activity such for example as immigration or tariff laws and regulations," and cannot be extended "to matters which in any degree involve external operation or application." [50] The Court, upholding the British plea as to the jurisdiction, pointed out that "the question to be considered is not whether one of the parties to the dispute is or is not competent in law to take or refrain from taking a particular action, but whether the jurisdiction claimed belongs *solely* to that party." [51] And the answer to that question "depends upon the development of international relations." [52] For, thought the Court, "it may well happen that in a matter which like that of nationality is not, in principle, regulated by international law, the right of a state to use its discretion is nevertheless restricted by obligations which it may have undertaken toward other states. In such a case, jurisdiction which in principle belongs solely to the State, is limited by rules of international law. . . ." Then the plea of domestic

48. *Publications*, Actes et Documents, Series C, No. 2, Supp. Vol., pp.1–32.
49. *Ibid.*, pp.33–64.
50. *Ibid.*, p.64. "By reason of the interdependence of states, of their mutual solidarity, in fact, it frequently happens that questions which would appear most naturally to be matters of domestic sovereignty affect the interests of neighbouring states." Scelle,G., *Pacte de la Société des Nations*, p.312.
51. *Ibid.* Great Britain relied upon a treaty limiting France's right.
52. *Publications*, Series B, No. 4, p.24.

jurisdiction will not be sustained and "the dispute as to the question whether a State has or has not the right to take certain measures becomes in these circumstances a dispute of an international character. . . ." [53]

Just as the right of a state to confer nationality by naturalization is limited to those individuals resident in its territory, and may not be exercised towards non-resident nationals of another state, so the right to withdraw nationality is strictly limited by territorial considerations and the rights of other states to be free from injury and the burden created thereby.[54]

The German Government itself has consistently affirmed these principles. In its official Reply sent to the Questionnaire of the Preparatory Committee for the Conference on Codification of International Law [55] it declared:

> "The general principle that all questions relating to the acquisition or loss of a specific nationality shall be governed by the laws of the State whose nationality is claimed or contested should be admitted. *The application of this principle, however, should not go beyond the limits at which the legislation of one State encroaches on the sovereignty of another.*" (p.13.)

53. *Ibid.*, p.24. "Though, generally speaking, it is true that a sovereign state has the right to decide what persons shall be regarded as its nationals, it is no less true that this principle is applicable only subject to the Treaty obligations referred to above." Advisory Opinion of the Court in the case of the Polish Nationality Decrees, *Publications*, Series B, No. 7, p.10.
54. Article 2 of the Draft Convention on Nationality prepared by the Harvard Research in International Law reads: "Under international law, the power of a state to confer its nationality is not unlimited." *American Journal of International Law*, Supp. Vol. 23, April, 1929, p.24. In a resolution at its annual meeting in 1928, the *Institut de Droit International* declared itself "faithful to the principle that questions of nationality are not left to the exclusive decision of individual states, but submitted to the increasing competence of international law." *Annuaire de l'Institut*, XXXIV, 1928, p.760.
55. *League of Nations Document* C. 73, M. 38, 1929, V.

This general principle of international law, forbidding the abuse of power by a state in granting or withdrawing nationality, was not only freely recognized by the German Government. It was positively accepted by at least fifteen states in their replies to the Questionnaire.[56] The British reply mentioned "the possibility that the right of a State to use its discretion in legislating with regard to nationality may be restricted by duties which it owes to other States." The Note of the United States pointed out that

> "the scope of municipal laws governing nationality must be regarded as limited by considerations of the rights and obligations of individuals and of other States. The reason for this is that true nationality involves a reciprocal relationship."[57]

It is because these denationalizations have been generally applied to refugees, because they have been coupled with the forced emigration of these thousands of individuals, that their effect is immediately and directly felt in the territorial domains of the states of refuge. In casting this additional burden upon neighboring states, the German government has, in the words of its own Reply to the League Questionnaire, "encroached on their sovereignty." It has abused its power to denationalize by a wholesale imposition of thousands of stateless individuals upon other states; it has, in effect, denied the rights of the states of refuge to deport (if they so desire) these stateless individuals back to their land of origin; and it has not observed its signature of a specific international undertaking to direct its efforts toward the abolition of all cases of statelessness.

56. The states accepting this principle were: Germany, the United States, Great Britain and the Dominions, India, Japan, Czechoslovakia, France, Austria, Belgium, Switzerland, The Netherlands, Roumania and Finland.

57. *Document* C. 73, M. 38, 1929, V, pp.145–6.

(a) *The Burden Imposed upon Neighboring States*

It is evident that the withdrawal of state protection and the creation of thousands of stateless individuals by the German Government increases the weight of the burden imposed upon other states by the forced mass emigration from Germany. According to recognized prescriptions of international law, the denationalization by a government of thousands of persons, especially if they have been forced to find refuge in other states where the resultant statelessness creates special difficulties, is an abuse of power which gives the receiving state injured thereby grounds for protest and an appeal to the law of nations.[58]

For the act of denationalizing an individual after he has entered, and while he remains in, the territory of another state on the basis of a passport of his own state, directly violates the right of the receiving state to expel or deport him to his country of origin which has thus repudiated its national.[59] Consequently, international law recognizes as between states, if not as between an individual and his state, not only the right of diplomatic protection of nationals but the international duty of continuing protection until and unless it may be withdrawn without violating the rights of other states.

The arbitrary and wholesale denationalization of individuals residing on foreign territory is an abuse of power when its effects are felt within the territorial jurisdiction of other sovereign states. There is no right of "omnipotence," Sir John Fischer Williams wrote, which gives a state the unqualified right to "destroy the tie that links it to a subject or citizen." On the contrary, he points out, no state can "of its

58. Cogordan, G., *La Nationalité*, 2nd Edition, Paris, 1890, p.287; Lehr, E., *Traité de Droit International Privé*, I, p.492, p.366.
59. Every state is obliged to receive back its own nationals, but is not bound to admit aliens. Oppenheim, L., *International Law*, Vol. I, Section 294; Fauchille, P., *op. cit.*, I, Section 451.

own sole authority sever the link which binds it to its own nationals in such a way as to be no longer compellable to receive back the person denationalized if another state should wish to deport him." [60] For this would involve the consequence that a state in the exercise of its own right could deprive other states of their equally sovereign rights. The duty of continuing its protection is not a "duty which the state owes to the individuals concerned; it is an international duty which it owes to its fellow states" whose rights cannot be destroyed by the unilateral action of the denationalizing state without a breach of the "sound principles of international law." [61]

Professor Heinrich Triepel, authority on international law at the University of Berlin, wrote in 1929:

> "A legislating state does not have the unlimited right to choose the criteria for acquisition and loss of nationality, nor the unlimited right of naturalizing or denationalizing its own citizens." [62]

He declared that "an arbitrary extension of the ordinary criteria for the acquisition and loss of nationality is, if it works to the injury of another country, a violation of public international law." [63]

At the meetings of the First Committee of the Hague Codification Conference, the representatives of The Netherlands

60. *Chapters on Current International Law and the League of Nations* (London, 1929), p.137. "It is of the essence of the conception of international law that states are members of a community and therefore in the sphere of their mutual relations owe duties one to another." (*Ibid.*, p.136.)
61. *Chapters on Current International Law and the League of Nations* (London, 1929), p.188.
62. Triepel, Heinrich, "Internationale Regelung der Staatzangehörigkeit," *Zeitschrift für Ausländisches Offentliches Recht und Völkerrecht* (1929) I, pp.185–99 at p.195.
63. *Ibid.*, p.196.

Belgium, Portugal, Poland and Mexico, in particular, pointed out that an abuse of the right of denationalization was contrary to international law. The representative of Mexico said: "If the principle of the freedom of a state to legislate on a matter of nationality is stated in the Convention, it should be understood and it is conditional upon the principle that it should not abuse its right, and international tribunals shall decide . . . if a state has used or abused its right." [64]

In the course of the discussion before the League Council on January 24th, 1936, on the problem of the German refugees, M. Massigli, the representative of France, asserted this principle and recommended the establishment of a standard Convention defining and limiting the power of States to denationalize their citizens.[65] Subsequently, before the Sixth Committee of the last Assembly (1936) the French delegation referred to the difficulties created by the practice of Germany in withdrawing protection from its nationals residing abroad. It expressed the hope that the attention of all countries, both members and non-members of the League, would be drawn to this serious problem which might act as a disturbing factor in international relations.[66] Upon the recommendation of the Sixth Committee, the Assembly adopted a resolution noting the

64. The Conference for the Codification of International Law, 1930, *Acts*, Vol. 2, Minutes of the First Committee, Nationality, C. 351 (a), M. 145 (a), 1930, V, p.198. See also pp.20, 26, 197–9. It was in recognition of this fact that the Institute of International Law as early as 1896 at its Venice meeting adopted the principle that: "Denationalization can never be imposed as a penalty," and that "no person can lose his nationality without having acquired another." *Resolutions of the Institute of International Law*, published by the Carnegie Endowment for International Peace, "Nationality and Expatriation," Article 6, p.135.

65. League of Nations, Minutes of the 90th Session of the Council, Sixth Meeting, *Document* C.

66. *Cf.* the Report submitted by the Sixth Committee to the Assembly on "International Assistance to Refugees," *League Document* A. 73, 1936, XII, p.4.

serious difficulties which had been thus created and expressing "the earnest hope that this practice may be discontinued." [67]

This breach of international law in denationalization takes place, in normal cases, when the receiving state demands that the denationalizing state take back its former national. But if the receiving state, in accordance with its right to grant asylum and in harmony with its humanitarian sentiments, is unwilling to deport a denationalized individual to the country which is persecuting him, the breach of international law takes place immediately upon denationalization. For, by refusing to exercise their right of demanding that Germany receive back her denationalized refugees, and by extending asylum to these persons from the imprisonment and discrimination which would await them in Germany, other states are not thereby estopped from asserting that their right to deport has been effectively denied. It would be contrary to all principles of international law and equity if a state would be obliged to commit an act of inhumanity, or to give up its sovereign right to grant asylum, before it could maintain that its *right* to deport (whether or not it desires to do so) had been destroyed by the act of denationalization.

In fact, the right of a state to deport an individual is the more flagrantly denied when the person concerned has sought asylum from political or religious persecution; even in extradition proceedings, states are unwilling to hand over such individuals to the governments who seek to punish or persecute them. "In insisting upon its right to expel them [the denationalized refugees] to the parent state," writes a leading American authority, "the state of asylum would be violating a humanitarian duty." [68]

67. *Ibid.*, p.5.
68. Preuss,L., "International Law and Deprivation of Nationality," *Georgetown Law Journal*, January, 1935, p.274. See also p.55.

In carrying out its policy of wholesale denationalization the German Government has failed to honor both its freely undertaken international obligations and its elementary duties towards other states. It is the task of the League of Nations, in view of the Council's resolution taking note of the suggestions of the Hague Conference and of the Assembly resolution of 1936, to remind the German Government of the juridical principles which are being violated by it, and to take appropriate action to defend both the principles of international law and the fundamental rights of those states which are forced to bear the burden of this abuse of power.

(*b*) *The Breach of Undertaking*

At the Conference for the Codification of International Law which was held at The Hague in 1930, the representative of the German Government, Herr Hering, expressed "regret at the abusive use which has been made of denationalization since the war, with the consequent increase in the number of stateless persons." [69]

Inspired by the German plea, and in conformity with the expressions of other Governments, this Conference drew up a Convention on Certain Questions Relating to the Conflict of Nationality Laws [70] in the preamble to which the High Contracting Parties set forth their convictions on this question. "Being convinced," they agreed, "that it is in the general interest of the international community to secure that all its members should recognize that every person should have a nationality and one nationality only; recognizing accordingly that the ideal towards which the efforts of humanity should be directed in this domain is the abolition of all cases both of

69. Hague Conference for the Codification of International Law, *Acts*, Vol. I, *League Document* C. 351, M. 145, 1930, V, p.173.
70. *Ibid.*, p.81.

statelessness and of double nationality," they asserted in Article 1 the principle which the majority of states had stressed in their replies to the preliminary Questionnaire. Although this Article stated that "it is for each State to determine under its own law who are its nationals" other states need recognize this law only in so far as it is consistent with "international conventions, international custom, and the principles of law generally recognized with regard to nationality."[71] The German State, as well as thirty-three other states, has signed this Convention, a signature which under international law is not without legal force and creates a certain legal obligation toward the other signatories to work for "the abolition of all cases . . . of statelessness . . ."[72]

For, as the Turkish-Greek Mixed Arbitral Tribunal held in 1928, between the date of signature of a Treaty and its entry into force the contracting parties are under the obligation to do nothing which might impair the operation of its clauses or violate its intent and purpose.[73] The signature of a treaty, declared the League Committee on the Ratification and Signature of Conventions, "indicates an intention on the part of the Government of that country to make a full examination of the question with a view to putting the Convention

71. Thirty-four states signed this convention; and it was opened to accession by twenty-one others. *Official Journal*, No. 1, 1933, pp.79–80.

72. See Nisot, J., Member of the Legal Section of the Secretariat of the League, "La Force Obligatoire des Traités Signés, non encore Ratifiés," in *77 Journal du Droit International*, p.878. "La validité des accords internationaux n'est pas subordonnée à des conditions de forme; malgré que le traité, de par ses termes exprès, appelle des ratifications, il produira, avant le dépôt de ces dernières, les effets juridiques que ses stipulations indiquent comme devant intervenir alors" (p.819). Also see Wilcox,F.O., *The Ratification of International Conventions* (1935), p.27.

73. Decision of July 26th, 1928, in the case of *A.A.Megaladis* v. *Turkey*, reported in *Annual Digest of Public International Law Cases, 1927–28*, p.395. See also Fauchille,P., I, part III, p.320.

into force as far as it is concerned." [74] Having accepted such a limitation upon her right to aggravate further the problem of statelessness, having in fact acknowledged that "every person should have a nationality," the German Government has nevertheless repudiated its solemn signature.[75]

It should be noted, also, that the League Council in a resolution of May 15th, 1930, took note of the views expressed by the Conference on nationality questions and supported the suggestion that the League should "make efforts to contribute in so far as possible to the solution of the important and difficult problem of the stateless. . . ." [76] This gives the League the obligation of checking at the source the new fountain of statelessness created, even after the signing of the Hague Convention, by the German Government.

There is still another aspect of the breach by Germany of her obligations toward other states. Naturalization, and nationality itself, as the Reply of the United States Govern-

74. *League Document* A. 10, 1930, V, p.42.

75. The Final Act of the Hague Conference (*League Document* C. 228, M. 115, 1930, V) also declared that the states represented were "unanimously of the opinion that it is very desirable that states should, in the exercise of their power of regulating questions of nationality, make every effort to reduce so far as possible cases of statelessness," and urged the League to continue efforts in that direction. In fact, so anxious was the German Government to prevent the evil of statelessness that when in the First Committee on Nationality it was proposed by some delegations "to limit the grounds of denaturalization to faults of omission or commission—that is to say, grounds personal to the person who is denaturalized" (a limitation which would have rendered impossible the denaturalizations now being directed by Germany) the German delegation objected that such a rule would "give rise to new cases" and that "it does not sufficiently restrict the possibility of denaturalization." (*Acts of the Conference*, Vol. II, Minutes of the First Committee, *League Document* C. 351 [*a*], M. 145 [*a*], 1930, V, p.167.) In other words, the German Government in signing the Convention on the Conflict of Nationality Laws intended to restrict the possibility of denaturalization, even going so far as to refuse acceptance of a measure designed to that end because it was regarded as opening up possibilities of greater denaturalization.

76. *Official Journal*, June, 1930, p.547.

ment to the Questionnaire of the Codification Conference pointed out, "involves a reciprocal relationship,"[77] primarily between the individual and the state granting nationality, but also between the latter and the state of which the individual was formerly a national. Although the act of naturalization takes place *in form* between an individual and the state granting nationality, it implies in essence a tacit agreement between the naturalizing state and the state whose allegiance is renounced. The state whose allegiance is renounced may, for example, oblige the individual to perform certain unfulfilled obligations, may in fact refuse to regard the naturalization as binding it to any course of action. On the other hand, the acquiescence of the former state in the acceptance of a new nationality by an individual implies a tacit accord between the new and the former state of allegiance. This reciprocal nature of the naturalization process as it affects the rights and duties of states has been acknowledged in many instances: in the Minorities Treaties,[78] the nationality clauses of the Treaty of Versailles,[79] and in the great number of interstatal conventions regulating nationality since the war.[80]

The naturalization of East-European Jews by the German

77. See above, p.67.
78. Article 5 of the Treaty signed by Poland reads as follows: "Poland undertakes to put no hindrance in the way of the exercise of the right which the persons concerned have, under the Treaties concluded or to be concluded by the Allied and Associated Powers with Germany, Austria, Hungary, or Russia, to choose whether or not they will acquire Polish nationality."
79. Article 91, paragraph 3: "Within a period of two years after the coming into force of the present Treaty, German nationals over eighteen years of age habitually resident in any of the territories recognized as forming part of Poland will be entitled to opt for German nationality." Article 278: "Germany undertakes to recognize any new nationality which has been or may be acquired by her nationals under the laws of the Allied and Associated Powers . . . and to regard such persons as having . . . in all respects severed their allegiance to their country of origin."
80. See Flournoy,R., and Hudson,M.O., *op. cit.*, part II.

State after the war was an acceptance by Germany of an obligation both toward the naturalized individuals and toward the states of which they were until then nationals. Toward the individuals, who in order to become naturalized had fulfilled stringent tests of character and loyalty,[81] and who in fact had relied upon the official offer of the Imperial German Government as expressed in the Ludendorf Manifesto,[82] there was a tacit promise that naturalization would be withdrawn only upon the commission of some crime or other act incompatible with loyalty to Germany. Toward the states of Eastern Europe, the naturalizing act on Germany's part changed their relations with thousands of their nationals and therefore directly affected their most vital interests.[83] The act of the German State in revoking this promise of protection is, therefore, a breach of trust toward the states of Eastern Europe whose former nationals have thus been left stateless. Furthermore, in the form that it has taken, the German denationalization is contrary to certain basic principles of international law.

International law recognizes as legitimate grounds for loss of nationality: (1) the acquisition of another nationality (by voluntary expatriation or naturalization, by option or otherwise as a result of the territorial transformation of the state and by the marriage of a woman to an alien); (2) fraudulent naturalization; (3) some voluntary act in violation of law or in disobedience to governmental orders, if such act or omis-

81. See p.64.
82. General Ludendorf, Commander of the German forces in the Eastern war zone, issued a proclamation in 1914 to the "Jews of Poland" assuring them that "the equal rights of the Jews will be built up on a firm foundation."
83. "Every naturalization of a foreigner affects the interests of the state to which he previously belonged," Triepel, Heinrich, "Internationale Regelung der Staatzangehörigkeit," *Zeitschrift für Auslandisches Offentliches Recht und Völkerrecht* (1929), 1, p.196.

sion to act clearly indicates a desire to renounce allegiance to a country. The laws on the loss of nationality promulgated by the Governments of the Union of Socialist Soviet Republics, Italy, or Austria, which may be taken as examples of the most severe legislation, do not fail to require at least some act of omission or commission on the part of the individual thus penalized.[84] The German Law is unprecedented in modern times.[85] For it applies to a whole class of persons who have been guilty of no violation of law, no intent to renounce allegiance, but solely by reason of their origin. In making race

84. The Soviet Decree of October 15th, 1921, provided for forfeiture of citizenship by those who *left* Russia after November 7th, 1917, *without authorization* of the Government (Article 1, b); those who *voluntarily* served in counter-revolutionary armies (c); those who had the right to opt for Soviet citizenship under an international treaty, *and did not exercise this right* within the period prescribed (d); and those who, residing abroad, *did not register* with the Soviet representatives within a certain period (e). The Soviet Federal Law of October 29th, 1924 (Article 12) provided for forfeiture of citizenship by those who, being abroad, *refused* to return home upon order of the Government. Several decrees of amnesty and "demobilization" (November 3rd, 1921; July 4th, 1923, etc.) facilitated the return of those who were desirous of recovering citizenship; the Law of 1924, in fact, provided for the restitution of citizenship (Article 10) and the naturalization (Article 8) of the repatriated. The Law of 1924 also provided for forfeiture of citizenship by decision of a Court of Law (Article 12, d) *as a penalty for a crime.*

The Italian Law of January 31st, 1926, forfeited the nationality of those who *committed acts abroad* which damaged the Government. The Austrian law of August 16th, 1933, permitted the Government to forfeit the citizenship of those nationals who, being abroad, take part in hostile *action* against the Government.

85. Even in Roumania, Jews under the Civil Code of 1864 (Articles 8 and 16) and the Constitution of 1886 (Article 7) were treated as foreigners, but were eligible to naturalization. The Treaty of Berlin (1878) in Article 44 provided for equality in civil and political rights without discrimination on account of creed. The Treaty between the Central Powers and Roumania signed at Bucharest on May 7th, 1918, provided that the Jews should be admitted to citizenship. See Laws of December 29th, 1918, and May 22nd, 1919, which were confirmed by the Treaty of December 9th, 1919, with the Allied Powers as well as by the Constitution of 1923 (Articles 7 and 133) and the Naturalization Law of February 23rd, 1924 (Article 56[3]).

or national origin grounds for loss of nationality and in being directed against persons who acquired nationality by naturalization—that is to say, on the strength of the promise of the state to continue to protect them until and unless by some individual act or failure to act, in violation of law or governmental orders, they were deemed personally disloyal to their pledge of allegiance—the German action is unique in the history of international affairs.[86]

Naturalization, affecting as it does the rights and duties of another state, may not according to international law be revoked arbitrarily or upon the whim of a new government. For the naturalizations granted by previous German Governments between 1918 and 1933 are acts of state which are binding upon the present National Socialist *régime*. The abuse of this right to revoke naturalizations freely granted is subject to review by other states whose rights are thus affected, who may weigh the grounds for such denationalization and hold the German Government responsible for whatever damage they have suffered thereby.

3. Violations of the Territorial Sovereignty of Neighboring States

The lives of the refugees from Germany have been filled with fear as a result of a system of espionage and terrorism directed against them from within Germany. Numerous incursions into the countries where refugees have fled, particularly Czechoslovakia, Switzerland, and The Netherlands, have taken place and have therefore violated one of the most well-established principles of public law and morality, the right of a State to grant asylum. But, whereas the right of asylum is usually associated with persons who have com-

86. See the editorial note by Professor James W. Garner of the University of Illinois in 30 *American Journal of International Law*, pp.96–9.

mitted crimes, the objects of terrorism in these instances have been innocent individuals whose philosophies, however, in some instances led them to express opposition toward the prevailing *régime* in Germany. In order to silence them, or to punish them for their utterances, they have been subjected to constant espionage and have been placed in fear and in danger of their lives. No less than nine of these acts of terrorism against refugees from Germany have come to public attention, six of them during the first five months of 1935:

(1) August 30th, 1933. The murder of Professor Theodore Lessing, formerly of Hanover, one of the outstanding philosophers and pacifists of Germany, who was forced to take refuge in Czechoslovakia because of his philosophical views, and who was murdered by emissaries from Germany.

(2) April 3rd, 1934. An attempt to chloroform and kidnap Reinhold Rau, a refugee in Ketten, Bohemia (Czechoslovakia) failed, but after official inquiry Czechoslovakian authorities established the fact that the German Secret State Police were involved.

(3) January 24th, 1935. Rudolf Formys, former technical manager of the West German Broadcasting Station at Muehlacker, was a member of the opposition within the National Socialist Party and fled to Czechoslovakia. He was trailed to his refuge and shot dead by three Germans, soon after the official National Socialist press had placed a price upon his head. Five previous attempts to abduct or murder him were declared to have been made.

(4) February 4th, 1935. A Memorandum sent by a Member of the Parliament of The Netherlands established the fact that Herr Gutzeit, a German refugee, was overpowered and taken in an automobile across the German frontier, at Gronau, where the gates were left open so that the car might pass. Gutzeit was then arrested and

imprisoned by German authorities. The Government of The Netherlands filed a strong protest.

(5) March 9th, 1935. Berthold Jacob Salomon, a journalist who had predicted the re-armament of Germany, was lured from France to Switzerland by a spy acting under directions from the German Secret State Police. He was seized in Swiss Territory, driven in an automobile across the frontier according to a pre-arranged plan, arrested and imprisoned for treason against the Reich. The Swiss Government vigorously protested and declared that the kidnapping had been carried out "with the aid of German authorities." [87]

(6) March 23rd, 1935. Herr Kurtzke, his wife and child, who had been living as refugees in Oberalstadt, Czechoslovakia, were kidnapped when, after receiving a note allegedly from relatives in Germany to go to the border near Lubau, they were placed in an automobile and driven across the frontier into Germany.

(7) April 5th, 1935. Fritz and Alfred Rotter, both refugees, had settled in Liechtenstein. They were invited to inspect a hotel in Gaslein, and upon arrival were attacked by seven men. Alfred Rotter and his wife were murdered, and their bodies were found in a woodland pond. The other brother Fritz, who had succeeded in wrenching himself free, was overtaken by the hotel proprietor (who, apparently, was working with the kidnappers) and induced to enter the car once more. When he realized that the same fate awaited him, he jumped from the car, fracturing his shoulder, but thereby effecting his escape. The car in which he was abducted carried a German license.

(8) April 29th, 1935. Joseph Lampersberger of Munich, formerly a member of the Social Democratic Party, who was a refugee in Czechoslovakia, was abducted by a kidnapping party, one of whose members was a German

87. See p.84 for a fuller treatment of the Jacob case.

police officer who protected the kidnappers with a drawn revolver. Lampersberger had arranged to meet relatives at a Czechoslovakian frontier station, and by means of espionage the meeting was made known to the abductors. He was beaten unconscious, dragged across the frontier and arrested by the German authorities. The German Government not only failed to deny the kidnapping, but even tried to defend the action as having taken place on German territory. The Czechoslovakian authorities on May 4th announced that they possessed photographs proving the falsity of this defense. A strong Note was sent to the German Government on May 9th, 1935.

(9) January 27th, 1936. Peter Christensen, a Danish worker, was lured across the German border from Soenderborg, South Jutland and arrested by the German State Police.

Apart from the sacred rights of the individual and of common humanity which have thus been trampled upon, these acts of violence and terrorism have resulted in the violation of the most fundamental principles of international law and one of the most jealously guarded rights of a state—that of territorial sovereignty. The rule *qui in territorio meo est etiam meus subditus est* establishes the sovereign jurisdiction of a state over all persons and things within its territory.[88] Even an alien is entitled to invoke this protection as long as he is in the territory of the state; for no state is required, except through the process of extradition, to permit its jurisdiction to be challenged upon its own territory.

When another state is responsible for this violation of territorial sovereignty, the matter becomes a serious question for international law; and, if the responsibility of the state is established, either by its own admission or through arbitral

88. Oppenheim,L., *op. cit.*, I, Sections 168–75; Phillimore,R., *op. cit.*, I, Sections 150–4; Heilborn, *System des Völkerrechts* (1896), pp.5–36.

procedure, the state whose territorial immunity has not been observed is entitled to satisfaction.[89]

This responsibility may exist both in law and in fact. In fact, a state may have directly planned this violation or may have made it possible through indirect encouragement. In law, however, the state may be held responsible for the acts of its agents who in pursuance of their general official duties have committed such a violation, even though they did not act upon governmental orders. "When the state invests an individual with its authority his acts become the acts of the state itself for which the state must accept responsibility under international law." [90]

Furthermore, if the agent is acting in general pursuit of his official duties, the fact that his action is a wanton one or that he is merely a minor functionary is no defense against the responsibility of his state.[91]

In the light of these general principles of international law and the established rules on state responsibility, the German

89. The Savarkar Case (1911), Scott,J.B., *Hague Court Reports*, p.276; Moore,J.B., *Digest*, IV, p.328; Colinje Claim (1933), *American and Panamanian General Claims Arbitration*, p.733. Cf. also Draft Convention on Jurisdiction with Respect to Crime, Harvard Law School Research, *A.J.I.L.*, Supp. Vol. 29, No. 3, July, 1935.

90. Eagleton, Clyde, *The Responsibility of States*, New York, 1928, p.45. "When we speak of an illegal act committed by the State, we mean an act done by the organs through which the State performs its functions and which enable it to fulfill its international duties. . . ." League of Nations Committee of Experts for the Progressive Codification of International Law, *Questionnaire* No. 4, "Responsibility of States for Damages Done in Their Territory to the Person and Property of Foreigners," p.6.

91. Hall,W.E., *International Law*, 8th Edition, Oxford, 1924, p.268; Strupp,K., *Das Völkerrechtliche Delikt*, Stuttgart, 1920, p.61. The state may even be held responsible under international law for the actions of individuals which violate the sovereignty of other states; for, as John Bassett Moore wrote, "from the supremacy and exclusiveness of the territorial jurisdiction, it follows that it is the duty of the State within the bounds of legal responsibility to prevent its territory and territorial waters from being used to the injury of another State." (*Digest*, II, p.446.)

Government is bound by law to answer for the violations of territorial sovereignty which have resulted in the kidnapping and murder of certain refugees. We shall see also, and this accusation is made with full realization of its gravity, that the German National Socialist Government itself has been directly responsible *in fact as well as in law* for these acts of terrorism and these grave violations of the sovereign rights of other states.

There is no doubt possible as to the unity of the National Socialist Party in Germany with the German Government. The responsibility of the German State for acts performed by the Party is unquestionable. This identification of Party and State has been amply confirmed and cemented by law. A statute of July 14th, 1933, for example, declared that: "In Germany the sole political party is the National Socialist Party." [92] Another law of December 1st, 1933, provided that "after the victory of the National Socialist Revolution, the National Socialist German Workers' Party is the bearer of the German idea of the State and is indissolubly united with the State." [93] Therefore, as one authority on international law has concluded in considering the responsibility of the German State for "hostile propaganda and subversive activities" against other states, "there is no basis for making any distinction between acts of the Government and of the National Socialist Party." [94]

92. *Reichsegesetzblatt*, I, p.479.

93. *Ibid.*, p.1016. "As a guarantee of the close co-operation of the agencies of the Party and the S.A. with the public authorities," Section 2 of this Law ran, "the Deputy of the Leader (i.e. Chancellor Hitler) and the Chief of Staff of the S.A. become members of the Government of the Reich." This provision was amended on July 3rd, 1934 (*Reichsgesetzblatt*, I, p.529) so that only the Deputy of the Leader is now a member of the Reich Government.

94. Preuss,L., "International Responsibility for Hostile Propaganda against Foreign States," *A.J.I.L.*, XXVIII, No. 4, October, 1934, p.667.

As to the special position of the *Gestapo*, or Secret State Police, the basic law from which it derives its powers establishes its direct and intimate connection with the Government. The Law of April 26th, 1933, for the creation of a Secret State Police provided that the *Gestapo* "has the position of a State Police authority and comes directly under the supervision of the Minister of the Interior" who regulates its "practical and local competence." [95]

The case of the kidnapping from Swiss territory of Berthold Jacob Salomon, a German refugee,[96] demonstrated the complicity and direct responsibility in fact of the German National Socialist Government for this violation of international law and territorial sovereignty. Jacob had been seized in Swiss territory on March 9th, 1935, by three kidnappers and had been transported into Germany where he was placed under arrest. The Swiss Government, incensed over this desecration of its territorial immunity and right of asylum, vigorously protested to the German Government in a Note of March 23rd, 1935.[97] On March 25th the German Government replied that "the German authorities are not in possession of information which would lead to the supposition that Jacob had not come into German territory of his own free will." The Swiss Minister at Berlin countered on April 1st, 1935, with a detailed Note of the facts of the kidnapping, concluding with the demand " . . . that Jacob be immediately returned to the Basel authorities and that the Government functionaries who had taken part in the kidnapping of a person enjoying Swiss hospitality be duly punished." [98] To which the

95. *Preussischegesetzsammlung*, 1933, No. 29, p.122. A law of November 30th, 1933 (*ibid.*, No. 74, p.413) provided that the President of Prussia was the acting head of the Secret Police.
96. See above, pp.79–81, for other similar cases.
97. *Documentation Internationale*, May 15th, 1935, p.203.
98. *Ibid.*, p.204.

German Government replied on April 13th, that "the official German authorities were not associated directly or indirectly" in the kidnapping and that since Jacob was "a traitor of the worst sort" he would be punished. Failing thus to receive satisfaction, the Swiss Federal Council in its Note of April 27th demanded that the dispute be decided by arbitration on the basis of a Treaty of December 3rd, 1921, and a protocol of August 29th, 1928, which provided for such settlements of disputes between the countries. To this end, an arbitral agreement (*compromis d'arbitrage*) was signed between Germany and Switzerland on July 26th, 1935, which set up an arbitral panel and empowered it "to establish the circumstances under which Berthold Jacob Salomon came upon Swiss territory and from there on March 9th, 1935, into the hands of the German authorities" as well as to decide the question "whether, thereby, the territorial sovereignty of Switzerland has or has not been violated under circumstances which obligate the German Government to make reparation."[99]

But, while the arbitral tribunal was still engaged in fulfilling its mandate, and just as it was about to make its report, on September 17th, 1935, the German Government released Jacob to the Swiss authorities.[100]

Thus the diplomatic history of the Jacob case was closed by Germany's acknowledgment of its *legal* responsibility. But the significance of this case in establishing the responsibility *in fact* of the German Government for this grave violation of international law, as well as the circumstances which make further violations probable in the future, must for the security of neighboring states and for the future safety of the refugees be pointed out.

99. *Documentation Internationale*, September 15th, 1935, pp.250–1.
100. *Journal des Nations, Geneva*, September 19th, 1935, p.2.

The Swiss Note of April 1st, 1935, must be taken as a complete and accurate description of all of the details of the kidnapping, for the response of the German Government to the Swiss charges before the arbitral tribunal acknowledged the facts as set forth in the Note.

Now, according to the Swiss Note, the direct responsibility and participation of the German Government in this illegal seizure is evident from the following facts: the Secret State Police (*Gestapo*) of Loerrach had known as early as the 8th of March that the kidnapping was to take place; the barriers at the German frontier were opened during the night in anticipation of the seizure; Wesemann, who lured the victim to Basel and who was also an *émigré* and "apparently occupied in anti-German propaganda" together with his accomplices, were not arrested although they should have been suspect if they were innocently in the company of Jacob (Wesemann when he re-crossed the border into Switzerland was arrested by the Swiss police and later sentenced to prison as a spy); the automobile license card carried the German frontier entry mark and departure seal, although the German frontier had been crossed at an excessive speed and without stopping, which proves that it was validated later by the German authorities.

These facts gave the Swiss Government a right to conclude that the kidnapping was carefully planned by the *Gestapo*, the Secret State Police, and that Wesemann was a spy chosen by them to seize Jacob. Moreover, in holding Jacob from March 9th to September 17th, a period of over six months, and in turning him over without awaiting the judgment of the arbitrators; in pleading guilty at law by placing the blame upon the *Gestapo* itself; and in confessing that Dr. Walter Richter, and other officials of that body, had planned the seizure, the German Government confirmed its own culpability in the kidnapping.

For, the *Gestapo* which confessedly directed this seizure and violation of territorial immunity is more than an irresponsible police force. As we have seen, it is charged with the execution of some of the most fundamental laws of the Reich, and is under the personal direction of General Wilhelm Goering, Minister of the Interior, Minister of Air, Premier of Prussia, and one of the principal members of the German National Socialist Government.

Besides this intimate connection between the Government and the Secret State Police, the *Gestapo* in planning and carrying out the kidnapping of Jacob, as well as of other refugees, has acted not in violation of German law but pursuant to its legal duties under the terms of a Statute enacted on April 24th, 1934. Thus this kidnapping, and other violations of territorial sovereignty, find their source and immediate inspiration in the legislative will of the German Government. Furthermore, it is the existence of this law which makes almost inevitable the repetition of similar acts of terrorism and kidnappings in the future and which places in jeopardy the rights of other states and the lives of refugees.

The Law of April 24th, 1934,[101] provides (Articles 3 and 4) that the following persons may be prosecuted under the penal laws of the German Reich whether or not the action in question was performed within Germany and whether or not the person so acting is a German national or an alien:

(1) Any person, whether a German or an alien, who has committed an act of high treason against the German Reich;

(2) Any person, whether a German or an alien, who has committed a treasonable (*landverratische*) act against the

101. *Gesetz zur Anderung von Vorschriften des Strafrechts und des Strafverfahrens* (*Reichsgesetzblatt*, I, p.341).

German Reich or an attack upon the President of the Reich [i.e. Hitler];

(3) Any person, whether a German or a foreigner, who makes a public statement concerning an official announcement or proceeding in a treason case without permission of the authorities (Section 92d).

This law has certain important characteristics. First of all, it applies to citizens of foreign states: aliens as well as Germans. Secondly, it provides for penal action by the German State for acts which have taken place within the territorial jurisdiction of other states and which according to the *lex loci* were legal in those countries. Thirdly, its wide terms bring every individual in the world who expresses criticism of the National Socialist Government or of President Hitler within the scope of its penalties. In addition, the application of this law is in the hands of the *Gestapo* and a People's Court (*Volksgericht*) of five members, only two of whom are required to possess the qualifications necessary for judicial office (Article 3, Section 1, paragraph 2, of the Law of April 24th). Nor are there any legal safeguards for persons suspected of having come under the terms of the law: the seizures and actions of the *Gestapo* are not subject to any appeal, review or suit for damages on the grounds of false arrest or abuse; and the People's Court has both original and final jurisdiction, from which there is no further recourse.

It is upon the strength of this law, with its extra-territorial application, that the *Gestapo* carried out the kidnapping of Jacob and that other refugees have been victims of similar espionage and seizure. It should be remembered that Jacob was not a German national, nor was any criticism of the National Socialist Government expressed by him within the territorial jurisdiction of Germany. He had departed from

Germany in 1932, had never returned and had been deprived of his nationality on August 23rd, 1933, by the German Minister of the Interior.[102] He was thus an alien within the meaning of the law. But neither that consideration nor the fact that his writings were published outside of German territory since 1932, nor the sovereign jurisdiction of Switzerland, stood in the way of the application of this law to him.[103]

Apart from the responsibility incumbent upon the German government for its attempt to apply this law by violating the sovereignty of neighboring states (as in the Jacob and other similar cases), the Law of April 24th itself is an unprecedented invasion of the sovereign rights of neighboring states. Although many states have laws providing for the punishment of foreigners who, even outside of their territory, commit criminal acts which endanger the security of the state, the German law exceeds this limit and infringes upon the jurisdiction of other states. First, it applies to "treasonable acts," without further definition; secondly, the concept of "treason" has been so extended by the National Socialist Government that any expression of opinion which dissents from that of the present dictatorship may be regarded as "treasonable," even a criticism of Chancellor Hitler; thirdly, in no other similar law has this limited right of non-territorial

102. See *Reichsanzeiger*, August 25th, 1933, No. 199, p.1, where a list of thirty-two others denationalized at the same time will be found.

103. In addition to the Law of April 24th, Section 3 of the *Verordnung zur Abwehr des Angriffes gegen die Regierung der nationalen Erhebung* of March 1st, 1933 (*Reichsgesetzblatt*, I, p.135) applies to any foreigner as well as a German national who on German territory "intentionally makes or spreads an untrue or grossly misrepresented statement of a factual nature which is apt to prejudice gravely the interests of the Reich or of a German State, or the prestige of the Government of the Reich or of a German State, or of the parties or associations standing behind these governments. . . ." This especially concerns foreign journalists who may thus be imprisoned for their writings up to two years, even though the objectionable "statement of a factual nature" be printed outside of Germany.

jurisdiction been so distorted and extended to include the right to punish unauthorized statements by foreigners outside of Germany *concerning treason cases;* and, finally, the operation of such a law with its vague and all inclusive terms would abridge the rights of free speech and free press guaranteed in civilized countries to all within their territories and would thereby violate their sovereignty.

The territoriality of criminal law was well established by the Permanent Court of International Justice in its Judgment No. 9 in the case of the S.S. Lotus.[104] The Court held that "the first and foremost restriction upon a state is that—failing the existence of a permissive rule to the contrary—it may not exercise its power in any form in the territory of another state. In this sense, jurisdiction is certainly territorial." [105] In this particular case, which concerned the extension of jurisdiction by Turkey to an act committed on the high seas, the majority of the Court held that international law granted Turkey such jurisdiction. The dissenting judges, particularly Lord Finlay of Great Britain and John Bassett Moore of the United States, raised the further question whether Article 6 of the Turkish Constitution was not fundamentally contrary to international law. Article 6 was analogous to the German Law of April 24th in that it applied to foreigners and to acts committed outside of Turkish territory, and provided punishment for "any foreigner who . . . commits an offense abroad to the prejudice of Turkey or of a Turkish subject." Although the judgment of the majority expressed no opinion as to the conformity of this article with international law, Lord Finlay believed it to be a vital issue.[106]

104. *Publications*, Series A, No. 9.
105. *Ibid.*, p.15.
106. The Court was asked by the parties, France and Turkey, to decide whether Turkey had properly exercised criminal jurisdiction over a crime committed on the high seas, outside of her territorial bound-

He expressed the categorical judgment that " . . . the Law of Nations does not recognize the assumption of jurisdiction for protection." [107] As he said, "a country is no more entitled to assume jurisdiction over foreigners than it would be to annex a bit of territory which happened to be very convenient to it."

M. Weiss, the French Judge, cited the maxim *extra territorium jus decenti impune non paretur* [108] and declared that by an "indisputable principle of international law the criminal jurisdiction of a state is based on and limited by the territorial area over which it exercises sovereignty." [109]

Judge Loder also expressed the view that "no municipal law . . . can apply or have binding effect outside the national territory," nor can the criminal law of the state "extend to offences committed by a foreigner in foreign territory, without infringing the sovereign rights of the foreign state concerned." [110]

aries. Because it held that the rules of international law specifically applicable to jurisdiction on the high seas granted Turkey this right, it did not find it necessary to go into the question whether Article 6 of the Turkish Penal Code giving Turkey extra-territorial jurisdiction on land and sea was or was not *per se* contrary to international law. The "point at issue," believed the Court, was not whether Turkey was acting on the basis of a statute illegal in international law, but whether it had a right so to act under whatever article it did. The dissenting opinions, therefore, merely differed from the majority in their interpretation of the rules of international law applicable to the high seas; the opinions did not clash, in fact they did not even meet, on the question whether Article 6 of the Turkish Constitution was contrary to international law. On that point, only the dissenting judges made pronouncements, the majority considering it irrelevant to the particular issue involved.

107. "The passing of such laws to affect aliens is defended on the ground that they are necessary for the 'protection' of the national." *Ibid.*, p.56.

108. *Publications*, Series A, No. 9, p.44.

109. *Ibid.*, p.45.

110. *Ibid.*, p.35. This was so, he believed, even if the foreigner who committed the illegal act in foreign territory was apprehended in the punishing state; for an act which is permissible according to the

Judge Moore was even more specific. As to Article 6 of the Turkish Penal Code (which, it will be remembered, was analogous to the present German law) he said: "I cannot escape the conclusion that it is contrary to well settled principles of international law." [111] "No one," Moore declared, "disputes the right of a State to subject its citizens abroad to the operations of its own penal laws if it sees fit to do so . . . but the case is fundamentally different where a country claims either that its penal laws apply to other countries and to what takes place wholly within such countries or . . . that it may punish foreigners for alleged violations, even in their own country, of laws to which they were not subject." Judge Moore concluded, therefore, that Article 6 of the Turkish Penal Code was in conflict with international law, in particular with the principles that "the jurisdiction of a state over its national territory is exclusive" and that a state cannot rightfully assume to punish foreigners for alleged infractions of laws to which they were not, at the time of the alleged offense, in any wise subject.[112]

Judge Moore cited the Cutting case,[113] in which Secretary of State Bayard wrote to the American Minister to Mexico on July 20th, 1886:

"The proposition that Mexico can take jurisdiction of its author [of a libel] on account of its publication in

lex loci cannot by a change of residence subsequently be made illegal and extend jurisdiction *ex post facto.*

111. *Ibid.*, p.91. He quoted Hall as an authority for the general principle that "to assert that this right of jurisdiction covers acts done before the arrival of the foreign subjects in the country is in reality to set up a claim to concurrent jurisdiction with other states as to acts done within them, and so to destroy the very principle of exclusive territorial jurisdiction to which the alleged right must appeal for support." Hall, W.E., *International Law*, 8th Edition, 1924, pp.261, 263.

112. *Ibid.*, p.96.

113. Foreign Relations, 1886, p.700; 1887, p.751; 1888, II, pp.1114, 1180.

Texas is wholly inadmissible and is peremptorily denied by this government."

But, continued Secretary Bayard, "there is another ground on which this demand may with equal positiveness be based." And he said:

"By the law of nations no punishment can be inflicted by a sovereign on the citizens of another country unless in conformity with those sanctions of justice which all civilized nations hold in common."

Referring to the Cutting incident, President Cleveland, in his annual message on December 5th, 1886,[114] said:

"The admission of such a pretension would have serious results invasive of the jurisdiction of this government and highly dangerous to our citizens and to our land. . . ."

He asked, therefore, that the statute in question be modified so "as to eliminate the present possibilities of danger to the peace of the two countries." After an exchange of diplomatic notes on the subject, a Convention was signed limiting the criminal jurisdiction of the signatories to acts committed upon the territory of the punishing state.

Thus the principles of international law do not permit the submission to a non-territorial jurisdiction of the very class of crimes, those of a political nature, which states by common consent exclude from extradition.[115] Moreover, as the legislative basis and inspiration for the numerous offenses against the territorial sovereignty of neighboring States, this Law of April 24th, with its extra-territorial effects, must be considered as encouraging the acts of terrorism, kidnapping and espionage against refugees which have in fact been carried on by

114. Foreign Relations, 1886, VII.
115. Brierly, J.L., "Report on Extraterritorial Crime," *League of Nations Document* C. 50, M. 27, 1926, V, 7, p.3.

means of the Secret State Police of Germany. Therefore, both in law and in fact, the German National Socialist Government is responsible for these violations of the law of nations, for these offenses against the sovereign rights of other States and for this repudiation of the sacred right of asylum.

B. *Germany's International Obligations*

In addition to these infringements upon the rights of other states, the National Socialist Government has by its system of discriminatory legislation toward "non-Aryans" failed to observe a specific international agreement embodied in an exchange of notes between Germany and the Allied Powers in 1919. Although this international undertaking was not given the form or the force of a minorities treaty (such as those signed by Poland, Czechoslovakia, Austria, etc.), it nevertheless constitutes a valid obligation binding the German State to observe within its territory the same principles of equality as those embodied in these formal treaties.

In exchange for the protection of those German nationals who, after the Peace Treaties had fixed the boundaries of the new states, would be under foreign jurisdiction, the German Government in 1919 solemnly promised that it would observe the same principles of equality toward those minorities within its own territory.[116]

The German Government, desirous of ensuring the protection of its nationals in Poland, in a Note on the Conditions of Peace which on May 29th, 1919, was handed to the

116. In fact, the German project for a "League of Nations" mentioned as one of the particular purposes" of the League "the protection of national minorities" (paragraph d. of Section 2). Section 54 of the project stipulated that the League should draw up a special convention to have the rights of minorities brought before the League organs. See Kraus,H., and Roediger,G.: *Urkunden zum Friedensvertrag*, pp.209ff.; Schucking,W., and Wehberg,H.: *Die Satzung des Völkerbundes*, B.I., 1931, p.139.

Peace Conference, forcefully expressed its concern over the oppression of minorities which had in the past characterized Poland. This Note declared, after pointing out the necessity of the protection of minorities that:

"Germany advocates in principle the protection of national minorities. The protection may be settled to the best purpose within the scope of the League of Nations. *Germany on her part, however, must demand such assurances as are already fixed by the Peace Treaty for those German minorities which, by cession, will pass over into alien sovereignty.* Such minorities must be afforded the possibility of cultivating their German characteristics, especially through permission to maintain and attend German schools and churches, and to publish German papers. A still more extensive cultural autonomy based on national registration would be desirable. *Germany on her part is resolved to treat minorities of alien origin in her territories according to the same principles.*" [Italics ours.] [117]

The Allied and Associated Powers, in return, replied to this Note on June 16th, 1919, that they were:

"Prepared to accord guarantees, under the protection of the League of Nations, for the educational, religious, and cultural rights of German minorities in territories transferred from the German Empire to the new States created by the Treaty."

Furthermore, the Allies' reply ran:

"*They take note of the statement that Germany is determined to treat foreign minorities within her territory according to the same principles.*" [Italics ours.]

117. Kraus,H., *Das Recht der Minderheiten*, p.42; translated in "International Conciliation," October, 1919, No. 143, p.30, entitled "Comments by the German Delegation on the Conditions of Peace."

Twelve days later, on June 28th, 1919, the Treaty of Versailles was signed between Germany and the Allied Powers. Article 93 of the Treaty is evidence of the intent of the Allies to fulfil their promise made to Germany, for it provided that Poland would "embody in a Treaty with the Principal Allied and Associated Powers such provisions as may be deemed necessary by the said Powers to protect the interests of inhabitants of Poland who differ from the majority of the population in race, language or religion." On that very same day, June 28th, Poland accepted specific international guarantees for the protection of her minorities, a guarantee which was motivated by the fact that (as the preamble stated) "under the Treaty of Peace concluded with Germany, a Treaty of which Poland is a signatory, certain portions of the former German Empire will be incorporated in the territory of Poland."

The fact that Poland's obligation to protect minorities within her territory was inserted as Article 93 into the Allies' Treaty of Peace with Germany, as well as the fact that Poland was a signatory thereto, demonstrates the intent of the Allied Powers to carry out their promise made in response to the German pledge. Article 93 of the Peace Treaty which gave Germany as signatory certain legal rights as against Poland, also a signatory, was in conformity with the German request of May 29th; it was in fact the transformation by the Allies of their preliminary promise of June 16th into a specific action.[118]

118. Germany, in fact, has made use of the right granted to her as against Poland, and before her admission into the League, defended her interest in a plea before the Permanent Court upon Article 93 of the Treaty of Versailles. *O.J.*, IX, No. 11, p.1291. "The German Government," her memorandum to the Permanent Court ran, "believes it may manifest its right and its interest in the execution of the system of minorities protection, guaranteed to Germany by Article 93, paragraph 1, of the Treaty of Versailles . . . (which) . . . signifies without a doubt that Poland undertakes with respect to Germany to conclude with the Principal Allied and Associated Powers a

This promise of the Allies, moreover, was in acceptance of an offer made in the form of a request and a pledge by the German State. Therefore, the exchange of Notes on May 29th and June 16th, coupled with the performance on the part of the Allies of their obligation to require minorities' guarantees from Poland and other states, may rightly be considered as having established an international contract under which Germany was bound to certain obligations which she had undertaken, those obligations forming the consideration for the Allies' performance of their promise.

Germany, therefore, is obliged, in the words of her offer, "to treat minorities in her territories according to the same principles" as those embodied in the Treaties with states containing German minorities.

It was not necessary, in order to constitute a binding international obligation, that this agreement between the German State and the Allied Powers be formalized by a minority treaty. For, it is a recognized principle both of international law and diplomatic usage that, as Westlake wrote, "The contracts of states are not tied to any form." [119] Forms of international engagements other than treaties have been

Treaty for the protection of minorities of race, language and religion. It is not therefore a question for Germany of a *res inter alios gesta.*" *Publications*, Series C, No. 3, Vol. 3, Part 2, pp.956–1033 at p.981. See also House, E.M., and Seymour, C., *What Really Happened at Paris*—"The incorporation of this undertaking in the Treaty with Germany had the effect of obligating these states to each of the other signatories to the Treaty, and it gives even Germany a *locus standi* that the guarantees accepted are performed" (p.211). The Permanent Court has also established the connection between Article 93 and the Minorities Treaty with Poland (*Publications*, Series B, No. 7, p.14), and has had recourse to the terms of the former in order to interpret the obligations assumed by Poland towards minorities. See also the Mello-Franco Report, *League Document* C. 24, M. 18, 1929, I, p.30.

119. Westlake, J., *International Law* (Cambridge, 1904, 6), I, p.290; see also Satow, E., *Guide to Diplomatic Practice*, 3rd Edition (London, 1932).

acknowledged as binding a state which is party to them.[120] The test would seem to be only the mutual consent of the parties,[121] irrespective of the form of its expression. Nor, without a stipulation to that effect, is ratification a necessity when engagements are undertaken by the competent state authorities.[122]

An exchange of diplomatic notes is sufficient to constitute an international agreement.[123]

Mr. Foster, Secretary of State, in a report to the President of the United States, stated: "An exchange of diplomatic notes has often sufficed without any further formality of ratification or exchange of ratifications, or even of proclamation, to effect purposes more usually accomplished by the more complex machinery of treaties." [124] Between the binding force of such contracts, Hall says, and those couched in solemn form, there is no difference.[125] Tacit ratification of this undertaking exists when upon knowledge thereof this exchange of notes is not repudiated by the ratifying authority.[126]

120. See *Field* v. *Clark* (1892), 143 U.S. 649; *Altman* v. *U.S.* (1912), 224 U.S. 583. Neither *pollicitations* (promises unaccepted), nor *punctationes* (negotiations looking towards a future treaty) are binding. But these are not to be confused with either a preliminary agreement or a *pactum de contrahando*, looking towards later formal incorporation into a treaty. Oppenheim,L., *International Law*, 4th Edition, McNair, ed. (London, 1928), I, p.710.

121. Oppenheim,L., *op. cit.*, I, p.715.

122. *Ibid.*, p.721.

123. Satow,E., *op. cit.*, pp.379–90; see also Crandall,S., *Treaties, Their Making and Enforcement* (Washington, 1916), p.6. The important Rush-Bagot agreement between Great Britain and the United States for the limitation of naval forces on the Great Lakes was arrived at by an exchange of Notes and was never embodied in any formal instrument. Moore,J.B., *Digest of International Law* (Washington, 1906), V, p.204; see *Compilation of Treaties in Force*, U.S. Senate Doc. No. 318, 58th Cong., 2nd Sess. (1904), p.312.

124. Quoted in Devlin,R.T., *The Treaty Power* (San Francisco, 1908), p.73.

125. Hall,W.E., *A Treatise on International Law* (8th edition, Oxford, 1924), p.383.

126. *Ibid.*, p.385. By means of an exchange of notes between General

In addition to these precedents [127] the Permanent Court of International Justice, as the decisive authority, has determined the manner in which an international agreement may be constituted and an international obligation be born without the formality of a treaty. Indeed, in its Judgment No. 20 on the legal status of Eastern Greenland the Court went so far as to hold [128] that a unilateral oral declaration given by a Minister for Foreign Affairs within his sphere of competence is binding upon his State. It mattered not, the Court believed, whether the agreement had been incorporated into a treaty, nor that the promise was oral. The Court was called upon to decide whether Denmark or Norway possessed sovereignty over certain portions of Eastern Greenland. The Danish Government sought to have the Norwegian claim declared "unlawful and invalid." One of the principal supports of the Danish case, as well as the decisive point for the Court, was the oral declaration of Mr. Ihlen, the Norwegian Minister for Foreign Affairs, to the Danish Minister at Oslo. The Danish Government, wishing to obtain an acknowledgment from Norway of its undisputed title to Eastern Greenland, had instructed its Minister to obtain an assurance to this effect from Norway. In the course of a conversation with Mr. Ihlen, the Danish Minister promised that Denmark would not press

D.E. Sickles, the American Minister to Spain and Señor Don Christino Martos, the Spanish Minister of State, on February 11th and 12th, 1871, an arrangement was made with Spain for the settlement by arbitration of claims of American citizens in Cuba. Moore,J.B., *International Arbitrations* (Washington, 1898), pp.1019–53.

127. The agreement declaratory of the policies of the United States and Japan arrived at by means of an exchange of Notes on November 13th, 1908, may also be cited as a precedent. Malloy,W.M., *Treaties of the United States*, 1776–1909 (Washington, 1910), I, p.1045, cited in Hyde,C.C., *International Law* (Boston, 1922), II, p.489. Later, the Lansing-Ishii agreement of November 2nd, 1917, was made by the same process. Hyde,C.C., *op. cit.*, II, p.33.

128. Judgment of April 5th, 1933, Series A/B, No. 53.

its claims to Spitzbergen before the Peace Conference and asked that Norway in return recognize Denmark's title to Eastern Greenland. Mr. Ihlen, as evidenced by his own memorandum of the conversation, promised that Norway "would not make any difficulties in the settlement of this question." This memorandum of the conversation was then sent to the Danish Minister over the initials of Mr. Ihlen.

Now, called upon to interpret this oral promise,

> "The Court considers it beyond all dispute that a reply of this nature given by the Minister for Foreign Affairs on behalf of his Government in response to a request by the diplomatic representative of a foreign Power, in regard to a question falling within his province is binding upon the country to which the Minister belongs." [129]

It regarded this promise as "unconditional and definitive" and interpreted it as resulting in an obligation on the part of Norway not to press any further its claims to Eastern Greenland. It mattered not, thought the Court, that Norway later refused to put the Ihlen declaration in writing, nor that, in fact, it later disavowed the promise by asserting that its Minister for Foreign Affairs had acted *ultra vires*. The promise given and received was sufficient in law immediately to constitute an internationally binding agreement. The Norwegian contention that such a promise was a mere diplomatic assurance and needed to be in writing and ratified in treaty form to be legally binding was not sustained.

It is highly significant, also, that neither the dissenting opinion of Judge Anzilotti nor that of Judge Vogt of Norway expressed opposition to the Court's interpretation in this respect. Judge Vogt agreed that "such a promise, made by the Minister for Foreign Affairs is, in principle, valid and

129. *Ibid.*, p.72.

binding." [130] Judge Anzilotti was even more specific than the Court:

> "As regards the form [in which the legal obligation was embodied], it should be noted to begin with that, as both parties are agreed as to the existence and tenor of these declarations, the question of proof does not arise. Moreover, there does not seem to be any rule of international law requiring that agreements of this kind must necessarily be in writing in order to be valid. . . . I consider that the agreement which was validly concluded in 1919 has retained its force."

Furthermore, both the majority of the Court and Judge Anzilotti agreed that the interdependence of the Norwegian promise with regard to Eastern Greenland and the Danish promise respecting Spitzbergen need not have been proved in order to render the former binding. The Court believed that if these mutual promises were dependent one upon the other (which was not necessary to establish, granting the validity of the unilateral promise), they "would have created a bilateral engagement." [131] *A fortiori*, then, having established the binding force of the unilateral promise of Norway by itself it was not necessary to prove the existence of a *quid pro quo* on Denmark's part. Judge Anzilotti, for example, even though denying the interdependence of the promises, nevertheless regarded the unilateral declaration as sufficient to constitute an international obligation.

Therefore, applying the judgment of the Permanent Court to the pledges made by the German Delegation to the Allied Powers in 1919, we find an exact parallel which is rendered even more forceful by certain features of the German declaration placing it upon an even firmer legal basis than the Nor-

130. Judgment of April 5th, Series A/B, No. 53, p.118.
131. *Ibid.*, p.70.

wegian promise. Firstly, both the German promise and the reply of the Allies were in written form. Secondly, they were more specific undertakings than the rather vague Norwegian assurance that no "difficulties" would be placed in the way of the disputed claim. Thirdly, the German declaration was made by a representative delegation of plenipotentiaries, rather than by a Foreign Minister on his own responsibility. Furthermore, it was not, as was the Norwegian promise, later disavowed by the Government. Fourthly, the German pledge contained both a promise and a request which may be considered interdependent; the German request having been immediately fulfilled on the part of the Allied Powers, the obligations of the German Government assumed in the 1919 pledge are from the viewpoint of international law and according to the decision of the highest international tribunal incumbent upon the present National Socialist Government. Even if it be considered that the reply of the Allies was not a promise dependent upon the German pledge, the decision of the Court in the Eastern Greenland case would seem to establish the binding force of the German pledge as a unilateral declaration.

The fact that the Allied Powers merely "took note" of the German promise, does not of itself imply the existence of a unilateral rather than a bilateral undertaking. For, the same language was used in the Treaty of Berlin (1878) wherein the Powers "took note" of the assurances given by the Sublime Porte that religious minorities in the Ottoman Empire would be treated on a basis of equality and justice. Hence, the words "took note" have by precedent a meaning which fully supports the view that they have a contractual and not merely a declaratory force.

Nor may it be maintained that, because the obligation of Germany to protect minorities was not incorporated into the

Treaty of Versailles or made the object of a special minorities treaty, the exchange of pledges and promises for this reason constitutes only an imperfect legal obligation. The question whether an accord created by an exchange of notes unincorporated into a later treaty is legally binding is, as the Permanent Court held in another case,[132] one of fact. The Court believed that the declaration inserted into the *Procès-Verbal* of a Conference between the Finnish and Russian Peace Delegations at Dorpat on October 14th, 1920 would be legally binding upon Russia if it formed part of the agreement with Finland. The fact that it was not embodied into the final Treaty was of no consequence; for if it constituted an agreement, "it would stand for this purpose on the same footing as the Treaty itself." [133]

Has the National Socialist Government violated Germany's freely accepted international obligation in this regard?

The German State promised, in essence, to guarantee the protection of the rights of those individuals of "foreign stock" (*fremdstaemmige Minderheiten*) resident in German territory. It was pledged that these individuals were to be treated according to the same principles as those established by the Peace Treaty and by the League of Nations for the protection of German minorities in other countries.

May the "non-Aryans" in Germany then be considered as included in this pledged protection? The Committee of Jurists

132. The request by Finland for a Judgment against Russia on the Status of East Carelia (*Publications*, Series B, No. 5).

133. *Ibid.*, p.26. Another recent decision upon the international legal validity of an agreement arrived at in a fashion similar to the 1919 understanding was made by the League (Lytton) Commission of Enquiry in Manchuria. The Commission decided that certain conversations recorded in the *Procès Verbaux* of a Conference between China and Japan in Pekin in 1905, but not included in the final Treaty, possessed legal force and were binding upon China. They possessed, the Commission declared, "the force of a formal agreement." *League Document* C. 663, M. 320, 1932, VII, p.44.

(Huber, Bourquin and Pedroso) appointed by the Seventy-third Session of the Council on the basis of its resolution of May 30th, 1933, to decide upon the "receivability" of the Bernheim Petition held that "a German national of Jewish origin" residing in Upper Silesia "must be regarded legally as belonging to a minority within the meaning of Article 147 of the Convention." Since Article 147 speaks without further definition merely of "members of a minority" (and their right to petition the Council) we may conclude that a German national of Jewish origin is a member of a minority in Germany. In the opinion of the Jurists, a person of "non-Aryan" origin belongs to a minority in view of the "discriminations enacted against the non-Aryan section of the population."

Therefore, it is not material whether in psychology, culture or personal feeling the "non-Aryan" desires to be a member of a minority; both the League of Nations and the Permanent Court have chosen to apply an extrinsic rather than an intrinsic definition of minority status.

The Court in its opinion regarding the protection of the German minority in Polish Upper Silesia pointed out that the term "minority applies to all those who differ from the majority of the population in race, language or religion. "It is to be observed," decided the Court, "that the two clauses which served as a basis for the provisions embodied in the Minorities Treaty . . . considerably extended the conceptions of minority and population, since they allude on the one hand to the inhabitants of the territory over which Poland has assumed sovereignty and on the other to inhabitants who differ from the majority of the population in race, language or religion." The Court was referring to the definition embodied in Article 93 of the Treaty of Versailles, the very Article which, as we have seen, was inserted by the Allies in accordance with their promise made on the basis of the German pledge.

The jurisprudence of the League has also adopted an extensive view of the minority definition. M. Politis, the distinguished Greek jurist and diplomatist, in addressing the Sixth Committee of the Assembly on October 5th, 1933 explained the apparent paradox that "the same people can be a minority in one country and not in other countries," or a minority at one period and not at another. When a minority are allowed to be fused with the majority, and enjoy exactly the same rights as the rest of the population, they have no desire to be regarded as a minority, and, in fact, they are not one. But, in M. Politis's words, "they are still latent minorities—sleeping minorities as one might say—ready to awaken at any moment when their moral union with the rest of the population may be relaxed." And it may be relaxed when the state discriminates between them and other sections of the population, imposes upon them from without, so to speak, a minority status.

Concluding, therefore, that the "non-Aryans" in Germany must now be considered a minority, is it material that the German State in 1919 did not specifically mention the protection of "non-Aryans" in its pledge, or that it could not then have envisaged the guarantee of the rights of those of Jewish origin? In order to answer this question, we must examine the terms of the pledge. The German State undertook a general obligation toward the Allies to adopt a certain course of action not toward any specific group of its inhabitants which was then defined, but toward all who at that time or at any time thereafter (while the League continued to protect those of German origin) might be regarded as "minorities of foreign stock" (*fremdstaemmige Minderheiten*). Even in the formal Treaties signed by States such as Poland and Roumania the specific minorities to whom the guarantee was to apply were not listed or defined. The guarantees were made so general that even the most recently created or obscure minority could appeal to their terms without first having to prove that the protecting State undertook guarantees on its particular behalf. The protective obligation exists as a bar to governmental abuse and not as a limitation upon those for whose benefit it was undertaken.

Although in 1919 the Jews of Germany, possessing the full rights of citizenship, were not considered a "minority of foreign stock," they have now been legally defined as such by the system of legislative discrimination enacted against them, and particularly by the Law of September 15, 1935, promulgated at Nuremberg. This Law deprived those of non-German or cognate blood of citizenship and membership in the State on the grounds of their foreign origin or ethnic "stock." But, this was merely the culmination of a whole program of discrimination by which the German National Socialist Government has set "non-Aryans" apart as individuals of "foreign stock." For example, inter-marriage between "Jews" and Germans is forbidden by the "Law for the Protection of German Blood and Honor"; "non-Aryans" are excluded from public service, the professions and many other occupations. They are regarded by the Courts as "unwelcome guests," as aliens of a different blood and mentality whose rights are on a plane inferior to those of the German majority.[134] The official writings of the National Socialist Party and of Chancellor Hitler leave no doubt that "non-Aryans" are categorized as individuals of a foreign, non-German stock. Even the official commentary on the Nurem-

134. See particularly, Chapter 3 of the Annex to Letter of Resignation addressed to the Council of the League by the High Commissioner for Refugees (Jewish and Other) Coming from Germany (London, 1935).

berg laws, written by two members of the Ministry of Interior, concluded that the German Jews were a racial (*voelkische*), though not a national, minority.[135] The 1919 exchange of notes, as well as the Minority Treaties, however, make no distinction between a "racial" and a "national" minority; both are equally protected from discrimination. The only test, as the Permanent Court has pointed out, is that individuals differ from the majority in race, language or religion. The individuals in question need not prove that they were specifically recognized as a minority at the time the obligation was undertaken by their State; for that obligation is a continuing one. If for example a large number of French individuals were now to settle in Poland they would have the right if they were subjected to discrimination to invoke the protection of the minorities treaty, even though they were not in 1919 residents of Poland and were not then envisaged as a protected minority. In the case of the German agreement with the Allies, concluded in 1919, having now defined "non-Aryans" as of alien and foreign stock, Germany is bound to treat them according to the principles of equality embodied in the Minority Treaties.

Does the system of legislative discrimination applied by the National Socialist Government to "non-Aryans" violate the terms of the German pledge? The Rapporteur of the Council on the Bernheim Petition has already pronounced upon this question with regard to the Upper Silesian Convention.[136] He concluded that "the mere perusal of the laws and the administrative orders mentioned in the petition . . . shows that . . . this application cannot have taken place without

135. Loesener, Bernhard, and Knost, Friedrich, *A Commentary on the Nuremberg Laws and Executory Decrees Concerning Citizenship and the Protection of German Blood and Honor*, Berlin, 1935.

136. *League Document* C. 351 (1), 1933, I. See p.112 for a fuller treatment of the Bernheim Petition. This was a petition addressed to the Council seeking to prevent Germany from applying the racial discriminations in Upper Silesia.

conflicting with a number of clauses of the third part of the Geneva Convention." Since the 1919 pledge obliges the German Government to apply within Germany the same principles as those contained in the Geneva Convention, it is clear that the laws cited in the Bernheim Petition also violate the 1919 pledge. The essence of the treatment accorded "non-Aryans" in Germany is, as we have seen, civil, political and cultural inequality solely by reason of their origin. Furthermore, the systematic program of discrimination towards "non-Aryans" is not, as Herr von Keller defended the action of his Government in Upper Silesia, merely the result of a "misconstruction of internal laws by subordinate authorities." On the contrary it is, as Senator Bérenger has said,[137] "the categorical affirmation of principles which are in themselves at variance with the principles laid down in the Minorities Treaties."

In so acting, the German Government has deliberately violated a solemn international agreement and has incurred a grave responsibility for this purposeful breach of her obligations. This violation of international law especially concerns the principal Allied and Associated Powers—Great Britain, the United States, France, Italy and Japan—towards whom the obligation was primarily undertaken. But, it is also of profound importance to the entire society of states, the basis of whose honorable relations has come to be the sanctity of treaties; and to the League of Nations whose preamble enjoins it to ensure respect for the understandings of international law.

* * *

It is clear, therefore, that the German National Socialist Government is responsible for numerous and flagrant viola-

137. Before the Sixth Committee on October 3, 1933, *O.J.*, Sp. Supp. No. 120, p.28.

tions of recognized principles of international law. In enacting its system of discrimination against hundreds of thousands of its nationals solely by reason of their origin, it has failed to observe its freely accepted obligations towards other states, embodied in the 1919 Agreement at the Peace Conference. In making conditions unbearable for a whole section of its population, and in imposing the burden of thousands of stateless, impoverished refugees upon neighboring states, it has violated their territorial sovereignty and immunity by its gross abuse of power. In attempting, through forcible seizures and espionage, on the basis of the Law of April, 1934, to extend its jurisdiction over other states, it has acted in defiance of all principles of international law and has disturbed the orderly and honorable relations between states.

CHAPTER THREE

THE TASK OF THE LEAGUE OF NATIONS

For more than a decade following the Paris Peace Settlement, the German Government, in keeping with its pledges, made a sincere attempt to assure equality to all inhabitants irrespective of race, language or religion. By word and deed it made manifest its conviction that wisdom and good government, as well as justice and humanity, required fair treatment to all. Germany insisted that the guarantee of the rights of minorities by the League of Nations and the assent given to the Assembly resolution of September 21st, 1922[1] imposed a duty upon all members of the League not only to observe a high standard of "justice and toleration" in dealing with their own minorities, but also to intercede whenever the stipulated guarantees were violated or ignored. Repeatedly the German representatives pointed an accusing finger at those states which ignored the spirit of the Minorities Treaties, and even at the League of Nations, when that body did not adopt the vigorous measures which Germany proposed for the protection of minorities.[2]

The Bernheim Petition: Action of the Council in 1933

In 1933, the accuser was itself brought to the bar of international justice. The National Socialist Government had violated the spirit and letter of the German *pledge* of 1919, and of the Assembly resolution of 1922. A large body of German citizens had been declared "non-Aryans," and on that pretext had been deprived of equal rights. Vast numbers of innocent men, women and children had been obliged to

1. See above, p.31.
2. See above, pp.32–40.

flee to adjacent lands and had become a burden upon the neighboring peoples and states.

The action of the Nazi Government so outraged public opinion throughout the civilized world that indignant protests were voiced by religious leaders and church assemblies, in parliaments and in the press, and at public meetings.[3] All eyes turned toward the League of Nations which was clearly responsible for the maintenance of the "laws of humanity" and the observance of German solemn assurances. The League acted at once, expressing in unmistakable terms its disapproval of the Nazi policies. But it chose first to call Germany to account, not on the broad issue of persecution in the Reich, but on the application of the discriminatory measures in one small area, namely, German Upper Silesia. This was done because, in respect to Upper Silesia, German guilt was evident beyond question, legally as well as morally. In enforcing the exceptional laws and the oppressive extralegal measures in Upper Silesia, Germany not only violated the "laws of humanity," the German *pledge* of 1919 and the Assembly resolution of 1922, but it likewise reduced to a scrap of paper an absolutely binding international commitment—a solemn treaty to which it was a party.

The industrial region of Upper Silesia was divided between Germany and Poland, after a plebiscite had been held in March, 1921. But the ethnic problem was not solved completely thereby, because minorities remained on both sides of the new frontier. Were Germans in Polish Upper Silesia to suffer discrimination at the hands of the Polish authorities, they might seek redress by appealing under the all-embracing Polish Minorities Treaty[4] which was meant to protect all minorities resident within the confines of the Polish Republic.

3. See Appendix III.
4. See above, pp.28–29.

For the Polish minority in German Upper Silesia, however, there was no international guarantee against maltreatment. The Council of the League of Nations therefore recommended that the German and Polish Governments agree to a Convention ensuring, among other things, the protection of minorities in Upper Silesia "upon the basis of an equitable reciprocity." Both governments accepted the recommendation and signed the Geneva Convention relating to Upper Silesia on May 15th, 1922.

By its acceptance of the Geneva Convention of May 15th, 1922, the German Government undertook, "at least for a transitional period of fifteen years," to assure absolute equality to all minorities resident in the German part of Upper Silesia. It agreed that all German nationals of that region "shall be equal before the law and shall enjoy the same civil and political rights without distinction as to race, language or religion." The substance of these rights was described minutely; the rights of the Jews as a minority were expressly guaranteed; and the provisions of the agreement were declared "obligations of international concern" and placed "under the guarantee of the League of Nations." [5]

This international commitment was absolute and unequivocal. Therefore, when the Nazi régime of discrimination was installed in German Upper Silesia, Franz Bernheim, an Upper Silesian refugee of the Jewish faith, submitted a petition, dated May 19th, 1933, to the League of Nations. The petition was declared *urgent* and at once placed before the Council of the League.

The German Government, called upon to defend its policy of persecution before the Council of the League of Nations, resorted to technicalities. Less than five years previously

5. See League of Nations, *Protection of Linguistic, Racial and Religious Minorities by the League of Nations, op. cit.*, pp.64–87.

von Schubert, the German delegate, had declared before the League Council that

> ". . . the German Government in its interpretation of the Geneva Convention, was not accustomed to base its action solely on formal grounds, but that it regarded the contractual rights of the minorities as a minimum which should be granted to them." [6]

In May, 1933, when confronted with its own wrong-doing, Germany resorted to technicalities. It no longer was concerned with the "spirit" and "general moral idea of minority rights," but sought to stifle the discussion of its policy of persecution by questioning the right of Bernheim to bring the matter before the Council. Von Keller, the German representative, expressed doubt as to whether Bernheim was a member of a minority and hence qualified to address himself to the Council. He denied to Bernheim the right to raise general questions respecting the application of the German laws in Upper Silesia because, in his view, the petitioner was not the "qualified representative of the interests of the Upper Silesian population." Finally he declared the petition not admissible because "no definite *de facto* situation" had yet arisen in Upper Silesia as to the application of the "Aryan" decrees.[7]

The technical points raised by Germany were referred to

6. League of Nations, *Official Journal, Minutes of the Council*, 1928, p.1675. Also von Neurath, the *present Foreign Minister of Germany*, in denouncing Polish agrarian laws which affected the German minority adversely, told the Council on December 9th, 1932, only a few weeks before the National Socialists became the rulers of Germany, that ". . . No less was at stake in the present case than the question whether it was allowable to apply the internal legislation of a country in a manner so discriminatory that a large part of the members of the minority lost their land or found themselves faced with economic difficulties so great as to force them to abandon their homes. . . ." *Ibid.*, 1932, p.1980.
7. *Ibid.*, 1933, pp.839–40.

a Committee of Jurists, but the members of the Council, notably Paul-Boncour, the French delegate, made certain that such action would not result in undue delay or procrastination. What is more, Paul-Boncour raised the general question of persecution in Germany, the "moral" issue which the Germans had so eloquently invoked on behalf of minorities at previous sessions of the Council. The Bernheim petition, he said, was "only one aspect of a more general and more moving problem" and the League of Nations which had so often shown "legitimate anxiety" for the welfare of minorities could not really ignore the rights of the Jews. Paul-Boncour also reminded Germany of her pledges. He recalled the fact that

> "In the discussions on the Peace Treaties it was Germany that had desired the minority treaties. She had at the same time insisted very strongly . . . that she would herself, in her own territory, ensure respect for the rights of minorities. . . ."

Other members of the Council willingly followed the lead of Paul-Boncour and enlarged upon the flagrant contradiction between the German promise and its performance. Count Raczynski, the Polish delegate, pointed out that Germany had reversed its former policy; no longer concerned with the "spirit" of the minority guarantees, the Reich could hardly continue to pose as the champion of racial, religious and linguistic minorities. The other members of the Council, he continued, could not fail to exercise "at least a moral right to make a pressing appeal to the German Government to ensure equal treatment for all the Jews in Germany." And Lange of Norway disposed of the objection which Germany was certain to raise against the discussion of its "internal affairs." No nation, he said, "could agree that these were exclusively internal questions. . . . Any problem that arose in a country might have, and in most cases had, such effects outside the country as to make of it an international problem."

The Committee of Jurists, consisting of Huber, Bourquin and Pedroso, to which the German objections had been submitted, were of the opinion that, as a German national of Jewish origin, domiciled (until his flight) in Upper Silesia, Bernheim must be regarded as belonging to a minority within the meaning of the Geneva Convention relating to Upper Silesia, and therefore qualified to petition the Council of the League. The other contentions of Germany were likewise denied, and the Council proceeded to adopt a report prepared by Sean Lester of Ireland, which clearly stated that in enforcing the "Aryan" decrees in Upper Silesia Germany had violated the Geneva Convention of May 15th, 1922. The report said in part:

> "The mere perusal of the laws and administrative orders mentioned in the petition, the texts of which are appended to it, shows that, in so far as some at any rate of their stipulations have been applied in the territory of Upper Silesia, this application cannot have taken place without conflicting with a number of clauses of the third part of the Geneva Convention."

The determined position of the Council of the League compelled the Nazi Government to promise—a promise which has not been fulfilled—that the provisions of the Geneva Convention would be observed. The Council took note of the declaration of the German Government that its internal legislation could not affect the fulfillment of international obligations and called upon the German authorities to reinstate the "non-Aryans" who had lost their employment through the application of the "Aryan" decrees.[8]

8. On this discussion see League of Nations, *Official Journal*, *Minutes of*

Action of the Assembly in 1933

The Council's action with respect to the Bernheim petition was limited to the specific problem of Upper Silesia. It was perhaps hoped that the frank expressions of disapproval of Germany's policy of discrimination might have a moderating influence upon the National Socialists. But the appeals to justice and humanity were disregarded by Germany's new rulers. When, therefore, the Assembly of the League of Nations convened in September, 1933, the issue had to be raised again.

In his opening address Mowinckel, the President of the Council, pleaded, in the presence of Goebbels, the Reich Minister of Enlightenment and Propaganda, for a return of

> ". . . mutual understanding and co-operation in our torn and divided Europe, where the words *equality* and *fraternity* are relics of a bygone day and where even the most sacred rights of liberty—liberty of thought and personal liberty—are not everywhere secure."

Similar hopes and pleas were expressed before the Assembly by other delegates, but the words of Sandler, Swedish Minister for Foreign Affairs, are particularly noteworthy. He declared that the conception of the equality of men and nations is the foundation upon which the League of Nations rests. Therefore any attempt to "divide humanity into separate species, . . . to proclaim the principle of unequality in the world is, in effect, to renounce the League." [9]

An even more outspoken condemnation of National Socialist persecution occurred in the Sixth Committee of the Assembly, when it considered the question of the protection of

the Council, 1933, pp.823, 833, 835, 838–49, 934–5. For the text of the Bernheim Petition, see *ibid.*, pp.929–33.

9. League of Nations, *Official Journal*, *Records of the Fourteenth Ordinary Session of Assembly* (1933), *Plenary Meetings*, pp.29, 44.

minorities. Von Keller of Germany opened the discussion with a long discourse on the rights and duties of a state, based on the ideal of racial homogeneity, with respect to minorities of its own race living abroad. Evidently able to reconcile the persecution of the "non-Aryans" in Germany and the violation of the Geneva Convention by his Government with the right of the Third Reich to pose as the champion of minorities, he asserted that Germany had ". . . always been prepared to advocate, within the League, not only the protection of the German minority, but that of all other minorities likewise." His position as champion of the rights of *all* minorities was rendered ludicrous when he sought to deny to the Jews such protection. With Nazi logic he declared that ". . . the Jewish question is a peculiar problem of race, and must not be connected with the general question of minorities. . . . It is a problem *sui generis*, for which, accordingly, a special settlement will have to be found. . . ." What settlement the Nazis intended for the "problem" of the "non-Aryans," the world already knows.

Once broad questions of principle with respect to the rights of minorities had been raised, the representatives of the various states seized upon the opportunity to condemn the segregation and persecution of the "non-Aryans" in Germany. Bérenger, the French member, pointed out that in cases involving an infraction of the rights of minorities the League had usually been called upon to prevent "an indirect breach, due to the tendentious interpretation of a law" which in its general implications was in conformity with the minority guarantees. The violation of the Upper Silesian Convention by Germany, however, constituted a *direct* breach, because the principles underlying the "Aryan" decrees were "in themselves at variance with the principles laid down in the Minorities Treaties." Moreover, in the consideration of the Bernheim petition, the Council was called upon to examine general laws which were being applied not only in Upper Silesia but throughout the Reich as well. Therefore, when the Council found that Germany had violated the *letter* of a minorities treaty in Upper Silesia, it followed *ipso facto* that the *spirit* of minority rights had been set at nought in the rest of Germany. The Council had limited its action to the specific problem raised in the Bernheim petition. But the Assembly, said Bérenger, possessed a wider mandate because it acted in minority questions under Article 3 of the Covenant.[10] And recalling the resolution passed by the Assembly in 1922, Bérenger pointedly asked the German delegation how it reconciled "the laws of the Reich, which the Council has had to examine in connection with the Bernheim case, with the treaties on which the League is founded. . . ."[11]

Ormsby-Gore of Great Britain attacked vigorously the basic doctrine of racial homogeneity on which National Socialist discrimination rested. "We reject absolutely," he said, "this conception put forward by the German delegate yesterday regarding the racial homogeneity of political units and States." The British Empire, he declared, "does not conceive itself in terms of racial solidarity, but in terms of the free association of free people, encouraged to develop their national consciousness within the greater unity and, above all, bound together by what is the real guarantee for

10. See below, p.124 and Note 17.
11. When von Keller objected to the consideration of the "Laws of Germany," Bérenger, in one of the most vigorous speeches heard in the Assembly, retorted that the discussion was "worthy of the international mission of justice and toleration which had always been and should always remain the chief perogative of the League of Nations." See League of Nations, *Official Journal, Records of the Fourteenth Ordinary Session of Assembly* (1933), *Minutes of Sixth Committee*, pp.41–2, 49.

all minorities all over the world—free self-governing institutions. . . ."

Nor did the members of the League fail to challenge and refute von Keller's assertion that the discrimination against German Jews was a problem "*sui generis*" and must not be viewed as one affecting the rights of minorities. Beneš of Czechoslovakia recalled the fact that the Minorities Treaties specifically guaranteed the rights of Jews as a racial or religious minority and added that

> ". . . any action which has hitherto been undertaken either by the Council, the various organs of the League or the Assembly, and which dealt with the Jews as citizens of any European State, has been based on the legal and political doctrine that the Jews should be considered as a racial or religious minority. . . ."

Ormsby-Gore warned the Germans that if they desired fair treatment for Germans in Czechoslovakia or Poland, they could not "have it both ways." The Jews, too, he concluded,

> "form a racial minority which deserves the same treatment everywhere as all other minorities in all countries. What is that treatment? Above all, equal rights of citizenship and fair treatment as loyal citizens of the nation to which they have been attached."

The French delegation reiterated these views and added that "as soon as there is legal discrimination a minority exists within the meaning of modern law." The French, English, or American Jews do not consider themselves minorities because they are assured full equality as citizens. If the National Socialists had not repudiated the traditions of a century, the German Jews, too, would not wish to look upon themselves as anything but Germans. But a Jewish minority was created in Germany by the "Aryan" decrees which segregated the

Jews from the rest of the population. "There is no escaping this dilemma," concluded the French delegate, "and, once we find ourselves in this position, the German delegation must understand that we cannot . . . fail to feel for the Jewish minority that same sentiment of human solidarity, that same spirit of equity which the German delegation asks of us when other national minorities outside Germany are involved. . . ."

The Sixth Committee of the Assembly of the League which witnessed this debate, comprised in its membership representatives of every state of the world which participates in the work of the League of Nations. But not a single voice, other than that of the German representative, was raised in defense of the Reich; and the Committee recommended that the Assembly reaffirm the obligation resting upon all states to assure justice and equality to their minorities. The Assembly of the League acted on the recommendation and passed unanimously the following resolution on October 11th, 1933:

> "The Assembly,
>
> Reiterating the recommendation which it passed on September 21st, 1922: [12]
>
> Expresses the hope that the States which are not bound by legal obligations to the League with respect to minorities will nevertheless observe in the treatment of their own racial, religious or linguistic minorities at least as high a standard of justice and toleration as is required by any of the treaties and by the regular action of the Council."

This resolution, adopted after a vigorous attack upon racial discrimination, must be regarded as a clear expression of disapproval of the German policies on the part of the League

12. See above, p.31.

of Nations. The Assembly, moreover, rejected the German contention that the obligation to respect the rights of minorities did not extend to the Jews. Every member of the League, save Germany, voted in favor of a second resolution which read:

> "The Assembly considers that the principles expounded in resolution I, which reaffirms the recommendation of 1922, must be applied without exception to all classes of nationals of a State that differ from the majority of the population in race, language or religion." [13]

The Need for Further Action

Thus within one year the League of Nations twice fulfilled its task by protesting against the policies of the National Socialist Government. The action of the Council resulted in the assurance by Germany that her obligations in the limited area of Upper Silesia would be observed; and the Assembly censured the denial of human rights throughout the territory of the Reich. However, the intercession of the League of Nations in 1933, and the world-wide protests, have not brought relief to the oppressed. In fact, the persecution of the "non-Aryans" has become even more intense: new regulations have extended the range of racial discrimination; Jews, and Christians of Jewish ancestry, are being boycotted and systematically deprived of their property; the courts have ceased to safeguard their elementary civil rights; they have been deprived of citizenship; and, as unwelcome strangers, their very presence in their native land is resented.

13. Technically this resolution was not adopted by the Assembly because unanimity was required and Germany refused to agree to the proposal in any form. For this discussion see League of Nations, *Official Journal*, *Records of the Fourteenth Ordinary Session of Assembly* (1933), *Minutes of Sixth Committee*, pp.22–57, 59–60; *Plenary Meetings*, p.88.

Hundreds of thousands of human beings are being driven to despair and destruction, and the League is in duty bound to intercede again on their behalf.

Nor is this matter solely humanitarian in character. Self-interest obliges the members of the League of Nations to protest against the program of the German Government. The savings and financial reserves of the German "non-Aryans" are being rapidly depleted, and within a short time the world will be burdened with an even greater relief and refugee problem. Masses of human beings, broken in spirit and impoverished, are being forced to flee from persecution and to throw themselves upon the generosity of adjacent lands. Action must be taken not only to uphold the "laws of humanity," but also to prevent a catastrophe which must inevitably have far-reaching international effects.

The policies of the German Government have already violated the principles of international law. International obligations, freely undertaken, have been ignored. The sovereign rights of other states have been infringed both by the attempt to extend jurisdiction beyond the borders of Germany and by the withdrawal of nationality and state protection from thousands of refugees. The League of Nations is authorized by the Covenant to bring the German Government before the bar of international justice.

The very foundations upon which the League rests are threatened. The persecution of minorities has long been recognized as one of the most dangerous causes of international bitterness and conflict,[14] and members of the Council

14. In the days when the League of Nations was being founded, President Wilson, in speaking of minorities, said, "Take the rights of minorities. Nothing, I venture to say, is more likely to disturb the peace of the world than the treatment which might in certain circumstances be meted out to minorities. . . ." Temperley, *op. cit.*, V, p.130.

and Assembly have on numerous occasions stressed the obligation of the League to protect minorities in order to safeguard peace and good understanding. In 1930, Motta of Switzerland, in summarizing a discussion on the question of minorities by one of the Committees of the Assembly, said that all the delegates had agreed that the protection of minorities "is one of the problems which may affect the peace of the world. All emphasized the fact that the problem is worldwide and concerns the whole of mankind." [15] At that session, and at others, the German representatives in particular emphasized the danger to the peace of the world inherent in the oppression of minorities. Curtius of Germany, for example, declared:

> "I should like to emphasize once more from this platform that, in the whole treatment of the minorities question, the point at issue is not so much the safeguarding of the particular interests of individual countries as of providing an important factor for safeguarding peace,

15. League of Nations, *Official Journal*, *Records of Eleventh Ordinary Session of Assembly* (1930), *Minutes of Sixth Committee*, p.86. The following are typical statements made before the Assembly or its Committees:

Professor Gilbert Murray, before the Third Assembly:—

". . . The question of minorities is not merely a humanitarian question. It is not merely that there are certain people suffering from oppression whom we wish to help; it is that the new condition of Europe is threatened with extreme danger if in any one of the new States there is a permanently disaffected element allowed to continue. . . ." Murray also said prophetically, "Have we made sure that the Jews can live like ordinary free citizens as long as they obey the laws in every part of Europe? I do not think we have." *Ibid.*, *Records of Third Assembly* (1922), *Plenary Meetings*, pp.37–8.

Mgr. Seipel, of Austria, before the Ninth Assembly:—

"The feeling of political insecurity which pervades the world is due to many causes. One of the most important and the most dangerous of these, in my opinion, is the intolerance caused by the inflation of the nationalist spirit in all that that term implies. . . ." *Ibid.*, *Records of Ninth Ordinary Session of Assembly* (1928), *Plenary Meetings*, p.67.

with which all Members of the League are equally concerned." [16]

Since the oppression of minorities is avowedly a danger to world peace, the persecution of the "non-Aryans" in Germany calls urgently for League action. There can be no two weights or two measures in the matter of the protection of human rights. If the League suffers one group differing from the majority in race, language or religion, to be hounded to destruction, the whole structure of minority protection collapses, and Europe is plunged again into the virulent hatreds and conflicts of irredentism. Irredentism has embittered international relations in the past and inevitably will do so in the future.

The mandate of the League of Nations is clear, and its organs, the Council and Assembly, are authorized by the Covenant to intercede on behalf of the "non-Aryans." Article 4, paragraph 4, of the Covenant reads:

> "The Council may deal at its meetings with any matter within the sphere of action of the League or affecting the peace of the world."

A similar grant of power to the Assembly is contained in Article 3, paragraph 3, and in 1930, the Assembly agreed unanimously (and the German delegate strongly approved of this action) that the League could deal with the question of minorities under this Article.[17] Moreover, Article 11, paragraph 2, affords the means by which the problem created by

16. League of Nations, *Official Journal*, *Records of the Eleventh Ordinary Session of Assembly* (1930), *Plenary Meetings*, p.101. See also *Minutes of Sixth Committee*, p.15; *Minutes of the Council*, 1929, pp.520, 522.

17. Motta's Report which was adopted by the Assembly, declared that ". . . All the delegates agreed, however, that the question of minorities could be discussed by the Assembly in virtue of Article 3, paragraph 3, of the Covenant of the League." *Ibid.*, *Records of Eleventh Ordinary Session of Assembly* (1930), p.531.

Germany may be brought to the attention of the League of Nations.

> Article 11, paragraph 2. "It is also declared to be the friendly right of each Member of the League to bring to the attention of the Assembly or of the Council any circumstance whatever affecting international relations which threatens to disturb international peace or the good understanding between nations upon which peace depends." [18]

Under this Article the League has the most extensive competence, and the Council may intervene in any situation affecting non-members as well as members of the League. Nor is it necessary to establish that an actual threat of war exists before invoking the second paragraph of Article 11. It was decided by a Committee of the Council in 1927, and reaffirmed in the Rutgers Report of 1928, that when "some circumstance threatens to disturb the good understanding between nations upon which peace depends," even though there may be no threat of war, that circumstance may be brought to the attention of the Assembly or the Council, so that action may be taken to restore international good will.[19] The persecution of "non-Aryans" in Germany has created international friction because of the denial of human rights and the consequent protest in the parliaments and press of various countries, because of the refugee problem which has imposed an intolerable burden upon other states, and because of the international disturbances occasioned by denationalization and the kidnapping of refugees.

Action under Article 11 on behalf of the "non-Aryans," who have been segregated as a racial minority, would con-

18. See *Ibid.*, *Official Journal*, 1920, pp.3, 4, 6.
19. *Ibid.*, *Minutes of the Council*, 1927, pp.832–3. See also 1924, pp.1367–8; 1928, p.674. The Rutgers Report was submitted to the Committee on Arbitration and Security. See *Ibid.*, 1928, pp.648–9, 670, 674–6.

stitute no innovation. Appeals to resolve difficulties arising from infringements of the rights of minorities have on numerous occasions come before, and been dealt with by, the Council under Article 11, paragraph 2. A notable precedent was established when the British Government brought before the Council, under this paragraph, the grievances of the population of the Åland Islands against the Finnish Government which was not then a member of the League of Nations. Finland argued that the issue was a domestic one involving a difference of opinion between a people and its Government. It denied that "an internal question relative to the protection of ethnical minorities could, and by the desire of a third party, be transformed into an international question." The Council rejected this contention and proceeded with the consideration of the question under Article 4, paragraph 4.[20]

In 1923–1924, the assistance of the Council was invoked in a situation not unlike the present one. At the Conference of Lausanne, when the Greek and Turkish Governments signed a convention providing for the exchange of populations, Caclamanos, the Greek delegate, made a declaration that the Albanians of Epirus would not be included in the exchange. Like the German pledge of 1919, this declaration was not incorporated in a formal treaty. Albania was neither a party to the Greco-Turkish convention, nor was it the recipient of the Greek "pledge." When convinced, however, that the Greek Government was forcibly removing Albanians from Epirus, the Albanian Government appealed to the Council under Article 11, paragraph 2. It maintained that the friendly relations with Greece were endangered by the indignation which "the martyrdom of wholesale expulsion"

20. See *Procès-Verbal of the Seventh Session of the Council*, July, 1920, pp. 35, 47, 59.

aroused, and by the great difficulty of providing for the large number of refugees. In December, 1923, the Council heard the Albanian claims under Article 11, paragraph 2, and resolved to call the attention of the Mixed Commission (for the Exchange of Greek and Turkish Populations) to the problem in the hope that a settlement might be reached. The decision of the Mixed Commission did not meet with the approval of Albania; it therefore proceeded to bring the matter again to the attention of the Council. This time the Council decided to consider the question under the minorities procedure. But the reason given is significant. The de Leon report, which the Council adopted, declared that "the juridical situation with regard to the Council of the League of Nations has recently changed owing to the entry into force, on August 6th last, of the Minorities Treaty signed by the Greek Government. . . ." It was this new juridical situation which led the Council to apply the minorities procedure to the issue raised by Albania. Since, however, the minorities procedure cannot be applied to the problem of the "non-Aryans," the Council or Assembly if seized under Article 11, paragraph 2, would be free to act under Article 3, paragraph 3, or Article 4, paragraph 4.[21]

The German Government has itself maintained that Article 11, paragraph 2, may be invoked in cases affecting minorities. It was not a member of the League of Nations in 1920 and 1924, when the Åland Islands and Greco-Albanian questions were considered; but, when a similar case arose in 1928, the German representative was one of the most in-

21. League of Nations, *Official Journal, Minutes of the Council*, 1924, pp.364–8, 1353–5, 1367–8, 1600–3; Ladas,S., *The Exchange of Minorities, Bulgaria, Greece and Turkey*, N.Y., 1932, pp.380, 384f. For other appeals under Article 11 in cases affecting the rights of minorities, see *Official Journal, Minutes of the Council*, 1923, pp.573ff.; 1924, pp.1678–9; 1925, p.579; 1927, pp.350ff.

sistent advocates of the right of a state to seize the Council in minorities questions under Article 11.[22]

Moreover, Article 11 was meant to cover such a contingency as has risen through the denial by the German Government of justice and equality to all persons of the Jewish faith and to those whose ancestors were of that faith. In 1919, President Wilson proposed that a clause be inserted in the Covenant binding all states not to "discriminate, either in law or in fact, against those who practice any particular creed, religion or belief . . ." Difficulties were encountered and the project had to be abandoned, but before the clause was dropped, Bourgeois, the French member of the Commission which drafted the Covenant, said:

> ". . . the possibilities envisaged in the Article under consideration have already been provided for in Article 9 [now Article 11 of the Covenant] which deals with international developments which may disturb the peace." [23]

Finally, an appeal to the League of Nations under Article 11, paragraph 2, does not constitute an unfriendly act. The application of that paragraph involves not a threat but an invitation to join with other states in a sincere attempt to find the solution of a difficult international problem. In that Article, declared the Rutgers Report, "the moral factors and the solidarity of the Members of the League are most clearly

22. Von Schubert, the German representative, expressed satisfaction with the decision of the Council to permit the application of Article 11 in grave cases affecting the rights of minorities. In 1929, the German Government, in a communication to the Council, reiterated its approval of the decision and added, "This fact proves at least that the League of Nations attaches to minorities problems an importance which considerably exceeds that of mere petitions." See *ibid.*, 1928, pp.868ff., 944; 1929, p.1157.

23. *La Documentation Internationale: La Paix de Versailles*, Paris, 1929, II, p.153.

brought out. Article 11 is the essential expression of the League and is designed to protect the interests of all."[24] The interests of the German "non-Aryans" cannot become a matter of indifference to the League of Nations.

24. See League of Nations, *Official Journal*, *Minutes of the Council*, 1928, p.675.

APPENDIX I

LETTER OF RESIGNATION OF

JAMES G. McDONALD

High Commissioner for Refugees (Jewish and Other)

Coming from Germany

ADDRESSED TO THE SECRETARY GENERAL OF THE

LEAGUE OF NATIONS

WITH AN ANNEX

Containing an Analysis of the Measures in Germany against "Non-Aryans," and of their Effects in creating Refugees

LONDON, DECEMBER 27TH, 1935

The Secretary General of the
League of Nations,
Geneva, Switzerland.

SIR,

On October 26th, 1933, the President of the Council of the League of Nations did me the honour to appoint me High Commissioner for Refugees (Jewish and Other) Coming from Germany, to "negotiate and direct" the "international collaboration" necessary to solve the "economic, financial and social problem" of the refugees. I hereby beg to submit through you to the Council of the League my resignation from this office, to become effective as from December 31st, 1935.

2. In the period of over two years since the establishment of the office, conditions in Germany which create refugees have developed so catastrophically that a reconsideration by the League of Nations of the entire situation is essential. The legislation and administrative and Party action against "non-Aryans" were steadily intensified, and culminated in the autumn of 1935 when a series of new laws and decrees initiated a fresh wave of repression and persecution of a character which was not envisaged in 1933.

The intensified persecution in Germany threatens the pauperization or exile of hundreds of thousands of Germans—men, women and children—not only Jews but also the "non-Aryan" Christians treated as Jews, and Protestants and Catholics who in obedience to their faith and conscience dare to resist the absolute will of the National Socialist State.

3. Apart from all questions of principle and of religious persecution, one portentous fact confronts the community of states. More than half a million persons, against whom no charge can be made except that they are not what the National Socialists choose to regard as "Nordic," are being crushed. They cannot escape oppression by any act of their own free-will, for what has been called "the membership of non-Aryan race" cannot be changed or kept in abeyance.

Tens of thousands are to-day anxiously seeking ways to flee abroad; but except for those prepared to sacrifice the whole or greater part of their savings, the official restrictions on export of capital effectively bar the road to escape, and the doors of most countries are closed against impoverished fugitives. Nevertheless, if the present pressure is not relieved, it is inconceivable that those who can flee will remain within Germany.

The task of saving these victims calls for renewed efforts of the philanthropic bodies. The private organizations, Jewish and Christian, may be expected to do their part if the Governments, acting through the League, make possible a solution. But in the new circumstances it will not be enough to continue the activities on behalf of those who flee from the Reich. Efforts must be made to remove or mitigate the causes which create German refugees. This could not have been any part of the work of the High Commissioner's office; nor, presumably, can it be a function of the body to which the League may decide to entrust future administrative activities on behalf of the refugees. It is a political function, which properly belongs to the League itself.

4. At the last meeting, on October 16th, 1935, of the Permanent Committee of the Governing Body of the High Commission, at which my intention to resign was fully discussed, action was taken to liquidate the office of the High Commissioner at the end of January, 1936, or sooner if before that date the Council of the League had made other provision for the co-ordination of the activities on behalf of the refugees coming from Germany. It was the expectation of the Permanent Committee that the Committee of Experts provided for by the Assembly of 1935, to study the re-organization of the activities on behalf of the "German" and of the "Nansen" refugees, would complete its investigations in time to present a plan for consideration, and it was hoped for action, by the Council at its meeting in January, 1936.

It has been the sense of the Governing Body that the work of assistance in the countries of refuge could be better carried forward by an organization directly under the authority of the League. It is now clear that the effectiveness of the High Commissioner's efforts was weakened from the beginning by the compromise which was agreed upon at the time his office was set up—that is, the decision to separate it definitely from the League. This compromise was accepted in order to avoid the veto of Germany, which was then an active member of the League.

5. Progress has been made during the last three years in settling the refugees from Germany. Of the more than 80,000 who have already left the Reich, approximately three-fourths have now found new homes—more than half of these in Palestine—or have been repatriated to their countries of origin. This accomplishment has been primarily the work of the refugees themselves and of the philanthropic organizations—Jewish and Christian—whose devoted labours have been ceaselessly carried on in many parts of the world. Probably not more than 15,000 refugees now remain unplaced. (An account of the work done for the refugees since April, 1933, is being published.)

6. The care and the settlement of these remaining thousands of refugees could and would be borne by the already heavily burdened private organizations, were they not fearful that the number of refugees may be increased many times by new flights from Germany.

The facts which arouse these apprehensions are indisputable. They are evidenced clearly in the German laws, decrees, judicial decisions and Party pronouncements and practices during the last two years. The culmination of these attacks on the Jews, the Christian "non-Aryans," and the political and religious dissenters was the new legislation announced at the Party Congress at Nuremberg last September. The core of that enactment was the law limiting citizenship to those who are "of German or cognate blood," and who also conform to the National Socialist conception of loyalty to the State. As the direct result in Germany not only the Jews, who now number about 435,000, but also tens of thousands of Christian "non-Aryans" who are classified as Jews, lost their citizenship, were disfranchised, and made ineligible to hold public office. Indirectly, through this new law, a constitutional basis was laid for unrestricted discriminations against all those whom the Party may wish to penalize.

The denationalization by the German Government of thousands of German citizens has added to the hardships both of those remaining in Germany and of the refugees, and is an increasing burden on States which have admitted the refugees while in possession of German nationality.

7. Relentlessly the Jews and "non-Aryans" are excluded from all public offices, from the exercise of the liberal professions, and from any part in the cultural and intellectual life of Germany. Ostracized from social relations with "Aryans," they are subjected to every kind of humiliation. Neither sex nor age exempts them from discrimination. Even the Jewish and "non-Aryan" children do not escape cruel forms of segregation and persecution. In Party publications, directly sponsored by the Government, "Aryan" children are stirred to hate the Jews and the Christian "non-Aryans," to spy upon them and to attack them, and to incite their own parents to extirpate the Jews altogether.

8. It is being made increasingly difficult for Jews and "non-Aryans" in Germany to sustain life. Condemned to segregation within the four corners of the legal and social Ghetto which has now closed upon them, they are increasingly prevented from earning their living. Indeed more than half of the Jews remaining in Germany have already been deprived of their livelihood. In many parts of the country there is a systematic attempt at starvation of the Jewish population. In no field of economic activity is there any security whatsoever. For some time it has been impossible for Jewish business men and shopkeepers to carry on their trades in small towns. The campaign against any dealings with Jews is now systematically prosecuted in the larger towns. Despite

the restrictions upon migration from the provinces into the few largest cities where Jewish economic activity is not yet completely excluded, the Jews are fleeing to those cities because there only can they hope to escape, at least for a time, from the more brutal forms of persecution.

This influx has exhausted already the resources of the Jewish philanthropic and educational institutions in Germany. The victims of the terrorism are being driven to the point where, in utter anguish and despair, they may burst the frontiers in fresh waves of refugees.

9. Again, as so often during their long heroic and tragic history, the Jewish people are used as the scapegoat for political and partisan purposes. The National Socialists level against them charges of the most outrageous and untenable kind. They ignore all of the facts of the continuous loyalty of the Jews in Germany: for example, during the Empire when Jews helped to unify Germany and to make it strong; during the War when a percentage of Jewish youth as high as that of any other religious community in the Reich gave their lives for the Fatherland, and Jewish scientists and men of affairs helped so notably to enable Germany to prolong the struggle; and under the Republic when Jewish leaders aided in saving Germany from some of the worst effects of defeat. Instead, it has been found useful to attribute to the Jews the responsibility for the misery and dejection which the German people suffered during the last years of the War and the decade that followed. Though less than a one-hundredth part of the total population, the Jews are held responsible for all the adversity which the German people had to undergo. As in the Middle Ages, when they were massacred and expelled from German States as the cause of the Black Death, so to-day they are eliminated from the economic and cultural life of Germany and degraded on the

ground that they were the cause of the German humiliation. So far does this hatred extend that even the Jewish war veterans who fought and were wounded in the front line trenches have been forced from their positions in the public services, and the names of the Jewish war dead may no longer be engraved on war memorials.

10. The attitude of the German Government is based not only on the theory of "Nordic race" supremacy and the desire to eliminate "foreign racial" elements from the life of the country; it rests also on the conception of the absolute subordination of the individual to the State. An influential section of the Party is actively promoting a revival of neo-Paganism which sets itself against both the Old Testament and parts of the New Testament. The conceptions of "blood, race and soil," propagated with fanatical enthusiasm, menace not alone the Jews, but all those who remain defiantly loyal to the old ideals of religious and individual freedom.

Party leaders violently attack religious freedom in the State, and threaten the Church with political domination. Outstanding thinkers of the two great Christian communities in Germany and abroad raise their voices in protest against this attack which threatens to increase the number of refugees.

11. The developments since 1933, and in particular those following the Nuremberg legislation, call for fresh collective action in regard to the problem created by persecution in Germany. The moral authority of the League of Nations and of States Members of the League must be directed towards a determined appeal to the German Government in the name of humanity and of the principles of the public law of Europe. They must ask for a modification of policies which constitute a source of unrest and perplexity in the world, a challenge to the conscience of mankind, and a menace to the legitimate

interests of the States affected by the immigration of German refugees.

12. Apart from the Upper Silesia Convention of May, 1922, Germany does not appear to be expressly bound by a treaty obligation providing for equal citizenship of racial, religious or linguistic minorities. But the principle of respect for the rights of minorities has been during the last three centuries hardening into an obligation of the public law of Europe. That principle was recognized in some of the most important international instruments of the nineteenth century. I may refer to the provisions of the Congress of Vienna, the treaty of guarantee following upon the Union of Belgium and Holland, the collective recognition of the independence of Greece, the creation of the autonomous principalities of Moldavia and Wallachia. It was affirmed at the Congress of Berlin in 1878 in relation to newly recognized states. It was deliberately reaffirmed in the Peace Settlement of 1919 and in a series of special minorities treaties as a vital condition both of international justice and of the preservation of the peace of the world. In the case of newly-created states its express recognition constituted a condition of admission to the League of Nations.

Neither was the attitude of Germany in this matter open to any doubt. During the Peace Conference, the German Delegation, in urging the adoption of the principle of protection of minorities for the German population in the territories detached from Germany, declared spontaneously that "Germany on her part is resolved to treat minorities of alien origin in her territories according to the same principles." The Allied and Associated Powers expressly took note of that declaration. From the moment of her admission to the League Germany took the lead in securing the effectiveness of the principles of international protection of minorities.

13. The Assembly of the League in 1922 adopted a resolution which expressed the hope that "states not bound by specific legal obligations in the matter of minorities will nevertheless observe in the treatment of their own minorities at least as high a standard of justice and toleration as is required by the treaties in question." The Assembly in 1933, when considering the question of the persecution of Jews in Germany in connection with the discussion on minorities, reaffirmed that resolution; and in order to dispel doubts whether it applied to the Jews in Germany, voted, with the single dissent of Germany, in favour of a further resolution that the principle "must be applied without exception to all classes of nationals of a state which differ from the majority of the population in race, language or religion."

The German Jews, although not claiming or desiring to be a minority, are within the scope of this principle because, as was stated at the Assembly, as soon as there is legal discrimination, a minority exists within the meaning of modern law.

14. It is not within my province to state to what extent the practice in this matter of the community of nations in the last hundred years and of the League of Nations has become a rule of customary international law; neither am I called upon to judge how far the declarations and the conduct of Germany prior to 1933 are in themselves sufficient to establish legal presumptions. But both, I believe, are sufficient to establish an appeal to those broad considerations of humanity and of international peace which are the basis of the public law of Europe in the matter of racial and religious minorities.

The growing sufferings of the persecuted minority in Germany and the menace of the growing exodus call for friendly but firm intercession with the German Government, by all pacific means, on the part of the League of Nations, of its Member-States and other members of the community of nations.

Pity and reason alike must inspire the hope that intercession will meet with response. Without such response, the problems caused by the persecution of the Jews and the "non-Aryans" will not be solved by philanthropic action, but will continue to constitute a danger to international peace and a source of injury to the legitimate interests of other states.

15. The efforts of the private organizations and of any League organization for refugees can only mitigate a problem of growing gravity and complexity. In the present economic conditions of the world, the European States, and even those overseas, have only a limited power of absorption of refugees. The problem must be tackled at its source if disaster is to be avoided.

This is the function of the League, which is essentially an association of states for the consideration of matters of common concern. The Covenant empowers the Council and the Assembly to deal with any matter within the sphere of activity of the League or affecting the peace of the world. The effort of the League to ensure respect for human personality, when not grounded on express provisions of the Covenant or international treaties, has a sure foundation in the fact that the protection of the individual from racial and religious intolerance is a vital condition of international peace and security.

16. I am appending to this letter a comprehensive analysis of the German legislation, administrative decrees and jurisprudence, as well as of their effects on the problem of refugees.

17. I feel bound to conclude this letter on a personal note. Prior to my appointment as High Commissioner for Refugees

Coming from Germany, and in particular during the fourteen years following the War, I gave in my former office frequent and tangible proof of my concern that justice be done to the German people. But convinced as I am that desperate suffering in the countries adjacent to Germany, and an even more terrible human calamity within the German frontiers, are inevitable unless present tendencies in the Reich are checked or reversed, I cannot remain silent. I am convinced that it is the duty of the High Commissioner for German Refugees, in tendering his resignation, to express an opinion on the essential elements of the task with which the Council of the League entrusted him. When domestic policies threaten the demoralization and exile of hundreds of thousands of human beings, considerations of diplomatic correctness must yield to those of common humanity. I should be recreant if I did not call attention to the actual situation, and plead that world opinion, acting through the League and its Member-States and other countries, move to avert the existing and impending tragedies.

I have the honour to be, Sir,

Your obedient servant,

JAMES G. MCDONALD,

High Commissioner for Refugees
(Jewish and Other) Coming from Germany.

ANNEX

INTRODUCTION

There was no German refugee problem before 1933. It is the general, and particularly the racial policy of the German Government which has created that problem, and it is the persistent pursuit of that policy which aggravates it and renders its liquidation well-nigh impossible. For three years this policy has found expression in legislation, in decisions of the courts, in the interpretation and application of the law by local officials and in extra-legal measures taken by the National Socialist Party and its leaders who direct the central and local governments of the country. The result has been to deprive hundreds of thousands of German citizens of all standing in the community and even of the means of livelihood.

More than 80,000 persons were obliged to leave Germany during the past three years and to seek refuge abroad. The vast majority of those affected, however, remained in their native land in the hope that the programme of racial discrimination would be abandoned or moderated. This hope has been dispelled by the action of the Reichstag which met in extraordinary session at Nuremberg on September 15th, 1935, and approved legislation which withdraws citizenship from persons of "non-German blood." The new law reads:

§1

"1. A German national (*Staatsangehöriger*) is one who belongs to the protective association of the German Reich to which he is therefore especially pledged.

"2. Nationality (*Staatsangehörigkeit*) shall be acquired in accordance with the prescriptions of the Reich and State Nationality Law.

§2

"1. He only is a citizen who is a national (*Staatsangehöriger*) of German or cognate blood and has shown by his behaviour that he is willing and fit loyally to serve the German people and Reich.

"2. Reich citizenship shall be acquired by the bestowal of a letter of patent of Reich citizenship.

"3. A Reich citizen is the sole bearer of full political rights in accordance with the law.

§3

"The Reich Minister of the Interior, in co-operation with the Deputy of the Leader, shall issue the legal and administrative stipulations for the execution and completion of the law." [1]

Even more ominous was the declaration of the German Chancellor to the Reichstag that the new legislation constituted an attempt of the Government at legal regulation of the Jewish problem so as to enable "the German people to find tolerable relations with the Jewish people." Should, however, the attempt at legal regulation fail, the Chancellor continued, then the problem must "be turned over to the National Socialist Party for a final solution." [2]

The new legislation has altered the entire complexion of the refugee problem. At least half a million people have been deprived of political rights, their civil status has become that of "guests or wards of the State," and a threat of even more drastic action against them has been pronounced before the Reichstag. It is inevitable that these outcasts should seek to emigrate from the land which has disowned them. They have become a reservoir from which more and ever more refugees will flow into neighbouring lands. It is therefore imperative to examine the fundamental cause of the refugee problem, namely the racial policy of the National Socialist Government.

A considerable number of persons have suffered persecution or been forced to emigrate for "political" reasons. They aroused the displeasure of the new rulers of Germany because of hostility to National Socialism prior to 1933, when the latter strove to seize power, or because they disregarded the doctrines of a strident nationalism and sought to further international co-operation and peace. Far more numerous, however, have been the victims of the "racial" policy of the new Germany,—a policy which requires elucidation.

The "racial" policy is not a passing phenomenon. As far back as February, 1920, the National Socialist Party proposed in its programme that:

> "None but members of the nation may be citizens of the State. None but those of German blood, whatever their creed, may be members of the nation. No Jew, therefore, may be a member of the nation."

This definition would deny German citizenship to persons of Jewish or of other "non-German blood." The National Socialist programme did not stop there. It demanded that

> "Anyone who is not a citizen of the State may live in Germany only as a guest and must be regarded as being subject to foreign laws."

Thus having proposed the reduction of all German citizens of Jewish ancestry to an inferior status, the National Socialist programme found no difficulty in urging the denial of all political rights to them, and, in particular, their exclusion from public employment.

This, however, has not been the final objective of the National Socialists with respect to the German Jews. They demanded in their programme the immediate expulsion of "all non-Germans," who entered Germany subsequent to August 2nd, 1914, and had in view a similar fate for all persons of Jewish origin, no matter how long they or their ancestors had lived in the country, or how devoted and useful they had been to the Fatherland. Point 7 of their 1920 programme reads:

> "We demand that the State shall make it its first duty to promote the industry and livelihood of citizens of the State. If it is not possible to nourish the entire population of the State, foreign nationals (non-citizens of the State) *must be excluded from the Reich.*" [Italics ours.]

In brief, then, the objective of the National Socialists, the present rulers of Germany, has been threefold: (1) to deprive all who have displeased them, and particularly Germans of Jewish ancestry, of citizenship and political rights; (2) to eliminate them from the political, cultural, social and economic life of the country; and (3) to force them to emigrate. This objective has been pursued relentlessly by the present Government of Germany without regard either for the human suffering occasioned by their policies or for the welfare of the states in whose domains the victims have been obliged to seek refuge.

NOTES

1. *Reichsgesetzblatt*, 1935, p.1146. The Reichstag sanctioned also the "Law for the Protection of German Blood and Honour" which prohibited intermarriage between Jews and German "nationals of German or cognate blood." *Ibid.*, pp.1146–7.
2. See *Westfälische Landeszeitung Rote Erde*, September 16th, 1935.

Chapter I

DISCRIMINATORY LEGISLATION:

THE "ARYAN" DECREES

HERR HITLER, the leader of the National Socialists, became German Chancellor on January 30th, 1933, but no legal action was taken immediately to realize the programme of the Party. The National Socialist leaders felt free to act only after the Reichstag, the deliberative and representative parliament of Germany, had been prorogued on March 23rd, 1933, and they had assumed dictatorial power. Then, however, decrees followed each other in rapid succession, and within a relatively short time liberals, pacifists, Jews and Christians of Jewish ancestry, were swept from public office, from Government employment, from the social services, and from the liberal professions.

The foundation of the entire structure of National Socialist legislative discrimination consists of sections 3 and 4 of the Law for the Restoration of the Professional Civil Service, issued on April 7th, 1933. Section 4 relating to "political" opponents prescribes that

> "Officials who, judged from their previous activity, do not warrant that they will always unreservedly exert themselves for their national country, may be dismissed. . . ." [1]

and subsequent decrees applying this test to professions other than the civil service, have made little effort to define or limit the meaning of this sweeping provision.

To be sure, a clause has generally been inserted designating as "politically unreliable" those who engaged in communist or marxist activities.[2] Enquiries have also been made as to whether persons in Government employ belonged to organizations such as the Union of Republican Judges, the Union of Republican Officials, the League of the Rights of Man, the Iron Front, the Reichsbanner Black-Red-Gold, and the like.[3] But vague formulae have been preferred: to be a newspaper editor one has to "possess the qualities required for a task involving the exercise of a spiritual influence upon public opinion"; for cultural pursuits, the necessary "reliability and capacity" are indispensable. Moreover,

> "Candidates [for admission to practice as dentists with the 'National Health Insurance Service'] may not be admitted if there exist some important personal reasons against their admission." [4]

A strict definition of terms might provide a legal refuge for those who are regarded as politically undesirable. As it is, those who possess dictatorial power in Germany are enabled "legally" to proscribe practically anyone who momentarily displeases them.

It is difficult to determine the exact number of refugees and those who suffer discrimination within Germany, who owe their plight to real or imagined hostility to National Socialism. The overwhelming majority, however, are not of this category. A multitude of men, women and children, have been humiliated and impoverished, or compelled to seek refuge abroad for no other reason than their "racial" affinities. They have been guilty of no political, moral, or any other kind of heterodoxy. Their offence is merely the fact that they are "non-Aryans,"—an offence over which they have no control and to rectify which they can do nothing. It is, therefore, to this group, the most numerous element among the refugees, that particular attention must be devoted.

It is generally believed that the Jews are the only victims of this form of discrimination, but a mere glance at the Law for the Restoration of the Professional Civil Service indicates that such is not the case. Article 3, the basis of the "racial" disabilities, commences thus:

> "(1) Officials who are of non-Aryan descent, are to be retired (see section 8); as regards the honorary officials they are to be discharged from office."

It will be observed that the law speaks not solely of Jews but of "non-Aryans," a more comprehensive term which has disqualified numerous persons who are Christians and have had no relations with the Jewish community. To understand this action we must recall the fact that numerous German Jews abandoned Judaism and espoused Christianity during the course of the nineteenth and early twentieth centuries. Even more numerous, perhaps, was the class of Jews who had intermarried with German Protestants or Catholics and they, or their children, had severed all affiliations with the Jewish group and had completely identified themselves with the Christian community. These persons regarded themselves and were regarded by others as Christians. But the National Socialist leaders have shown little respect for traditional Christianity. They have sought to render even faith subservient to the purposes of an exclusive racialism. Therefore, legislation specifically directed against Jews would not have answered their purposes. It would have reached only the five or six hundred thousand Jews of Germany and not the additional hundreds of thousands [5] of German Christians who are descended from Jewish stock. The National Socialists would include them all, those of the Christian as well as of the Jewish faith. For that purpose, "non-Aryan" appeared more satisfactory because it was more comprehensive and more in consonance with the "racial" theory.

But who is a "non-Aryan"? This question proved troublesome and the National Socialist legislators were compelled to issue a number of decrees defining arbitrarily this vague and elusive concept. First it was decreed that

> "A non-Aryan is one who is descended from non-Aryan, particularly Jewish parents or grandparents. It suffices if one parent or one grandparent is non-Aryan. This obtains especially if one parent or one grandparent belonged to the Jewish faith." [6]

This definition was comprehensive enough, but it was soon discovered that some people had been left in doubt as to the purity of their "Aryanism." The Minister of the Interior thereupon ordained that illegitimate descent from a non-Aryan did not remove the stigma which entailed an inferior status, and that "Aryanism" could not be acquired or assumed through adoption. On the other hand, an "Aryan" lost his privileged position if he married a "non-Aryan." [7]

It has never been made clear why racial assimilation is achieved in three generations. Yet, the "parent or grandparent clause" posessed the virtue of definiteness and enabled all persons whose two parents and four grandparents had not been Jews to feel secure from molestation on racial grounds. New legislation, however, soon disclosed that the search for traces of "Jewish blood" was to be extended further into the past. The law regulating peasant holdings (September 29th, 1933) no longer spoke of parents or grandparents but declared that:

> "A person is not considered as of German or cognate blood if his paternal or maternal ancestors have Jewish or coloured blood in their veins,"

and then went on to fix the "first of January, 1800" as the day beyond which probing would be unnecessary.[8] A new regulation concerning the press which was issued in April, 1935,[9] likewise barred from the publishing business all persons who could not prove "their own Aryan descent and that of their consorts . . . up to 1800."

The decision to disqualify as "non-Aryans" even those whose grandparents had not been Jews, provided some Jewish ancestor could be discovered to have lived after January 1st, 1800, undoubtedly augmented the number of "non-Aryans" subject to discrimination. The German Government has not disclosed exactly how many Christians, in addition to the five or six hundred thousand Jews, were thus relegated to an inferior status by the "parent and grandparent clause" and by the decision to discriminate against the descendants of persons who had abandoned the Jewish faith subsequent to January 1st, 1800.[10] Nevertheless, the far-reaching character of these provisions may be observed from the genealogical tables on page 151.

It should be noted that for the sake of simplicity the genealogical tables limit the issue of each marriage to *one* child. More often several children resulted and married into different non-Jewish families, and with each succeeding generation the mixation of "non-Aryans" with "Aryans" was multiplied. The ramifications of the "Aryan" test must extend far indeed when one considers that each baptism and each intermarriage tainted with "non-Aryanism" all the descendants for at least two or three generations, possibly for more if the test of January 1st, 1800 is applied.

Moreover, National Socialist legislation does not consider a person free of the stigma of "non-Aryanism" unless proved otherwise. The onus of proof is thrown upon the individual who desires to hold public office, engage in a liberal profession, or contribute to the intellectual and cultural life of the country. With respect to office-holders who have fallen under

I. Descent from Baptized Jews

		Baptized Jew—marries—Baptized Jewess
1st generation	"Non-Aryan" because parents and grandparents were Jews	child—(m. "Aryan")
2nd generation	"Non-Aryan" because two grandparents were Jews	grandchild—(m. "Aryan")
3rd generation	"Non-Aryan" because one grandparent, descended of Jewish parents, was considered a Jew	great-grandchild—(m. "Aryan")
4th generation	"Aryan"	great-great-grandchild

II. Descent from Mixed Marriage

		Jew—marries—"Aryan"
1st generation	"Non-Aryan" because one parent and two grandparents were Jews	child—(m. "Aryan")
2nd generation	"Non-Aryan" because one grandparent was a Jew	grandchild—(m."Aryan")
3rd generation	"Aryan"	great-grandchild [11]

11. For the purposes of the laws regulating the publishing business and peasant holdings (see above, p. 149) the great-great-grandchild of Table I and the great-grandchild of Table II would not be considered "Aryan" if the mixed marriage or baptism had occurred after January 1st, 1800.

suspicion, the Prussian Ministry of Justice has summarily ordered that officials whose "Aryan" descent is questioned by "reliable sources," especially by associations of a national character, "must within three days, clarify their status," [12] and failure to produce the requisite evidence has resulted in dismissal from office.

Nor did the Government authorities wait until suspicion had been cast upon an individual. Officials, lawyers, doctors, and those engaged in educational and cultural work were ordered to submit proof in the form of documents, such as birth and marriage certificates, that they and their wives were of "Aryan" descent. Even those who had held office uninterruptedly for nearly twenty years (since August 1st, 1914) and whose "Aryan" origin had not been questioned, must make the following statement:

> "I declare officially herewith: I do not know of any circumstance—despite careful scrutiny—that may justify the presumption that I am not of Aryan descent; in particular, none of my paternal or maternal parents, or grandparents, was at any time of the Jewish faith.
>
> "I am fully aware of the fact that I expose myself to prosecution and dismissal if this declaration proves untrue." [13]

The State even provided for a "racial expert" to delve into the obscurities of "Aryan" antecedents and resolve doubtful cases.

> "If Ayran descent is doubtful [read a decree of the Reich Ministry of the Interior] an opinion is to be obtained from the expert for racial research attached to the Minister of the Interior." [14]

Thus, the aid of "scientific research" has been enlisted to make certain that not even a person of doubtful "Aryanism" would remain to contaminate the life of the new Germany.

Application to the Government Service

This was no theoretic question. The "Aryan" test was established to eliminate Jews, and Christians of Jewish ancestry, from participation in the life of the country. The first to be affected were those in the Government service against whom the basic Law for the Restoration of the Professional Civil Service was directed. This called for the elimination of officials of "non-Aryan" descent, and the term official was broadly defined:

> "According to this law the following are to be regarded as officials: immediate and mediate functionaries of the Reich, immediate and mediate functionaries of the States, and functionaries of the Communes and Unions of Communes, servants of public law corporations, as well as officers of similar institutions and establishments. . . . These provisions are also to be applied to functionaries of social insurance bodies who have the status of officials." [15]

It was the intent of the law to remove from Government employ all persons of "non-Aryan" descent (with certain exceptions) [16] whether occupying political office, administrative positions, honorary posts, or engaged in manual and menial labour. This objective was achieved by means of a series of decrees and ordinances which clarified and amplified the sweeping provisions of the basic law. The ban fell upon the "non-Aryan" members of the instructional staffs of all public educational institutions; upon the officials of judicial tribunals of every description; upon tax assessors, consultants and notaries; upon officials and employees of the Imperial Railway Administration, of municipal theatres, gas and electricity works, of public banks and insurance companies, of the postal service and public welfare institutions, and of other public or semi-public agencies; and upon police officers and civil employees of the army.[17] The only branch of the service which was unaffected by the general legislation was the military; ". . . officers, health officers, veterinary officers, non-commissioned officers, and soldiers" of the army were expressly exempted from the "Aryan" provisions of the laws respecting Government employment. It must not be supposed, however, that the National Socialist leaders were unconcerned about the "racial purity" of the most honourable institution of the German State. It is more likely that the effectiveness of the army would have suffered from the immediate retirement of many devoted and efficient "non-Aryans," and the army chiefs dared to insist that the welfare of the army should take precedence over the racial theories of the National Socialists. Subsequently, however (in May, 1935), when the new Conscription Law was issued, the "Aryan" test was applied to the army also. The Conscription Law provided that

> "(1) Aryan descent is a pre-supposition for active military service. . . .
>
> "(3) Only members of Aryan descent may be superiors in the army.
>
> "(4) Members of the army and of the reserve of Aryan descent are forbidden to marry persons of non-Aryan descent. Contraventions bring about the loss of any higher military rank." [18]

One provision of the new Conscription Law merits special attention, namely, "The service of non-Aryans during a war is reserved for special regulation." Man-power in war is a compelling necessity and it might prove desirable to call upon the "non-Aryans," untrained though they be, to defend the Fatherland which disowned and humiliated them.

Application to the Professions

The National Socialist legislators did not stop with the elimination of "non-Aryans" (and incidentally also of "Aryans" whose opinions they disliked), from Government service. They immediately reached out to "purge" the liberal professions. It might have been expected that the "Aryan" test would be applied to judges, arbitrators in civil and labour courts, jurors and court officials, because they were employees of the State. But the new legislation of Germany went further and declared that

> "The admission of lawyers who, according to the Law for the Restoration of the Professional Civil Service . . . are of non-Aryan descent, may be cancelled until September 30th, 1933. . . .
>
> "Admission to the bar may be refused to persons who . . . are of non-Aryan descent, even if there exists none of the reasons enumerated in the Regulations for Lawyers (*Rechtsanwaltsordnung*). . . ." [19]

This enactment made the practice of law impossible for "non-Aryans" [20] and additional laws and ministerial decrees were issued to close every branch of the profession to the proscribed group. Civil, criminal and patent lawyers; counsellors in administrative law and in social insurance; consultants on tax appeals and on cases brought before the labour courts; and candidates in training for the legal profession must all establish the pure "Aryanism" of their ancestry (and the acceptability of their political and social views) or be driven from the bar and the courts. It mattered not that professional and personal conduct had been beyond reproach, or that a lawyer had been an honoured and respected member of his profession. If he could not meet or subscribe to the narrow and exclusive standard of the National Socialists his usefulness to the community was at an end.[21]

Even more startling was the application of racial and political tests to medicine and dentistry. German physicians and dentists were not, like the lawyers, driven at one stroke from their professions. Their elimination was achieved in a manner more ingenious, but in the long run no less effective. In the first place, provision was made that no *new* "non-Aryan" physicians or dentists be certified. An announcement made by the Rector of the University of Berlin read:

> "The Prussian Minister of Public Instruction has announced that non-Aryan medical students cannot expect to receive authorization to practice. But, according to present prescriptions, diplomas in medicine and dentistry may be granted only to foreign nationals, regardless of the question whether and when a German official authorization to practice is granted";

and the Rector went on to advise that

> "the only recourse left to candidates of German nationality of non-Aryan descent, if they desire to obtain their diploma in medicine before securing authorization to practice as physician (dentist) in Germany, is to renounce German nationality. . . ." [22]

Physicians and dentists already in practice were not prevented by law from pursuing their callings, but, through expulsion from the National (and private) Health Insurance Service, they were deprived of their most numerous clientele and basic source of income. A decree of the Reich Minister of Labour read:

> "The work of panel doctors of non-Aryan descent, as well as of panel doctors who engaged in activities of a communistic nature, must cease. Further admission of such physicians as panel doctors to the National Health Insurance Service is forbidden."

Similarly,

> "The work of dentists and dental technicians in connection with the National Health Insurance Service . . . must cease if they are of non-Aryan descent or if they displayed communistic tendencies; such dentists and technicians are henceforth excluded from the practice."[23]

These laws were put into effect by a number of decrees, the most noteworthy of which were the regulations concerning National Health Insurance practice which were issued by the Commissioner of Physicians, Dr. Wagner. He declared that:

> "Aryan physicians may be substituted by Aryan physicians only. . . . The same principle applies in the case of employing an assistant.
>
> "Aryan physicians must assign their Aryan patients to Aryan specialists, physicians of hospitals, sanitaria, etc., and *vice versa*. Where local conditions render it absolutely necessary, Aryan physicians, especially those employed in hospitals, may accept assignments from non-Aryan physicians. . . .
>
> "Common practice between Aryan and non-Aryan physicians is prohibited."[24]

Thus collaboration, substitution and consultation between "Aryan" and "non-Aryan" physicians were prohibited. Apparently a specialist's superior knowledge or surgical skill must be dispensed with in order further to segregate the "non-Aryans."

One decree of the Reich Minister of Labour, that of February 3rd, 1934, is especially revealing as to what the moulders of the New Germany consider essential in the training of a Health Insurance officer. After announcing that employment in the National Health Insurance Service and promotion could be secured only on the basis of competitive examinations, the Minister went on to direct that the

> "subject matter of the examination in addition to the general and professional attainments must be civics (National Socialist view of life), as well as racial theory and eugenics.
>
> "The National Health Insurance Service must see to it that all officials, employees and labourers, even if they are not to pass an examination, acquire the necessary knowledge of civics, racial theory and eugenics." [25]

Application to Educational and Cultural Fields

But if National Socialist "civics, racial theory and eugenics" were essential in the Health Insurance Service, how much more so in the educational and cultural institutions! Accordingly, legislation was enacted to clear this field of all elements that might fail to subscribe to the National Socialist view of life. "Non-Aryans" and the politically undesirable were swept from their posts in schools, colleges, universities, even from professional and scientific schools. Instructors, lecturers, professors ordinary and extraordinary, salaried and honorary, were equally displaced. Nor were all young Germans permitted to come indiscriminately and drink freely at this purified fountain of knowledge. Schools in which attendance was not compulsory, colleges and universities, were ordered to reduce the number of their "non-Aryan" scholars to a maximum of 5 per cent. of the student body, and new "non-Aryan" pupils were not to be admitted in excess of 1.5 per cent. of the student body. Even the few "non-Aryan" students who were admitted were classed as outcasts and excluded from the Associations of Students that were formed in the universities. National Socialist legislative generosity appears to have been exhausted with the provision that

"If the number of new pupils admitted into a given school is so small that, according to the fixed percentage, no pupil of non-Aryan descent could be admitted, one pupil of non-Aryan descent may be admitted." [26]

The National Socialists were also greatly concerned about the welfare of the press. "Scandalous" elements were to be eliminated and the "independence of the press" was to be furthered by subordination to the Minister of Propaganda, and by ordering that

> "Only he may be an editor:
> "(3) who is of Aryan descent and not married to a person of non-Aryan descent;
> "(7) who possesses the qualities requisite for a task involving the exercise of a spiritual influence upon public opinion." [27]

Even more rigorous were the requirements for publishers, stockholders of newspaper firms, the members of boards of directors and employees. These must prove "their own Aryan descent and that of their wives . . . up to 1800." [28] Newspaper publishing firms were suppressed if their newspapers reported "on events in a form not commensurate with their importance for the public and which is apt to give offence to, or to prejudice the dignity of the press."

The cinema was regulated by the establishment of a Temporary Film Chamber, membership in which was compulsory for all those who produced, sold or presented films and for "film creators," a comprehensive term which included:

> "Production managers, stage managers, composers, scenario writers, musical managers, musicians, managers of photography, architects, camera men, sound masters, stars and minor artists, supers and the like."

And admission to the Film Chamber might be refused, or a member might be expelled, if the person in question "does not inspire the confidence necessary for carrying on the film profession." [29] Much light was thrown upon this vague standard by Dr. Goebbels, Reich Minister for Enlightenment and Propaganda, when he told the film producers on February 9th, 1934, that one of their chief tasks had been "the exclusion of the Jews" [30]—a task which was performed with despatch and thoroughness.

The most far-reaching measure taken to bend the cultural life of Germany to the purposes of an exclusive racialism was the establishment on September 22nd, 1933, of a Reich Chamber of Culture, with sub-divisions devoted to literature, the press, broadcasting, the theatre, music and the plastic arts. Membership was compulsory, for the Minister of Enlightenment and Propaganda ordered that

> "whoever participates in production, reproduction, spiritual or technical elaboration, dissemination, preservation, sale or commission of sale of a cultural product, must be a member of a branch of the Reich Chamber that appertains to his activity.
>
> "Dissemination also means the production and sale of technical means for dissemination."

Exclusion from membership in the Chamber of Culture involved a ban on the public pursuit of a person's artistic or cultural activities, and provision was made for the refusal of admission to former political opponents and particularly to "non-Aryans." [31]

As in the regulations respecting the cinema, the familiar "Aryan paragraph" gave way to vaguer formula which read:

> "Admission to a Chamber may be refused, and a member may be excluded, if facts justify the presumption that the

person in question does not inspire the confidence or possess the ability necessary for the carrying on of his activity."

But it sufficed, because the Minister for Enlightenment and Propaganda ruled that "non-Aryans" did not possess the necessary reliability and capacity for cultural work.[32]

The "Exceptions" from Discrimination

The campaign of the National Socialists to eliminate all "non-Aryans" from the public life of Germany encountered one obstacle, a self-imposed obstacle. For it was decided to make an exception of certain classes of war veterans and of those who had held office under the Empire. The basic Law for the Restoration of the Professional Civil Service provided that "non-Aryan" officials

> ". . . who were already serving as officials on August 1st, 1914, or who, during the World War, fought at the front for Germany or her allies, or whose fathers or sons [33] were killed in action in the World War"

were not to be removed from office.[34]

Similar provisions are to be found in the laws regulating the liberal professions,[35] but a careful reading of the "Aryan" decrees reveals a decided tendency to whittle down the concessions made. Thus the decree respecting physicians neglected to specify as exempt from discrimination those who had practised their profession since August 1st, 1914; while the law relating to editors does not exempt even those who served at the front during the World War, but merely permits an exception to be made.[36] The failure to disqualify by mention "non-Aryans" from participation in cultural activities (including the film industry) made it impossible for war veterans, even of the preferred variety, to claim exemption.

All could be eliminated indiscriminately as lacking the "reliability and capacity necessary" for cultural leadership.

Even more significant were the regulations respecting lawyers and doctors who had been exempted because of their war service. It was not enough that the war registers attested to the fact that a man had been in active service at the front. The administration of justice of a district was "authorised" to request the Minister of Justice of the Reich for a ruling

> " . . . if it hesitates to grant to an advocate the quality of a combatant at the front, despite the fact that it is so certified in the war registers."

And the Ordinance of June 23rd, 1933, regarding exempt doctors and dentists, speaks for itself:

§2

> "Even such physicians of non-Aryan descent for whom an exception is provided in . . . the Law for the Restoration of the Civil Service may not be appointed as physicians of trust or of verification of accidents or of similar functions.
>
> "In so far as non-official non-Aryan physicians have such a position at present, and do not lose it by virtue of the Law for the Restoration of the Professional Civil Service, their service contract must be rescinded. . . . This does not apply to physicians who are severely injured by reason of war wounds."

§5

> "In the Social Insurance and Reich Welfare, examination by a non-Aryan physician may be refused by anyone before the beginning of the examination. In this case care must be taken that the examination is made by a capable physician of Aryan descent." [37]

EXTENSION TO INDUSTRY, AGRICULTURE AND COMMERCE

Save, then, for the rapidly diminishing handful of "non-Aryans" still permitted to maintain a precarious hold upon their former positions, Jews, and Christians of Jewish ancestry, have been driven from the intellectual and cultural life of their country. Government officials, doctors, lawyers, educators, renowned artists and celebrated scientists, even those whose sole interest was the furtherance of human knowledge, have been or are being driven from their posts regardless of years of faithful service, of contributions made to science, to art and letters. The astronomer, the mathematician, the engineer, the chemist, the physicist, the musician, the painter, have not been spared. It matters not that their opinions have been orthodox. If a trace of "non-Aryanism" can be discovered by recourse to long-forgotten and wholly meaningless genealogical tables, the individual can no longer pursue his calling.

Thus far we have examined primarily the discrimination against what might be called the "non-Aryan" intellectuals. If this group alone had been affected, the refugee problem would not have assumed such staggering dimensions. In fact, National Socialist policy of the past three years has manifested a decided tendency to extend the application of the "Aryan" test to other human relations and activities, and the number of potential refugees has thereby been greatly augmented.

The economic opportunities of manufacturers and merchants of "non-Aryan" descent have been progressively curtailed. It was made difficult, if not impossible, for "non-Aryan" firms to secure concessions for public works. A decree of the central government merely ordered that

> "As regards firms, the proprietors or managing officers of which are of non-Aryan descent, the principle obtains

that Aryan firms are to be given preference if their offer is equivalent. The officers in charge of the public orders have discretion to decide. . . . "

But, in executing the order, a Prussian official said:

"I believe that the choice of contractors—as heretofore—must be left to the judgment of the responsible officers placing the orders. In placing the orders—I expect and assume this with certainty—even without special instructions everything possible will be done to have special regard to well-deserving National Socialists." [38]

The legislation respecting the "hereditary" peasantry indicated the desirability of excluding "non-Aryans" from agricultural pursuits. In the law of September 29th, 1933, regulating peasant holdings, it was decreed that

"(1) Only a person of German or cognate blood may be a peasant.

"(2) A person is not considered German or as having cognate blood, if his paternal or maternal ancestors have Jewish or coloured blood in their veins.

"(3) The first of January, 1800, is the day that decides whether the premises of paragraph 1 obtain. . . ." [39]

The Stock and Produce Exchanges were likewise purged of "non-Aryans." The *Völkischer Beobachter*, after declaring that it was not the intention of the Government to decrease the number of brokers, went on to say:

"The paramount consideration was the purging of the German Stock Exchange of all foreign and non-Aryan intruders, and making the vocation of brokers into a class of honest merchants who are suitable for their calling because of their national sentiments." [40]

Finally, the intention of the Government with regard to "non-Aryan" business establishments was revealed in the regulations respecting the expenditure of the sums received by loyal "Aryans" as "marriage loans." The Reich Minister of Finance ordered that

> " . . . As sales agencies are admitted . . . only those whose owners warrant that they will always unswervingly support the National Socialist Government,"[41]

a condition which could, of course, not be met by "non-Aryans."

It must not be assumed that these selected regulations exhaust the National Socialist discriminatory legislation with regard to the economic activities of "non-Aryans." They have been selected with the sole purpose of indicating that not only will the men and women who have been driven from the civil service and the professions find it impossible to employ their talents and earn a livelihood in commerce and industry, but also that the opportunities of "non-Aryan" business men and manufacturers are being progressively circumscribed. Is it then the intention of the National Socialist Government to reduce all "non-Aryans" to the status of manual labourers? For light on this question one must turn again to the basic law of April 7th, 1933, to which reference has repeatedly been made, and to subsequent legislation respecting employees and workers.

The Law for the Restoration of the Professional Civil Service specifically mentions "clerks and workers" of "non-Aryan" descent as subject to dismissal, a provision which must have cut deeply into the economic opportunities of "non-Aryans," since it has been applied not only in the agencies of the central government but also in those of the " . . . states, communes, unions of communes and of *other associations, institutions and foundations of public law.*" [Italics ours.][42] The Reichsbank, the State Railway Company, and "religious associations of public law and their federations" are specifically "authorized to issue similar provisions" —an authorization which is, of course, to be regarded as a mandate for immediate action.[43] Moreover, the term "institutions, associations and foundations of public law" includes also all

> "unions of corporations, associations and institutions more than half of whose income comes from public bodies, . . . enterprises more than half of whose corporate capital is owned by public bodies, . . . and all subsidiaries and intermediaries more than half of whose capital belongs to public bodies."

The service contracts of "non-Aryan" employees and workmen of these establishments, as well as of the central and local governments are to be annulled "within one month, to be effective at the end of the following month."[44]

Employment, then, even as clerks and manual labourers, is denied to "non-Aryans" in all establishments directly or indirectly endowed with a public character. One recourse would remain, namely, to work as artisans in private industry. But that avenue of escape has not been allowed to remain unencumbered with obstacles. Membership of Jewish artisans in guilds or trade unions has been discouraged by the Federation of German Handicraftsmen in the following instruction:

> "Membership of Jewish artisans in trade unions is admissible as far as binding legal provisions exist in regard to membership in the chamber of artisans and the compulsory guild. But it must be avoided at all events that the Jewish members of the trade unions hold offices or seats on the board. As far as membership in the trade unions is not legally required, the individual trade unions may decide at their own discretion whether they wish to admit Jewish members. But it goes without saying that

on principle, Jewish members should not hold offices or seats on the board." [45]

"Non-Aryan" Christians, as well as Jews, are excluded from the Labour Front, the only authorized labour organization, which embraces in its membership employers, employees and manual labourers. Technically, employment is not conditional upon membership of the Labour Front, but in practice "non-Aryans" are in constant danger of losing their jobs and, once out of work, a "non-Aryan" can entertain little hope of finding further employment.

* * *

The legislative disabilities of "non-Aryans" which have just been analysed prove that it is the intention of the National Socialist rulers of Germany to eliminate Jews and Christians of Jewish ancestry from all public and semi-public institutions, from the liberal professions and from intellectual and cultural life; to restrict their opportunities as business men, employees or labourers; and to segregate them as a group of outcasts. However, the full force of these laws and decrees, many of them quite loosely drawn and obscure, can be felt only when one examines the manner in which they have been interpreted by the courts and applied by local authorities. Nor must we fail to take into consideration the extra-legal measures employed both to remove "non-Aryans" from fields of endeavour not yet closed by legislation and to make the practice of their calling impossible for those who were expressly exempted from the disabilities because of war service or other reasons. We must remember that "Aryan" legislation has set a standard for National Socialist Germany, and those who feel strongly on the question of "Aryanism" and "non-Aryanism" cannot fail to draw their own conclusions and act accordingly. For example, if "non-Aryan" medical men are prohibited by law from practising as panel doctors and dentists, if even the few favoured and exempted persons must not be retained in "positions of trust," how can an "Aryan" come to such a person for private consultation? When "non-Aryan" lawyers and educators are ostracized, a war veteran cannot flaunt his war record before every client or pupil. If "non-Aryan" business men and labourers are denied all contact with public institutions, pure "Aryans" cannot fail to boycott their shops and avoid all intercourse with them. In short, we must examine the court decisions, the application of the laws by local officials and the activities of the National Socialist Party and its affiliates to obtain a true picture of the present status of "non-Aryans" in Germany.

NOTES

1. *Reichsgesetzblatt*, 1933, I, p.175.
2. See, for example, *Preussische Gesetzsammlung*, 1933, p.209 §3; *Reichsgesetzblatt*, 1933, I, pp.257 §2, 188 §3, 222 §1, 518.
3. See *Reichsgesetzblatt*, 1933, I, pp.195, 245.
4. *Reichsgesetzblatt*, 1933, I, pp.541 §27, 713 §5 (7). See also pp.483 §3, 797 §10.
5. Estimates of the number of "non-Aryans" vary from two hundred thousand to several millions. For a careful analysis of this question, see Wellisch, "Die Anzahl der Menschen Jüdischer Abstammung," *Zeitschrift für Rassenkunde und ihre Nachbargebiete*, Stuttgart, 1935, II, heft 2, pp.198–203.
6. Decree of April 11th, 1933, *Reichsgesetzblatt*, 1933, I, p.195.
7. Decree of September 28th, 1933, *Reichsgesetzblatt*, 1933, I, p.678.
8. *Reichsgesetzblatt*, 1933, I, p.685 §13.
9. *Frankfurter Zeitung*, April 26th, 1935.
10. The "Law on Citizenship and on the Protection of the Purity of German Blood" which was issued on November 15th, 1935, does not define the term "non-Aryan." Moreover, paragraph 6 specifically states that previous laws respecting the "purity of blood" remain in force. See *Völkischer Beobachter*, November 16th, 1935.
11. See p.151.
12. *Justizministerialblatt*, 1935, I, p.160.
13. Decree of May 23rd, 1933. *Justizministerialblatt*, p.160.
14. *Reichsgesetzblatt*, 1933, I, p.575. See also pp.195, 222, 541; *Justizministerialblatt*, 1933, pp.160, 164; *Deutsche Justiz*, 1933, p.729.
15. Law of April 7th, 1933, *Reichsgesetzblatt*, 1933, I, p.175.

16. See pp.161–2.
17. *Reichsgesetzblatt*, 1933, I, pp.245, 219, 257, 277, 397; *Justizministerialblatt*, p.151.
18. *Völkischer Beobachter*, May 23rd, 1935.
19. Law Respecting Admission to the Legal Profession, April 7th, 1933, *Reichsgesetzblatt*, 1933, I, p.188 §§ 1, 2. See also *Gesetzsammlung*, pp.195, 213.
20. For exceptions see p.162.
21. See, for example, *Reichsgesetzblatt*, 1933, I, pp.188, 277, 522, 217, 528, 669; *Deutsche Justiz*, 1933, p.729; *Preussische Gesetzsammlung*, 1933, pp.209, 367; *Justizministerialblatt*, 1933, p.164.
22. *Frankfurter Zeitung*, December 20th, 1933.
23. *Reichsgesetzblatt*, 1933, I, p.222 §1, p.350 §1. See also *Vossische Zeitung*, July 9th, 1933.
24. *Deutsches Ärzteblatt*, 1933, p.131. See also *Völkischer Beobachter*, August 22nd, 1933, November 24th, 1933; *Reichsgesetzblatt*, 1933, I, pp.541, 696, 983, 1118.
25. *Reichsgesetzblatt*, 1934, p.84.
26. *Ibid.*, 1933, I, pp.215, 225, 226. See also pp.175, 245; *Völkischer Beobachter*, December 24th, 1933, December 22nd, 1934.
27. *Reichsgesetzblatt*, 1933, I, p.713 §5.
28. Order for the Preservation of the Independence of the Press, April 24th, 1935, in *Frankfurter Zeitung*, April 26th, 1935.
29. *Reichsgesetzblatt*, 1933, I, p.483. See also pp.393, 531; *Reichsministerialblatt*, p.351.
30. *Frankfurter Zeitung*, February 11th, 1934.
31. For an instance of such exclusion see *Manchester Guardian*, April 6th, 1935.
32. *Reichsgesetzblatt*, 1933, I, pp.661, 797, 969. See also *Völkischer Beobachter*, March 7th, 1934; *Berliner Tageblatt*, February 8th, 1934.
33. Or husbands, see *Reichsgesetzblatt*, 1933, I, p.655.
34. *Reichsgesetzblatt*, 1933, I, p.175.
35. See, for example, *Preussische Gesetzammlung*, 1933, p.209; *Reichsgesetzblatt*, 1933, I, pp.188, 217, 225, 260, 350; *Justizministerialblatt*, p.164.
36. See Article 2 of the Ordinance of April 22nd, 1933, *Reichsgesetzblatt*, 1933, I, p.222, and Article 16 of the Ordinance of December 19th, 1933, *Reichsgesetzblatt*, 1933, I, p.1085.
37. *Reichsgesetzblatt*, 1933, I, pp.397, 528. Many exempted "non-Aryans" were eliminated through the application of Article 6 of the Law for the Restoration of the Professional Civil Service which authorized the retirement of officials for the purpose of "simplifying the administration." See *ibid.*, p.175. Paragraph 4(2) of the "Law on Citizenship and on the Protection of the Purity of German Blood," issued on November 15th, 1935, prescribes that *all* remaining Jewish officials be retired by December 31st, 1935. So far as Jews are concerned, the exception has been completely withdrawn. See *Völkischer Beobachter*, November 16th, 1935.

38. *Reichsanzeiger*, No. 180; MBLiV. I, p.1277 §2.
39. *Reichsgesetzblatt*, 1933, I, p.685 §§11–3. See also pp.118, 1096, and *Gesetzsammlung*, p.165.
40. See *Völkischer Beobachter*, October 6th, 1933, November 4th, 1933.
41. See *Reichsanzeiger*, No. 199 §II; *Reichsgesetzblatt*, 1933, I, p.377 §1.
42. *Reichsgesetzblatt*, 1933, I, p.175 §15; p.433 §6 (1).
43. *Ibid.*, 1933, I, p.175 §1 (4); p.433 §6 (2). See also p.622.
44. See Ordinance of May 4th, 1933. *Reichsgesetzblatt*, 1933, I, p.233 §§1, 3; Ordinance of September 28th, 1933, *ibid.*, 1933, I, p.678 §IX; Decree of August 7th, 1933, *Reichsbesoldungsblatt*, p.113 §§1, 2, 9.
45. *Völkischer Beobachter*, October 18th, 1933.

Chapter II

ADMINISTRATIVE MEASURES AND PARTY ACTIVITY

THE full picture of the straits to which the "non-Aryan" population of Germany has been reduced by legislative discrimination is not adequately portrayed merely by an analysis of the formal statutes enacted. The very organization of the Reich encourages legislation in the wider sense by administrative officials, both national and local, Party leaders, corporate Chambers and quasi-public bodies. As a result, it has been possible to apply the racial principle to the remotest nooks and crannies of German life.

Lacunae left in the laws, as well as daily applications of the statutes to specific instances not regulated thereby, are dealt with according to the discretion of administrative officials. The identification of Party with State, as well as the assumption of the functions of government by Party members rather than elected officers, gives to the orders and actions of National Socialist leaders a public legal character.[1] The organization of each branch of economic and cultural activity into a corporate Chamber upon the fascist model makes it possible for these quasi-autonomous bodies to legislate within the sphere of jurisdiction left to them. In addition, every local society, business, or private organization is encouraged to carry on the process of *Gleichschaltung* (i.e. "co-ordination" and the removal of "non-Aryans") of its own accord, assured as it is of the wholehearted support of the Government in such a programme.

Furthermore, even many "non-Aryans" who, because they come within certain exceptions, are still in theory allowed to practise their occupations,[2] are in actual fact forced from their positions, and ruined in their professions and businesses by the governmentally encouraged boycott. This further and final handicap has penetrated all fields of endeavour, but has been particularly noticeable in business life where the racial principle has not yet been completely applied by statute.

The manner in which the Government's programme of discrimination against "non-Aryans" has been extended and enforced in all branches of activity may be seen from the following typical instances relating to the professions, education, culture, commerce, artisanship and business.

Law and the Judiciary

As a result of the National Socialist revolution, the German Bar Association was dissolved and a National Socialist Lawyers' Society was set up to replace it. Even those "non-Aryan" lawyers who came within the exceptions of the law of April 7th, were refused membership in this "co-ordinated" association.[3]

Dr. Freisler, leader of the National Socialist League of German Jurists, protested as early as August 9th, 1933, against the use by "Aryans" of Jewish lawyers. "This conduct," he said, "is incompatible with the guiding principles of the national reconstruction." He gave warning that the National Socialist League would thereafter publish the names of all "Aryans" who employed Jewish lawyers to defend them.[4] Nor is the "non-Aryan" lawyer given an equal status before the Courts. The *Frankfurter Zeitung* of February 5th, 1935, reported a case before a Labour Court in which the Magistrate declared, following upon the speech of a Jewish lawyer, that "racial considerations" prohibited the Court from considering the case of the client of the Jewish lawyer on its merits. The Magistrate admitted that the fact that "the defendant had chosen this counsel proved his lack of instinct and was significant of his lack of racial and National Socialist sentiments."

The difficulties which Judges of "non-Aryan" descent who are allowed to retain their positions nevertheless face have been illustrated in numerous court decisions upholding their removal as being "prejudiced" and unfamiliar with the "National Socialist view of life." [5] In addition, an order enacted by the Minister of Justice as early as April of 1933 is still in force and prohibits even those "non-Aryan" Judges still allowed to sit from adjudicating upon cases of criminal law. This same prohibition still stands, without exception, for state's attorneys and public prosecutors of "non-Aryan" descent.[6]

An example of the thoroughness with which this "co-ordination" or removal of "non-Aryans" has taken place was given by an announcement in the *Juristische Wochenschrift* of August 5th, 1933, the organ of the new German bar association and formerly edited by Justizrat Magnus, one of the leading jurists of Germany, a "non-Aryan." The announcement read in part:

> "The *Juristische Wochenschrift* . . . can publish contributions only from persons who are 'Aryans.' Books written by 'non-Aryans' or published by 'non-Aryan' publishing houses will not be reviewed; advertisements regarding such books will not be accepted for the advertisement section."

Furthermore, the new editors announced that only such articles would be published as "unconditionally adhere to the platform and viewpoint of National Socialism." [7]

Nor has the Government reached the end of its programme for the dismissal of "non-Aryan" lawyers and judges. The Minister of Justice for the Reich and the Leader of the National Socialist Bar Association declared in May, 1935, that "it is our great task to take the necessary steps to remove these parasites and create a true German law." [8] This end is being attained through the boycott of "non-Aryan" lawyers which is carried out by the National Socialist Bar Association. Those who attempt to earn a pittance by assisting "Aryan" lawyers are faced with regulations laid down by the Bar Associations, both national and local, forbidding such relations.

Medicine

As in the case of lawyers and judges, "non-Aryan" physicians and dentists have been subjected to further discrimination even though they come within the exemptions laid down by law.[9] Nominally, "non-Aryan" physicians or dentists who were admitted to practice before 1914, who fought at the front, who served in a military hospital during the war, or who lost a father or husband in the war, may continue to serve as Panel physicians under the Health Insurance Service. In March, 1934, however, the Nationalist Club for Legal Information of Greater Berlin made public the fact that, since "non-Aryan" physicians may not be appointed experts in legal proceedings to obtain compensation and pensions under the Social Insurance regulations, claims certified by such physicians would not be honoured. "All patients, therefore," the announcement ran, "who owing to an illness, have a claim for a pension are cautioned that they must be treated from the very beginning by German Christian (Aryan) physicians only, because, as mentioned above, they alone are considered eligible as experts in court procedure." [10] Since many illnesses or injuries may eventually result in a claim for a pension or compensation, there is little likelihood that even "non-Aryan" physicians still allowed to retain their Health Panel or their Social Insurance practice, have greatly benefited from their right.

Furthermore, no "non-Aryan" medical student, even if he

completed his studies before 1933 and passed his examination, may be licensed to practice.[11] In certain exceptional instances, and under the following conditions, a "non-Aryan" may be licensed to practice after completing the examination; if he is only a "quarter Jew," that is, has only one grandfather or grandmother of Jewish blood; or if he fought in the war (most unlikely, of course, in the case of candidates for license at this date); and if his mental attitude and physical appearance are unobjectionable. Likewise, "non-Aryan" dentists and dental mechanics may not be admitted to the necessary examinations for the exercise of their profession.

Furthermore, according to rules set forth by the National Socialist Medical Association, "Aryan" physicians or dentists are forbidden to engage "non-Aryan" physicians or dentists as assistants, or substitutes, to have a joint consultation office, or to refer cases regarding expert treatment to specialists of "non-Aryan" descent. "Non-Aryan" physicians who come within the exceptions are also forbidden to employ "non-Aryans" who have been excluded.[12]

Education

According to a decree of Reich Minister Rust, no "non-Aryan" pupils may be admitted to German elementary public schools.[13] "Racial science," teaching that the "non-Aryan" is a perverse and traitorous creature has been made a fundamental part of the school curricula by order of the Prussian Minister of Education.[14] The Instructions issued by the Prussian Minister for Economy and Labour, for example, in March, 1934, setting forth the subjects recommended for "civic education" in professional and technical schools, contained suggestions for the study of "the new structure of the family and nation on a racial basis, and in this regard the Jewish question." [15]

Among the official school texts chosen by Reich Minister Rust for this racial study are the following: Adolf Hitler's *Mein Kampf;* Theodore Fritsch's *Handbook of the Jewish Question;* H. F. R. Gunther's *Racial Science of the Jewish People;* and A. Rosenberg's *Protocols of the Elders of Zion and Jewish World Politics.*[16] The instructions given to German school teachers on methods of lecturing schoolgirls on the Jewish question advise that "when raising the Jewish question with the girls, steps should be taken by the teachers to bring out the fact that Jews are of Asiatic descent and cannot mix with 'Aryans,' and that intermarriage with Jews is out of the question." [17] In the schools of Bavaria a text-book by von Fikenscher, *Aufbruch der Nation*, is used with the approval of the Minister of Education and is particularly devoted to reconstructing German history so as to portray the Jew as a villain.[18] *The Handbook of the Hitler Jugend* teaches the same doctrine.[19]

The central organization of the German students (*Deutsche Studentenschaft*) has taken a leading rôle in preventing even those "non-Aryan" professors exempt from dismissal from carrying on their teaching. Its proclamation of April 21st, 1933, called for the elimination of all Jews from Germany as "alien antagonists," and suggested the public burning of "un-German books." The student body of the University of Berlin ordered students not to enroll for or attend lectures delivered by "Jewish instructors." [20]

Further, Minister of Education Rust, on March 23rd, 1935, issued decrees which render it improbable, if not impossible, that "non-Aryan" children or those who refuse to accept National Socialist principles will be educated beyond the elementary school stage. Pupils of "Aryan" descent, even if intellectually inferior, are to be allowed to make up for this deficiency by their "bodily capacity," "ability to lead," and "personal character." In no case, the decree runs, may "Aryan" pupils be placed at a disadvantage in relation to "non-Aryan" pupils. In addition, children, who "through their attitude within or without the school sabotage the unity of People or State must be expelled." [21]

Artisanship

In the field of manual labour, also, the lack of specific legislation preventing "non-Aryans" from continuing their activity has been no obstacle to their exclusion in practice. Artisanship, like the cultural activities, the professions, and commerce, has been organized in the form of state associations, corporate groups which apply the racial principle to their jurisdictions.

This was clearly shown by the order of Dr. Hjalmar Schacht, Reich Minister of Economics, on March 12th, 1935, when he pointed out that for "non-Aryans" the "independent pursuit of a manual craft as a standing trade is contrary to the provisions of the Third Ordinance regarding the Preliminary Reconstruction of German manual trades, dated January 18th, 1935." [22] In actual fact, the Ordinance mentioned by the Minister of Economics contains no "Aryan paragraph." Nevertheless, his statement was a confession of a common state of affairs and accurately portrayed the reality that, without such a clause and on grounds of "unreliability," "non-Aryans" have been excluded from artisanship. In this field of activity, it has been decided that graduates of a Jewish manual training school course cannot, whatever their ability, become qualified for membership in the Manual Trades Guild, which is compulsory for all artisans. Furthermore, "non-Aryans" who have taken the regular manual craft training either find it impossible to obtain masters to whom they may be apprenticed, or, after their apprenticeship, may still be excluded from the Guild upon the protest of a single member. Furthermore, Jewish youth in Upper Bavaria, according to a decision of the Chamber of Commerce, may not be apprentices; for membership in the Hitler Jugend is required, an organization to which "non-Aryans" cannot belong.[23] Thus, for all practical purposes, in artisanship and the handicrafts, there is an unwritten "Aryan paragraph" which is effectively applied.

Commerce and Industry

The re-organization of commerce and industry along corporate lines has been directed towards the elimination of "non-Aryans" through the process of "co-ordination," and has been accomplished through the efforts of the Government as well as its instrument, the Party. The larger industrial associations and commercial unions have introduced "Aryan" clauses into their constitutions as requirements for membership.[24] The control exercised by the State over Chambers of Commerce and cartels has been used to this same purpose.[25]

In most large stores and factories, the Party has formed cells which through sabotage, intimidation, and official pressure agitate for the dismissal of all "non-Aryans," even though they be the proprietors.[26]

Among the state-controlled economic bodies which have been "co-ordinated" and from which "non-Aryans" have been dismissed are the following:

The Provisional Reich Economic Council (*Reichsgesetzblatt*, 1933, II, p.175).
The Reich Coal Council (*R.G.*, 1933, p.203).
The Reich Potash Council (*Ibid.*, p.205).
Executive Committee of Central Co-operative Societies Bank (*Ibid.*, p.227).
Board of Directors of Bank of German Industrial Bonds (*R.G.*, 1933, I, p.483).

Although in some instances the Reich Minister of Economics, sensitive to the economic dislocations which might result from too immediate an elimination of "non-Aryans" from business, has protested against the use of the racial principle,[27] the official campaign to eliminate "non-Aryans" has been no less effective though its tempo be somewhat slower than the more wholesale methods employed in other spheres.

The *Frankfurter Zeitung* of October 18th, 1935, reported just such an instance of the official governmental attempt to have Jews dismissed from business. A merchant complained that the dismissal of his "non-Aryan" employees had been demanded of him by the "official authorities."

It has already been pointed out that the Government, in certain laws and decrees, has given the signal for the elimination of "non-Aryans" from business and commerce.[28] Thus, "non-Aryan" firms receive no public contracts, and are excluded from accepting in payment the vouchers (*Bedarfsdeckungsschein*) of the unemployed for their purchases. Because of the magnitude of business affected by these prescriptions, this has been the first step in the programme to banish "non-Aryans" from commerce and industry. In order to save his firm from complete collapse, "the non-Aryan" is forced to take in "Aryan" partners, give them a majority share in the company, and to dismiss all "non-Aryan" employees. An example of this procedure was given early in 1934, when the Salamandar Shoe Company, a "non-Aryan" undertaking, was "co-ordinated," the shares passing into "perfectly Aryan hands." [29] Likewise, the Fuld Telephone Company was taken over by the Government in June, 1934, and "co-ordinated," the "non-Aryan" founders being retired from the board.[30]

Furthermore, industrial and commercial associations have been formed by "purging" existent bodies and excluding "non-Aryans." A German "Aryan" Clothing Manufacturers Society has replaced the former Association, and is dedicated to the elimination of "non-Aryans" by proving that "even in the clothing industry the monopoly of 'non-Aryans' has been abolished." All selling agents, brokers, and commercial representatives of "non-Aryan" origin have been excluded from the new Union of Commercial Representatives and Travelling Salesmen which has replaced the Central Union of German Commercial Representatives.[31] The same result has been obtained by the German Union of Exchange Bankers.[32]

The Government itself has sought, by further administrative orders, to restrict the economic opportunities open to "non-Aryans." On April 17th the Minister of Interior decided that no Apothecary's license is to be granted to any person of "non-Aryan" descent or to one who is married to a "non-Aryan." No exception is made for those who fought in the war.[33] The trade in antiques, which has among its leading merchants a great number of persons of "non-Aryan" descent, has also been made a closed field for them.[34] The German Railway, a semi-governmental corporation, published an order in May, 1935, confirming the fact that "advertisements of Jewish firms are no longer admissible within the precincts of the German Railway," and adding that proof of "Aryan" descent would no longer be required where from the name of the enterprise its "non-Aryan" origin was clear.[35]

Here, we find the most effective and ingenious method of co-ordination: the elimination of "non-Aryans" from commerce and business through boycott. For, even those "non-Aryan" firms which are able to resist "co-ordination" are forced to renounce the name "German business," to emphasize their "non-Aryan" nature, and thereby render themselves easy targets for the systematic and governmentally encouraged boycott. Since businesses employing Jews are considered to be "non-German," the boycott of such concerns invariably leads to the dismissal of all Jewish employees.[36] Thus, business, like the professions and other fields of activity, is made impossible for those of "non-Aryan" descent.

But, more than the mere hindrance of the business activity of "non-Aryans" is taking place, more than a curtailment of the means of livelihood for the more than 60 per cent. of the Jews of Germany engaged therein. The latest reports indicate that nothing less than the complete liquidation of all economic enterprises owned by Jews is the objective of National Socialist policy. The only sphere of economic activity left to Jews is to buy and sell among themselves in a veritable Ghetto. Pressure is being placed upon Jewish owners of corporation stocks to sell them at greatly reduced figures, in order that a concern may be known as thoroughly German. A plan has been advanced by the Party's Economic Information Agency for the liquidation of Jewish holdings through the creation of a central corporation which, backed by the power and the authority of the State, will compel Jews to sell their property at the lowest possible figure.[37] The achievement of this final expropriation of the property of Jews would seem to be only a matter of time; it has hitherto been slackened somewhat by the desire to avoid serious repercussions upon German economic life. But the aim of the Government has not been left obscure, and is rapidly being attained.

The Boycott of "Non-Aryans"

The deliberate and nation-wide boycott of Jewish business firms was first announced by the Government to begin on April 1st, 1933, and still continues with the greatest intensity. Previous to that date, the Party had prepared the groundwork by boycott propaganda and by demonstrations in which the members of the S.A. (*Sturm Abteilung*) took the leading part. General Goering, himself, then Prussian Minister of the Interior, as early as March 10th, 1933, confirmed the fact that the Government was encouraging Germans not to buy from Jews.[38] On March 27th, the National Socialist Party headquarters decided to transform these isolated boycott activities into a huge nation-wide demonstration.[39] The manifesto of the Party, proclaiming the country wide boycott of business conducted by Jews, as well as of Jewish professional men, appeared on March 29th, 1933.[40] Every local branch and unit of the Party was to appoint a Committee of Action to "popularize the boycott by propaganda and enlightenment." Herr Julius Streicher was appointed chairman and director. The Committees were urged to "penetrate into the smallest villages in order particularly to strike at Jewish rural traders," to organize "tens of thousands of mass meetings which shall reach into the tiniest hamlets." The Jewish origin of the victims was to be judged on the basis of race rather than religion [41] and picketing was to be coupled with the posting of placards announcing the race of the victim. In order to finance the campaign, contributions were to be solicited from "German business men." [42]

The suspension of the boycott was announced by a representative of the Government, Minister of Propaganda Goebbels, on March 31st, to commence on April 2nd.[43] Despite this official suspension, however, it is clear that the intent of the Government is to use the Party organization (they are, in fact, identical) to make the boycott of "non-Aryans" in Germany a permanent and systematic "humiliation of the Jews of Germany." [44] The original Party instructions called for a movement of long duration, and the current of events since April 1st, 1933, shows clearly how thoroughly successful this measure has been in removing and humiliating "non-

Aryans" whose existence was not already wiped out by statute.

The Committees of Action have drawn up directories of "non-Aryan" merchants which are distributed to the consuming public. "Aryan" stores are forced to place in their windows signs indicating their German origin; and no "non-Aryan" enterprise may do so without being called into court for unfair trade practice.[45] Hotels, restaurants, cafés, and even food stores and apothecaries' shops, are in various localities made to bear signs announcing that Jews may not even buy from them. Those who buy from "non-Aryans" are warned by the Party that they will be considered traitors to the people.[46] That these conditions are not accidental, but that they are on the contrary the very substance of the Government's programme, is shown by the express declarations of Party officials and Government leaders.

The Party has issued instructions to its members forbidding any contact between them and Jews, and providing for punishment of those who fail to "maintain an attitude of reserve towards Jews." [47] District Leader Grohe, speaking before the Hitler Youth at Aachen on July 22nd, 1934, declared that "anyone who buys of a Jew, or consults a Jewish physician, or a Jewish lawyer, besmirches German honour." [48] Gustav Giesecke, Peasant Leader for Brunswick, decreed on August 9th, 1935, that "any German peasant engaging in trade with a Jew or otherwise maintaining contact with him, commits treason to the blood and gives comfort to the deadly enemy of the German people, the Jew." [49] A similar warning was given by the Party Leader of Bretzenheim, Herr Lotz, on August 31st, 1934, pointing out the falsity of the "rumour" spread by "selfish persons," that "trade with Jews is now permitted." On the contrary, he declared, it is the duty of every German to deal with his folk-comrades and not with

Jews.[50] Sprenger, the National Socialist District Leader for Hessen (which includes the city of Frankfurt) and at the same time the Governor of the State and Province of Hessen, was reported by the *Frankfurter Zeitung* on March 19th, 1935, to have declared in a speech before a gathering of peasants:

> "The peril is still among us, for there are still Jews in Germany. . . . The way from the peasant to the townsman must be through the German and not through the Jew." [51]

The Mayor of Nuremberg, who in an order of May 19th, 1934, set forth rules for the purity of the German language, took the opportunity to point out that, as a matter of practical as well as of grammatical accuracy, "when discriminating between German and non-German businesses, the designation 'Christian' is totally unsuitable and should be avoided in principle." For, he declared,

> "There are no 'Christian' shops, physicians, cattle dealers, lawyers, etc. In contradistinction to the Jewish, there are only German physicians, German cattle dealers, German lawyers. . . . It is absolutely immaterial whether one or the other of the Jews in question is Catholic, Protestant, or otherwise baptized, he is and remains a Jew." [52]

It is this constant distinction between "German" and "Jewish" business which has been made the rallying cry for the boycott. The most active propagandist force, beside the National Socialist Party proper, has been the HAGO (*Handwerker und Gewerber-Organisation*), the official National Socialist Syndicate of Artisans and Merchants. It has been particularly successful in preventing retailers from continuing to purchase from Jewish wholesalers.[53] This end is being accomplished both by the compilation of lists of "non-Aryan" firms and by threats of official punishment. The National

Socialist Party district offices have also reached consumers by requesting signatures to the following "Solemn Declaration of Honour":

"I hereby declare on my word of honour that from now on and in the future I shall never do business of any kind with Jews, or with anyone connected directly or indirectly with Jews. I shall never enter a Jewish shop, and will turn away any Jews who enter my place of residence or estate.

"I shall not consult a Jewish physician or a Jewish lawyer. I shall also take care that nobody in my family, or my relatives or acquaintances, visits Jews.

"I am aware that I have the opportunity to consult the list containing the names of Jewish businesses in my residential district. I am also aware that if I fail to keep this promise, or if I try to evade it, I shall be expelled immediately from the Party, the S.A., the local Council, the National Socialist organizations (cross out those of which you are not a member), and that I may be branded, both orally and by writing, a man who has broken his word of honour and as a scoundrel."

To this relentless campaign, the Courts of Germany have given full sanction and support.[54] They have judicially declared boycott lists to be legitimate means of furthering the national interest; they have accepted the definition that a "Jewish business" can never be a "German business," and they have penalized and punished, as employing methods of unfair competition, "non-Aryan" merchants who have dared to lay claim to the title of "German."

In addition to the boycott adopted in the economic sphere, "non-Aryans" in Germany are subjected to a social boycott which is designed to ostracize them and confine them to a Ghetto. Over fifty-six German towns have either posted signs on their outskirts announcing that they exclude Jews from their territory, have forbidden them to buy real estate, or have threatened to discontinue public relief to any unemployed person associating with or buying from Jews.[55] Most of the German seaside and other holiday resorts and spas, such as Bad Duerkheim, Misdroy, Arendsee, Swinemuende, Neustrelitz, Lychen, Heringsdorf, Norderney, Borkum, Sylt, Garmisch-Partenkirchen to mention only the best known, exclude Jews. Recently, also, the boycott has been extended in the smaller towns particularly to prevent Jews from making purchases of food and medical supplies, as well as of other necessary products, in "Aryan" shops.

The social isolation and humiliation of "non-Aryans" is further stimulated by the persistent and relentless campaign of propaganda which is one of the principal activities of the Party and one of the foremost preoccupations of the Government. The Government itself has undertaken on the widest scale the encouragement and propagation of the beliefs that "non-Aryans" are sexual degenerates,[56] murderers of "Aryan" children,[57] and traitors to Germany.[58] This propaganda is consistently stressed in the public pronouncements of government officials, is hammered daily into the minds of all readers of the co-ordinated press, and is made a part of the daily instruction in the schools.[59]

It has been widely disseminated throughout Germany by means of *Der Stürmer* and the efforts of Herr Streicher, Member of the Bavarian Government and District Leader of Franconia. This paper has a weekly circulation of 480,000 and is distributed with the aid of the National Socialist Party. Its ritual murder number of May 1st, 1934, in which fourteen pages were devoted to details of an alleged "Jewish plot to murder Herr Hitler," was typical of the inflammatory nature of the propaganda which it broadcasts throughout Germany, and even into the elementary schools. Its pages are filled each week with stories designed to portray the Jew as a sexual degenerate and fiendish villain; and suggesting the most violent action toward them.[60] Each issue contains names of Jews and non-Jews who have been seen in public together, charging them with "Race Treason" and placing their names on the public pillory. In fact, all the National Socialist official newspapers make a regular feature of publishing names of non-Jews who are alleged to have had relations with Jews. In the following towns, among others, individuals have been placed in concentration camps on these grounds: Munich, Trier, Wesemuende, Nuremberg, Elbiag, Norden, Koenigsberg, Cologne, Nordhausen, Hanover, Stralsund, Karlsruhe, Dresden, Breslau, Halle, Brunswick, Juelich, Liegnitz, Goerlitz and Heidelberg.

As the *West German Beobachter* boasted, in its issue of August 21st, 1935, this propaganda of social ostracism has been successful. "The Jews' provocative behaviour has resulted in reports from numerous villages and towns indicating that Jews are barred from migrating to these localities. No property will be sold to them there, and all municipal facilities, such as municipal halls, baths, and theatres and also private places of entertainment, hotels, restaurants, moving picture theatres and cabarets are closed to them."

NOTES

1. They have at their disposal, in fact, a police force of their own, composed of the *Gestapo*, or Secret State Police, and the S.S. formations.
2. See pp.161–2.
3. Chapter 2, clause 4 of the Statutes of this organization specifies that all members must be of "German blood." *Frankfurter Zeitung*, November 21st, 1933.
4. Reported in the *Hessische Volkswirt*, August 10th, 1933.
5. See p.202.
6. Decree of the Minister of Justice, reported in the *Völkischer Beobachter* of April 12th, 1933.

7. *Juristische Wochenschrift*, August 5th, 1933.
8. *Völkischer Beobachter*, May 6th, 1935.
9. See p.162.
10. *Völkischer Beobachter*, March 14th, 1934.
11. See p.156.
12. See p.157. Decree of the Commissioner of Medicine, Dr. Wagner, August 22nd, 1933, *Völkischer Beobachter*, August 22nd, 1933.
13. *Völkischer Beobachter*, September 11th, 1935.
14. *Frankfurter Zeitung*, January 28th, 1935. Jewish pupils also must take the course in Raceology, for it is made a compulsory requirement in the final examinations. *Deutsche Allgemeine Zeitung*, September 20th, 1933.
15. *Völkischer Beobachter*, March 6th, 1934.
16. *Frankfurter Zeitung*, November 9th, 1934.
17. *Neue Deutsche Schule*, January 23rd, 1934.
18. It speaks of "inflation swindlers and Jewish profiteers" (p.14) and urges "away with the Jews and the traitors" (p.24). The Schools of Saxony, also, have been specially directed to emphasize the racial issue. *Völkischer Beobachter*, October 18th, 1935.
19. In a catechism, the following colloquy among others takes place and must be memorized:

    12. *Q.* Why are we Jew-Haters?

    A. The Jew is the scourge of humanity, the worm which eats up the nation and brings about its collapse.
20. *Völkischer Beobachter*, May 14th, 1933, where this announcement was made under the caption, "German instructors for German Universities."
21. *Frankfurter Zeitung*, March 24th, 1935.
22. *New York Times*, March 13th, 1935, p.13.
23. *Frankfurter Zeitung*, October 6th, 1935.
24. "As the industrial life of the nation is organized by the Nazis, it is virtually impossible to engage in business unless one is a member of an appropriate association or union. But many of these organizations, such as the Association of German Brokers, have introduced an 'Aryan' clause into their constitutions." Mr. John Elliott, Berlin Correspondent of the *New York Herald Tribune*, April 15th, 1934.
25. As reported in the London *Economist* of April 22nd, 1933: "Private organizations have also found it advisable to eliminate from leading positions in their offices those persons—Jews and members of the Parties of the Left—who are regarded by the Government as undesirable. The *Gleichschaltung* usually consists in the appointment of one or more Nazi Commissioners as members of the organization."
26. A case was reported on March 12th, 1935, in the *Frankfurter Zeitung*, of an action brought by a Jewess who was dismissed from a firm in Wiesbaden as a result of a letter received by her employer from the District Leader of the National Socialist Party. This communication threatened boycott if the employee remained.
27. These protests themselves have been official corroborations of the intense pressure which is being placed upon "non-Aryan" business

men, and are motivated rather by a fear of the dangerous consequences which may follow for the German economy than by a concern for the suffering of the Jewish merchant. See the statement of Dr. Schacht reported in the *New York Times* on August 20th, 1935; and on November 17th, 1934, in the *Frankfurter Zeitung*. These suggestions have fallen on deaf ears.

28. See p.163.
29. Reported in *Der Stürmer*, January, 1934.
30. *Frankfurter Zeitung*, June 3rd, 1934. Other "non-Aryan" firms are daily being forced to pass into "Aryan" hands; for example the firm of Dr. Paul Meyer, A.G. (reported in the *Frankfurter Zeitung* of August 26th, 1934); and the Tietz Chain Stores (reported in the *Manchester Guardian* of April 7th, 1933).
31. *Deutscher Handelsvertreter Zeitung*, March, 1934.
32. *Frankfurter Zeitung*, March 20th, 1934.
33. *Ibid.*, May 10th, 1935.
34. Jewish art dealers in Munich were ordered by the local police to close their stores; *New York Times*, September 12th, 1935.
35. *Westfaelische Landeszeitung;* quoted in *Jüdische Rundschhau*, No. 44, May 31st, 1935.
36. See *Frankfurter Zeitung* of May 8th, 1935, for a typical example of this result.
37. *New York Times*, September 24th, 1935.
38. "What more had happened than that we Germans said, 'Germans, don't buy from the Jews; buy from the Germans'?" General Goering's speech at Essen, reported in the *London Times* of March 11th, 1933.
39. *Völkischer Beobachter*, March 28th, 1933.
40. *Ibid.*, March 29th, 1933, Articles 3, 4, 7 and 9 of the Manifesto.
41. "Religion," ran the proclamation of the National Socialist Boycott Committee, "is immaterial"; business men of Jewish race who were converted to Catholicism or Protestantism "are also Jews in the sense of this Decree" (Article 11); quoted in the *Völkischer Beobachter*, March 30th, 1933.
42. Articles 7 and 13 of the Party Proclamation.
43. *Völkischer Beobachter*, April 1st, 1933.
44. As the official *Völkischer Beobachter* wrote on April 3rd, 1933.
45. See court decisions cited pp.206–7.
46. See p.206.
47. Ordinance of Rudolf Hess, Deputy of Chancellor Hitler, on August 16th, 1934, published in the *Völkischer Beobachter*, August 17th, 1934.
48. *Westdeutscher Beobachter*, July 24th, 1934.
49. Quoted in the *New York Times*, August 10th, 1935, p.6.
50. *Bretzenheimer Nachrichten* of August 31st, 1934.
51. Countless other similar declarations have been made. The District Leader for the Saar Territory, Buerckel, has published a proclamation declaring: "National Socialists, it is necessary to remind you that we have lost nothing in the rag-shop of the Jews, . . . and if you tell me that your wife does the shopping, it follows that in your

house no National-Socialist spirit prevails, and that you yourself are no real man, but a buffoon." (Quoted in *Rhein NSZ Front, a.d. H.*, December 18th, 1934.) The State Councillor of Hamburg was reported by the *Hamburger Tageblatt* on December 12th, 1934, to have declared that: "Just as you wish the German people to buy in German shops, even so do we demand that the German tradesmen buy only from the German manufacturers."

52. Quoted in full in *Der Stürmer*, May, 1934.
53. A typical boycott appeal by the HAGO Leader of Hanover is printed in the *Frankfurter Zeitung* of July 27th, 1933.
54. See pp.205–7.
55. Those announcements have, thus far, come from the following towns, among others: Ockenheim, Rommersheim, Udenheim, Schweisweiler, Koenigstatten, Dieburgstatten, Niederstein, Wuerzburg, Rotenburg (Hessen-Nassau), Hassfurt, Schotten, Frohnhofen, Adelshofen, Schriesheim, Asemissen, Greste, Bechterdissen, Bacharach, Bechtheim, Doddenheim, Bunzlau, Brilon, Delbrueck, Kreis, Detmold, Frankenberg, Frankfurt-on-the-Oder, Fraustadt, St. Goarshausen, Hangen-Weissheim, Neuss, Waldshut, Wallerstaedten, Westhofen, Arnsheim, Schoenebeck, Oppenheim, Teterow, Edenkoben, Coburg, Herborn, Freystadt, Osann, Hundsaugen, Pleutschbach, Weroth, Oberhausen, Wittlich, Bergzabern, Rosslau, Wimpffen, Breunigweiler.
56. The Law of September 15th, 1935 (see p.142) prohibiting "Aryan" female servants under the age of forty-five from holding positions in the households of "non-Aryans" shows that the writings of Chancellor Hitler (see p.70 of *Mein Kampf*), attributing sexual perversion to Jews are the very essence of official policy and public law.
57. The ritual murder number of *Der Stürmer*, a newspaper edited in Nuremberg by Herr Julius Streicher, the National Socialist Government Leader of Franconia, published on May 1st, 1934 the alleged records of ritual murders dating from 169 B.C. onwards.
58. Chancellor Hitler's speech at the Nuremberg Congress of September 15th, 1935, for example, spoke of "Jewish Marxists" as the primary cause for Germany's difficulties. "If," he wrote in his book, *Mein Kampf*, "at the beginning of the war twelve or fifteen thousand of these Hebrew corrupters of the people had been held under poison gas . . . then the sacrifice of millions at the Front would not have been in vain" (p.344). And, further, "Thus the Jew to-day is the great instigator of the complete destruction of Germany" (p.279).
59. See above, p.176.
60. The issue No. 7 of February, 1934, for example, declares that: "Our knowledge of the Jewish question has led us to the opinion that all Jews should, in fact, be castrated. They all have the same blood which leads them to violation. They all have the Talmud which permits the violation even of non-Jewish children." Other suggested punishments are too obscene to be repeated here.

Chapter III

Application of Racial Law by the Courts

The Courts of Germany have not only failed to safeguard the rights of equality and liberty which have become the basis of all civilized legal systems, they have even been transformed into instruments for the extension and application of the racial principle to matters unregulated by formal legislation or unreached by administrative decree.[1]

This development of their function has been made possible through the avowed abolition by the National Socialist *régime* of the three corner-stones of judicial morality: equality of all men before the law; independence of judges; and the doctrine that only those acts are to come under the prohibitions of the law for which the law specifically provides (the maxim, in criminal law, *nullum crimen nulla poena sine lege*). These fundamental guarantees of civilized justice [2] have been rejected as non-German,[3] "non-Aryan," [4] and as Judeo-Roman [5] in origin.

Therefore, in order to co-ordinate the administration of National Socialist law with the basic philosophy of the *régime*, equality before the law has been replaced by the doctrine of racial inequality; the independence of the judiciary has given way before the *Führerprinzip* that judges are agents of the Party and that tenure of office is dependent upon their administration of the political and moral standards of the Party, rather than upon the application of abstract justice; and the principle forbidding arbitrary judicial decisions has been abolished in favour of unlimited latitude given the Courts to adjudicate and penalize whether or not a law or a right has been violated.

1. The Doctrine of Racial Inequality before the Law

The Programme of the Party, adopted at Munich on February 25th, 1920, declared that:

> "Only those who are of German blood, irrespective of religion, can be members of the German national community (*Volksgenosse*). No Jew, therefore, can be a member of the national community." [6]

This syllogism is more than a mere party programme. It is the fundamental law of Germany to-day. The *National Socialist Correspondence*, an official publication, declared in August, 1935, that the Programme of the Party was *ipso facto* the constitutional law of the Reich and needed no further legislation to render it the supreme judicial code. This was especially so, the official statement ran, in its provisions respecting Jews who are "neither racial comrades nor citizens, but who rather stand under the law regulating aliens." [7] In fact this definition excluding Jews from membership in the national community has been taken over into the Law of September 15th, 1935, promulgated by Chancellor Hitler at the Party Congress at Nuremberg.[8] Establishing a distinction between German citizens and those entitled merely to formal registry as residents in German territory, this law provides that only citizens (that is, those of German "Aryan" blood and of the proper political views) may exercise civil and political rights.

Thus, the Courts are bound to apply as a fundamental law the principle of the inequality of race and blood as a decisive judicial rule in all cases brought before them. The rights of a German "Aryan" citizen must, necessarily, be accorded the greatest weight in any judicial proceeding, and must be given precedence over those claimed by "non-Aryans."

This method of administering justice is in conformity with

the definition of the law given by Alfred Rosenberg, Leader of the Department of Foreign Affairs of the National Socialist Party: "Law is what the Aryan man deems to be right; legal wrong is what he rejects." [9] The protection of the rights of the "Aryan" against the "non-Aryan" is, therefore, the principal purpose and function of the law and the Courts.[10] "The duty of justice consists in the preservation of the purity of species, the protection of race." [11] Therefore, even before the promulgation of the Laws of September 15th, 1935, which prohibited marriage between "Aryans" and Jews, as well as intimate relations between them, we find that the Courts acting in conformity with this injunction consistently fulfilled their function of protecting the "Aryan" race against such "non-Aryan" invasion, which, however, was not then forbidden by law.[12] The legislation of September 15th merely gives the Courts a statutory basis for the extra-legal action which they had previously taken of their own accord in applying the racial principle as a fundamental rule.[13]

2. Judges as Agents of the National Socialist Party

The *Führerprinzip*, namely, that all public officials must express the will of Adolf Hitler, has been applied to the German judiciary both in respect of tenure of office and of the content of the law which they are to apply. As the official commentary upon the centralization of the administration of justice in the Reich pointed out,[14] all judges in both civil and criminal courts are intended to be the personal appointees of Chancellor Hitler and may be dismissed at his will without reasons being given. "The Judge," declared Premier Goering of Prussia, at the ceremony celebrating this centralization, "must be an active supporter of the National Socialist viewpoint." [15]

This "viewpoint" which the Courts are bound to apply

and "actively support" with regard to the "non-Aryans" of Germany is that embodied in the will of Chancellor Hitler. For, as Minister Goering explained on July 12th, 1934, before the prosecuting officials of Prussia: "The law and the will of the *Führer* [Hitler] are one." [16] The "will of the Führer" as to the legal position of "non-Aryans" has been clearly expressed, and may be determined by reference to his published writings [17] and speeches.[18] On the basis of these declarations, it may be concluded that apart from any specific legal disabilities imposed by legislation, the judges of Germany are bound by law and by the terms of their office to regard "non-Aryans" as a dangerous and fundamentally criminal element, devoid of morality, biological and intellectual inferiors, and deserving of no protection for whatever civil or legal rights they may still dare to claim.[19]

3. Latitude Given to Judges through the Abolition of the Guarantees of a Fair Trial

The principle that only those acts are crimes or are to come under the prohibitions of the law for which the law provides, and its corollaries prohibiting punishment imposed on the basis of retroactive legislation and the use of analogy, are properly acknowledged as "general principles of law recognized by civilized nations." They have served as limitations upon the arbitrary power of judges, sovereigns, and even the law itself, to safeguard the humanity of the judicial process and the liberty of the parties before the Courts.[20] The abolition of these basic guarantees permits the Courts of Germany arbitrarily to punish whether or not a law has been violated and to deny civil rights to "non-Aryans" whether or not these rights be protected by law. It establishes a *régime* of ambulant justice.

The culmination of this revolution in legal administration

is the law passed by the German Reichstag on July 5th, 1935.[21] It replaces Section 2 of the former German Criminal Code by the following provisions:

> "Whoever commits an act which is declared a crime by law, or which deserves punishment according to the basic ideas of the Criminal Code, and according to the true feelings of the people, is to be punished."
>
> "Where no particular provision of the Criminal Code is directly applicable, the act will be punished by applying that provision, the underlying principle of which is the most appropriate to the act in question." [22]

Dr. Frank, Reich Minister of Justice, has interpreted these amendments to mean that judges can impose a sentence even if the act in question is not a penal offence, provided that it is similar to another act that is a penal offence, and provided that it merits punishment according to "healthy public opinion." [23]

Another departure from the traditional method of administering justice is the imposition of punishment by the application of laws passed after the act in question was committed; hitherto, this *ex post facto* punishment had been forbidden by the rule of non-retroactivity. Not only was this principle consecrated in Art. 116 of the Republican (Weimar) Constitution, it was at the head of the German *Strafgesetzbuch* (§2, par. 1). It was this Section which was repealed by the Law of July, 1935:

> "An act can be visited with a penalty only if the penalty was determined by law before the act was committed." [24]

These new and radical methods of administering justice have, as we shall see, profoundly affected even the minimal rights which have been left to "non-Aryans" by the legislation of the Reich. The almost unlimited power given the National Socialist judge; the abolition of judicial safeguards for the accused; the requirement that the judiciary serve the National Socialist viewpoint which regards "non-Aryans" as *prima facie* culpable and places their rights upon a plane inferior to those of "Aryans"; the replacement of objective legal tests by the subjective will of the judge [25]—all of these principles of the new German judicial administration have not only rendered useless appeals by "non-Aryans" to the Courts for the defence of even those few rights still left to them, but have also provided the means of extending the dogma of racial inequality to spheres and cases left untouched by legislation. The manner in which these rights are regarded and the method by which these doctrines are applied in specific instances will be seen from the citations which follow.

Marriage and Divorce

Although until September 15th, 1935, there existed no formal law forbidding marriages between "Aryans" and "non-Aryans," the German Courts in numerous instances upheld and justified local officials who had refused to perform such marriages, and granted divorce to the "Aryan" party on the grounds of the racial principle.[26]

The leading case on this subject was that decided by the *Oberlandesgericht* (Court of Appeals) of Karlsruhe.[27] An "Aryan" clergyman appealed to the Court to annul his marriage with a "non-Aryan" woman, who at his behest had been baptized as a Christian, arguing that the National Socialist *régime* had taught him the importance of racial distinctions and that, upon the strength of this new knowledge, he could no longer continue to live with his racially inferior wife. The Court granted the dissolution of the marriage, and in the course of its opinion wrote:

> "It has now been established that the Jewish race is something quite different from the Aryan race in regard to blood, character, personality and outlook on life, and that a connection with a member of this race is not only undesirable for a member of the Aryan race, but destructive, dangerous and contrary to nature. It estranges the Aryan as an individual, especially in his capacity as member of the racial community (*Volkstum*), from his nation and furthermore places him in the dangerous position of begetting children of a different species. . . . The contrast of races, as it has now been established, is so radical that in the future it will hardly ever lead to marriage between Aryans and non-Aryans."

Since, the Court concluded, the element of race is the decisive factor of personality, the "Aryan" man would not have contracted the marriage originally had he then known its importance. The marriage, therefore, should be annulled on the ground of error.[28]

Another decision to the same effect, annulling a marriage concluded seven years previously, was handed down by the State Court of Breslau in May, 1934. The Court declared that:

> "Personality is to a certain degree founded upon blood and race. Miscegenation between members of the Aryan and non-Aryan races produces a hybrid offspring." [29]

The same grounds for dissolution of marriage were given by the Superior Court of Celle in a decision of November 5th, 1934.[30]

A second category of decisions has served to sustain the refusal of local officials to perform marriages between "Aryans" and "non-Aryans." For example, on July 1st, 1935 the Municipal Court of Wetzlar dismissed an action brought by an "Aryan" against the local registrar (*Standesbeamter*) who refused to legalize a marriage between the complainant and a Jewess.[31] The registrar refused to perform the marriage on the grounds that as a National Socialist he would not agree to a mating between a man of German blood and a Jewess. The petitioner argued that no law was in existence forbidding such a marriage, and asked the court to order the registrar to fulfil his legal duty.

The Court, disallowing the appeal of the "Aryan" petitioner, acknowledged the fact that "the existing legal provisions do not prohibit marriage between a man of German blood and a Jewess." But, it held:

> "This argument shows a typically Jewish liberalistic mentality and legal casuistry. The principle that 'What is not expressly forbidden is permitted' would render German law and German morals more or less ineffective. The National Socialist conception of law and morality, on the contrary, is re-introducing the old, typically German rule of obedience as the duty of each individual. . . . The marriage of a man of German blood to a Jewess is absolutely irreconcilable with this principle."

In explanation of these new principles which, without a law to that effect, could be used to prohibit such a marriage, the Court declared:

> "When National Socialism seized power in Germany the foundation and underlying principles of the National Socialistic *Weltanschauung* immediately became the basis for the new political and social structure of the German Empire. . . . Similarly, the legal conceptions and methods of administering justice implicit in that viewpoint became as rooted in the new Germany as the new legislation of the Empire. The law concerning the purging of the civil service, the hereditary homestead act, and the conscription law

are the most striking expressions of this new spirit. These fundamental laws are permeated with the conviction of the direful effects, both physical and spiritual, of a blood-mixture of men of German origin with members of an alien race or foreign blood, particularly Jews. . . . In the light of these principles, embodied as they are in all parts of the legislation and all official and semi-official writings of the Government and the National Socialist Party, it would be a slap in the face to permit further inter-marriages. . . ." [32]

Children

The racial principle, as applied by the German Courts to the custody and upbringing of children, has without legislation to that effect established the rule that only on "Aryan" parent may care for an "Aryan" child, whatever may be the character, needs or respective rights of the parties in question. Thus, if a "non-Aryan" wife obtain a divorce from her "Aryan" husband on the grounds of his misconduct, and if, according to the law of racial heredity the child of that marriage be an "Aryan," [33] the mother will be refused the right to have the custody of the child because she is considered racially different from her offspring.[34]

This principle has been applied to the guardian-ward relationship, the Prussian Court of Appeals having decided that only an "Aryan" may be appointed guardian for an "Aryan" ward.[35] It has also been made a rule in adoption cases. The *Reichsgericht* in a decision of February 11th, 1935, expressed its doubt that a child (racial origin unknown) adopted by an "Aryan" mother and a "non-Aryan" father could be brought up to be a "German man." [36] In addition, the Berlin *Landgericht* has decided that the adoption by an "Aryan" of a "non-Aryan" child is null and void as contrary to the moral concepts of the National State when the purpose of such an adoption seems to be to change the name of the child and thus mask its racial identity.[37]

Even if mother, father and child be "Aryan," and the parent given the custody of the child after divorce contract a second marriage with a "non-Aryan," the child will be taken away and placed in a more suitable racial environment. This was decided by the *Landgericht* of Berlin on May 15th, 1934.[38] The "Aryan" mother and father of "Aryan" children having been divorced owing to the father's misconduct, the mother was given the custody of the children. Many years later, the mother married a Hungarian Jew. The father who had failed to contribute to the maintenance of the children since the divorce, asked the Court to take the children away from the mother on the ground that their physical and mental well-being was endangered by the "non-Aryan" origin of their stepfather. Despite the fact that the children wished to remain with their mother, the Court recognized the father's demand and transferred the children to him. The reason given by the Court was that "the German Reich needs every boy and girl of German origin." The allegiance of the children to the Reich would, the Court believed, be placed in peril by the "non-Aryan" environment of their new household.[39]

The judgments of the Courts with regard to the environment and upbringing of "Aryan" children would seem to imply that an "Aryan," even though he be fortified by the proper racial heredity, may through contact with "non-Aryan" influences be weaned away from the proper path. An example of this solicitude was given by the Municipal Court of Verden,[40] in a case where an "Aryan" guardian asked the Court to ratify an apprenticeship agreement which he had made in the name of his "Aryan" ward with a "non-Aryan" merchant (this ratification being required by law). The Court refused to sanction such an agreement as being contrary to the interests of the "Aryan" ward. The Jewish race, argued the Court, is in such sharp contrast to the German character that the education of a German minor should not be put into the hands of a Jew, where there would be no opportunity to become acquainted with the fundamental ideals of the National Socialist *Weltanschauung*.

Lawyers, Judges, Arbitrators, etc.

Lawyers, judges and arbitrators of "non-Aryan" descent having been excluded by statute from their position,[41] the Courts have been called upon to extend the racial formula to areas overlooked by the legislators. The manner in which their discretion has been exercised in extension of the law was well illustrated by the decisions of the Berlin Labour Court (*Arbeitsgericht*) [42] and the Superior Labour Court (*Landesarbeitsgericht*) [43] on June 20th and July 27th, 1933, respectively. Although there could be found no legal provision prohibiting a Jewish lawyer from representing an association of employers before the Berlin Labour Court, the Court refused to interpret the intent of the legislature as leaving to a Jewish representative of an employers' association more rights than a Jewish lawyer would have in an ordinary Court. The Superior Labour Court, to which an appeal was taken, sustained this decision by pointing out that a revolutionary legislature naturally leaves loopholes which the Court should fill in by applying the National Socialist viewpoint (*Weltanschauung*).

Even in cases where, by an exception of the law in favour of Front Soldiers, "non-Aryan" lawyers are still permitted to practice, their rights have been denied. For example, in May, 1935, the Labour Court of Magdeburg refused the right of such a Jewish lawyer still permitted to practice to appear before it.[44] According to the rules of the Court, it had the right to exercise its judicial discretion in admitting lawyers; consequently, since it was not compelled to admit the Jewish lawyer, it exercised its right to reject him. Similarly, the *Oberlandesgericht* of Frankfurt [45] decided on May 24th, 1935, that no Jewish lawyer, even if he be still allowed to practice, has any right or claim to be delegated by the judicial authorities as counsel to a poor person. The *Oberlandesgericht* of Hamm held on March 23, 1935, that "the spirit which has prevailed since the national uprising with regard to a justice closely connected with nation and race demands that German litigants shall not be represented by counsel of a foreign race." [46]

The residual rights of the few Jewish judges who were exempt from dismissal by virtue either of active war service or tenure of office before 1914 have similarly been compromised and denied. For, as numerous Court decisions have held, their impartiality and their judicial capacity may be challenged by any of the parties, and their right to try a case will be denied by a Court to which an appeal is taken. Thus, a National Socialist, bringing an action against a "non-Aryan" debtor, refused to have his case tried before a Jewish judge in Berlin. The *Landgericht* of Berlin, called upon to decide this question of the competence of the Judge, gave a judgment on November 10th, 1935, which, instead of restricting the right of the plaintiff to make libellous statements before the Court concerning the racial origin of the Jewish defendant and the Judge, confined itself to removing the latter as lacking the "necessary impartiality." [47] The Berlin *Kammergericht* on March 5th, 1934, also upheld this rejection of a Jewish Judge upon the plea of one of the parties that it was contrary to his National Socialist view of life to have his rights adjudicated by a "non-Aryan." [48]

The leading decision upon the validity of an arbitral award

handed down by a panel of arbitrators, one of whom was a "non-Aryan," was that given by the Hanover *Landgericht* [49] on March 26th, 1934. The "non-Aryan" arbitrator was appointed as early as 1930, and had been a Front Soldier during the war. The Hanover Court, acting on the basis of a law providing that either party may reject an arbitrator of "non-Aryan" descent (no exception being made for war service) set aside *the award* which had *already* been handed down by the arbitral panel on the grounds that one of the arbitrators was a Jew, and that therefore the whole award was void.

Furthermore, although no statute had been enacted forbidding "non-Aryans" from acting as Referees for the administration of estates (*Zwangsverwalter*), the Berlin *Landgericht* on October 5th, 1933, decided that a Jew (in this case one who had seen service during the war) could be immediately discharged from his position.[50] The Court based its decision upon the popular feeling aroused against the Jewish people which "made it seem inadvisable to retain a Jew in such an office, even without a special law to that effect."

The same disregard for acquired rights and the same method of extending the racial doctrine beyond the terms of the formal legislation have been shown in the decisions regarding "non-Aryan" executors of wills. On October 9th, 1933 the Berlin *Landgericht*, upon the application of one of the heirs, dismissed a Jewish Executor (*Testamentsvollstrecker*), who had been appointed by the testator after the Hitler *régime* had laid down the racial laws.[51] The Court explained that, despite the will of the deceased and his knowledge of the new political system, "it is the first fundamental principle of the new law to expel all persons of alien race from public offices and functions, such as the office of an Executor of a will, who has to rule upon the fate (*wohl und wehe*) of German men."

Yet, even where the "*wohl und wehe* of German men" is

not in question, the Courts do not hesitate to violate the expressed intent of the deceased and the terms of his will in order to extend the racial rule. Thus, there was reported in *Jugend und Recht* of July 15, 1935, an important case wherein a Surrogate Court, called upon by the executors to appoint a Jew to replace an executor who had died, refused to comply either with the demand of the executors or the terms of the will.[52] The original will had been made by a Jew who had died in 1900, and had established a trust of five million marks to foster artisanship and agriculture. The Testator had appointed a Board of Directors, composed entirely of his co-religionists, and a number of executors, also of his faith, with the stipulation that upon the death of any of the executors, the Surrogate Court should "appoint a suitable person from the members of the Board of Directors or, from other members of the Jewish community." Despite the clear wording of the deceased's will, the Court held that the new legislation of the National Socialist Government had now set forth the rights and duties of Jews; and that since it was nowhere expressly provided that Jews may be permitted to be executors, the Court in accordance with the prevailing legal principles would presume that the right did not exist. It therefore refused to appoint a Jew. This decision was, furthermore, supported by the Ministry of Justice, which acts as a final board of appeals on such trusts and endowments.

Business and Commerce

The only statutory provisions restricting the rights of "non-Aryans" to conduct their business and commerce are the Instructions Regarding the Granting of Public Orders of August 4th, 1933, for the Reich [53] and the Prussian Ordinance of August 30th, 1933.[54] But, the Courts without legislative authorization have consistently applied the "Aryan" paragraph to commercial contracts, employment agreements, unfair competition, debtor and creditor relationships, in addition to supporting and legalizing the boycott of Jewish business which has been conducted under the auspices of the National Socialist Party.[55]

The Court of Appeals of Marienwerder in June, 1935, was asked to decide whether the alleged assertion by a Jewish merchant of Schneidemuehl that a leading National Socialist had bought an overcoat in his shop constituted a slander. Although the Court of Appeals referred the case back to the lower court because of insufficient evidence that the statement had actually been made, it had this to say on the question of law involved:

> "Those German subjects who even to-day buy from a Jew cannot be considered as belonging to that part of the German people which represents public opinion. German public opinion condemns a purchase from a Jew as an immoral, unethical act." [56]

Therefore, in the Court's opinion, if the Jewish merchant had made such a statement about any member of "German public opinion," a cause of action for slander would arise.

A similar sanction was given the boycott of "non-Aryan" business by the decision of the Municipal Court of Eberswalde.[57] A "non-Aryan" owner of an Automobile Driving School attempted to obtain an injunction restraining the local Leader of the Party from continuing to post on a wall near the petitioner's place of business a list of Jewish shops and firms to be boycotted, among which was the name of the complainant's Automobile School. The Court refused the injunction on the grounds that under prevailing conditions in Germany every German had a right to learn whether or not a firm was Jewish.

Likewise, the Hamburg *Amtsgericht* decided on June 29th, 1935, that an "Aryan" woman whose "non-Aryan" husband had been forced to leave Germany as a refugee could not obtain damages against a member of the National Socialist Party who had publicly spread the warning that the complainant operated a "Jewish business" and who for that reason had urged a boycott of the shop.[58] Since, the Court argued, the plaintiff although an "Aryan" was still fond of her "non-Aryan" husband after living with him for fifteen years, and since he as a refugee could not be expected to be working for the glory of Germany abroad, the business of the complainant was properly designated a "Jewish" one.[59] Furthermore, according to the Program and orders of the National Socialist Party, the defendant was bound to call the attention of his fellow-comrades to the necessity of boycotting such an enterprise. The Court pointed out that the slogan "Don't Buy from Jews" had been adopted as a fundamental law in Germany, for "the objectives of the Party and the objectives of the State are one and the same." This was all the more true because, as the judge observed, "the German people have in the overwhelming majority accepted the principle that the Jews are mainly responsible for German suffering." Jews, conceded the Court, are not without rights; but their rights are only those of guests of the National Socialist State. Therefore, a German Court could not deny the right of a German to encourage the boycott of the shop in question.

Nor, according to the decision of the Prussian Court of Appeals, has a firm owned by "non-Aryans" or employing "non-Aryans" the right to call itself a "German business."[60] The Prussian Court decided that the designation "German" was understood to mean "Aryan," and that it would be unfair competition for a firm owned by "non-Aryans" to advertise without indicating the racial origin of its proprietors.

Even the *Reichsgericht* has sustained this distinction between a "German" and a "Jewish" business, and has forbidden as unfair competition the use of any company name unless it clearly indicates the "non-Aryan" origin of its owners. Thus, on July 12th, 1934, this highest judicial authority in the Reich,[61] forbade the *Dampfsäge und Hobellwerk Germaniamuhle Gmbh* from using the word "Germania" in its corporation name, because the stockholders were predominantly "non-Aryan" and the word "Germania," according to the Court, meant not only "non-foreign" but also "non-Jew."[62]

The Courts have, despite the hesitation of the *Reichsarbeitsgericht* and the *Reichsgericht* in two exceptional instances,[63] refused to grant judicial redress to "non-Aryans" whose contracts have been terminated without notification. In a typical and leading case the State Labour Court of Frankfurt confirmed the decision of the Labour Court of Weisbaden which had refused to grant redress to a Jewess, who had been dismissed from her position as a result of a threatening letter sent her employer by the National Socialist Party. The dismissed employee was the sole support of her aged father and of a brother who had been disabled during the World War. She brought action on the grounds that there was no law requiring the dismissal of Jews from business employment and that the agitation of the National Socialist district group to have her dismissed was an unwarranted interference in private business. Both Courts rejected this plea on the grounds that conceptions of right and wrong had undergone a change in Germany and that the majority of the German people would not consider it wrong for an "Aryan" firm to dismiss its "non-Aryan" employees.[64] The Berlin *Landgericht* on November 17, 1933, also declared when a Jewish Manager of an Estate unsuccessfully claimed damages before it for wrongful dismissal: "It is the intention of the present government to restrict and even expunge the Jewish influence, particularly in all branches of cultural life."[65] This "intention of the present government" also is used to justify the decisive weight given by the Courts to the claims of "Aryans," whatever may be the legal rights possessed by "non-Aryans." Thus, the Naumberg *Oberlandesgericht* on January 5th, 1935, held that a German firm has the right to refuse payment of an uncontested debt if, by such payment "German" money would fall into the hands of a "non-Aryan" foreigner.[66] This right to refuse payment to "non-Aryan" creditors was, the Court said, in harmony with the principles of National Socialism. For, in the words of the decision: "According to the actual purified conception of the law, a debtor is entitled to refuse the execution of an obligation even if the performance thereof is contrary neither to law nor to morals, but yet would have the effect of bringing parts of the national property, especially real property, into the hands of a 'non-Aryan' foreigner, thereby harming the national community."

This method of fitting the law to the racial origin of the parties was well illustrated in two leading cases decided by superior German Courts. The first decision was that of the Berlin *Landgericht* on December 3rd, 1934,[67] and is significant not so much for the intrinsic value of the question involved as for an appreciation of the methods of juristic logic now in vogue in the German Reich. Since Chancellor Hitler's assumption of power, the Courts have established the rule that the wireless now belongs to that class of personal belongings which is exempt from being garnisheed in payment of a debt, the reason being that in the Third Reich it is considered the duty of every German to listen to the political speeches and announcements of the Government which are broadcast. In the case in question, however, the receiving set of a "non-Aryan" was garnisheed and this action was upheld by the Municipal Court on the ground that the general rule forbidding garnishee of wireless sets did not apply in the case of a Jew, because he was not expected to have the same rights and duties as a German citizen. The *Landgericht*, however, refused to sustain the lower Court's exception to the rule on garnishee. It gave as the reason for its loyalty thereto, not the principle that Jews have the same rights as German citizens, but the pragmatic fact that a Jew should listen on his set to important political speeches so as to inform himself on the conduct demanded of him by the new Government. An instrument of such vital political importance could not therefore be garnisheed.

The second case came before the German Supreme Court of Finance (*Reichsfinanzhof*) and was decided on December 20th, 1933.[68] The statute imposing a special tax for those departing from the Reich contained a provision to the effect that this tax did not have to be paid in cases where such emigration was in the interests of the German people or German economics. It was argued that Jewish refugees from Germany should therefore be exempt from this tax since the Government had in numerous instances declared that Jews were a destructive and dangerous element whose influence should be stamped out from German life.[69] Their emigration, consequently, from the viewpoint of the Government, ought to be looked upon as desirable and in the interest of the Third Reich. The Court, however, decided that this tax would have to be paid for the reason that even if their departure were beneficial it could hardly be expected that a "non-Aryan" abroad would foster German thoughts and ideas. Although German industry encouraged exports, the departure of refugees was not considered particularly beneficial to the national economy.

* * *

These citations demonstrate the extent to which the dogma of "non-Aryan" inferiority and inequality before the law has permeated the legal system of National Socialist Germany. They explain why Jews and other "non-Aryan" elements can no longer look to the law for protection of their elementary civil rights, not to speak of their political liberties. Undoubtedly, the number of decisions of the same nature would have been multiplied, had not there arisen so early and so sharply the realization that no hope whatsoever existed for the safeguarding by the Courts of the most basic human rights, which have been incorporated into civilized legal systems as charters of freedom and public order. Whatever small minimal rights might still be claimed by Jews or "non-Aryans," however strong the evidence presented, or clear the terms of the laws to which appeal was made, the Courts of Germany have on racial grounds denied those rights, overlooked the evidence brought to sustain them, have, wherever possible, rendered the laws more harsh or have, wherever necessary, on their own authority filled the *lacunae* in the system of legislative discrimination.

NOTES

1. For a descriptive analysis of the laws which the Courts have been called upon to administer in application of the racial formula, see above, Chapter I.
2. "Out of this heterogeneous mass of prescriptions which make up the criminal law of the western world, there emerge a few general principles in the nature of limitations on arbitrary power, whether of the sovereign or of the law itself. The most important of these, inherited by the United States from the English law, may be stated in the language of the Bill of Rights of the American Constitution, viz. that no person shall be 'deprived of life, liberty, or property without due process of law . . .'

   "Analogous to these is the 'rule of certainty,' which prescribes that every act made punishable by law shall be so clearly defined as to leave no penumbra of uncertainty as to its applicability to a given case, and finally the rule denying any retroactive effect to a penal law. The last of these, embodied in the maxim *nullum crimen nulla poena sine lege* was the first rule laid down by Livingstone in his draft codes for Louisiana and the United States."

G. W. KIRCHWEY, "Criminal Law," *Encyclopaedia of the Social Sciences*, New York, 1931, IV, p.574.

3. *Denkschrift des Preussischen Justizministers*, Berlin, 1933, p.127 (hereafter cited as *Denkschrift*). See also Karlbach in *Juristische Wochenschrift*, 1934, p.2232. It would be an injustice to let such a gross misconception pass as a libel upon the true contribution of German culture to civilized jurisprudence. No less an "Aryan" authority than Prof. Carl Ludwig von Bar, of the University of Göttingen, wrote:

   "The significant bearing upon the world's history customarily ascribed to the Roman Law as a factor in assisting the individual human being to assume a position of importance 'per se,' and to acquire a position of independence towards the State is contrary to fact. These results were obtained only when the Germanic ideal of law had impressed itself upon the progress of humanity." *A History of Continental Criminal Law*, Boston, 1916, p.19.

4. Helmut Nicolai, *Die Rassengesetzliche Rechslehre* (Nationalsozialistische Bibliothek, Heft 35), Munich, 1933, *passim*. Also, Judge G. R. Schmelzeisen, *Das Recht im Nationalsozialistischen Weltbild*, Leipzig, 1934.
5. Programme of the National Socialist Party, Article 19, signed by Adolf Hitler in Munich, February 24th, 1920: "We demand that the Roman law which serves the materialistic world order shall be replaced by a popular legal system." Gottfried Feder, *Was will Adolf Hitler?* (Munich, 1932). See also H. Nicolai, in *Juristische Wochenschrift*, 1933, p.2315.
6. See p.144.
7. *New York Times*, August 11th, 1935, p.19.
8. For the text of this law see above, pp.142–3.
9. 2 *Deutsches Recht* (1934), p.233.
10. "The Police are not a defence squad for Jewish stores. . . . They tell me I must call out the police to protect them [the Jews, who were being boycotted through official instigation]. Certainly I shall employ the police, and without any mercy, wherever German people are hurt, but I refuse to turn the police into a guard for Jewish stores. . . ."—GEN. GOERING, March 10th, 1933, as then Minister of the Interior of Prussia, reported in the *London Times*, March 11th, 1933.
11. Nicolai, *op. cit.*, p.33. In order to carry out their function as protectors of the "Aryan" race, the Courts have been applying in wholesale fashion a sterilization law of unprecedented severity (*Reichsgesetzblatt*, I, p.529). It was officially announced in *Deutsche Justiz*, the organ of the National Socialist Lawyers Union, that during the

year 1934 no less than 56,244 sterilizations had been ordered by the German Courts, an average of over 1,000 each week. 6,550 individuals in Berlin alone were sterilized during the year; and the same fate was decreed for 2.56 of every 1,000 inhabitants of Karlsruhe and 2.22 of Hamburg. Furthermore, 96 per cent. of the sterilizations were ordered on mental grounds, rather than because of any heritable physical malady. Of all alleged causes for sterilization, mental aberrations are considered the least valid by scientific authorities, for it is doubted whether they may actually be transmitted to the offspring in all cases.

12. For instances of this type of judicial "legislation," see cases cited below, pp.196–9.

13. The leading legal officials of Germany have been preparing further legislation of this type, of which the Laws of September 15th are merely a foretaste. Thus, the official *Denkschrift* of the Prussian Minister of Justice, which establishes the outlines of a new penal code, contains a section entitled "Schutz von Rasse und Volkstum: Angriffe auf die Rasse," which provides for three new crimes: *Rassenverrat* (race treason); *Verletzung der Rassenehre* (violation of race honour); and *Rassengefährdung* (endangering the race). See also the discourse of Reichsminister of Justice Frank before the *Reichstagung des Bundes Nationalsozialistischer Deutschen Juristen*, September 30th, 1933, quoted in 1 *Deutsches Recht* (1933), p.195.

14. Dr. George Schroeder, member of the Ministry of Justice, in the Ministry's official organ, *Deutsche Justiz*, of April 18th, 1935.

15. "The final authority as to the principles of the German State and the German Law is the National Socialist Party." *Official Procedure for the German Legal Profession*, printed in the *Juristische Wochenschrift*, No. 29, July 21st, 1934, p.1763.

16. That this statement is no mere figure of speech is indicated by the fact that it was used to justify the assassinations of June 30th, 1934. For, at the same meeting, Goering explained: "Now that this action, which was law in itself, has in addition been formally legalized, no authority can claim the right to probe into it." (*New York Times*, July 13th, 1934.) Chancellor Hitler, explaining his actions before the Reichstag on July 13th, 1934, declared: "If someone questions me why we did not invoke an ordinary Court to deal with the men, I can only tell him: In that hour, I was responsible for the fate of the German Nation; therefore, the Supreme Court of the German people during those twenty-four hours consisted of myself." (*New York Times*, July 14th, 1934.)

17. In his work, *Mein Kampf* (My Struggle), Chancellor Hitler wrote: "When I defend myself against the Jew I fight for the work of the Lord"; "The black-haired Jewish youth lies for hours in ambush, a Satanic joy in his face, for the unsuspecting girl whom he pollutes with his blood and steals from her own race. By every means he seeks to wreck the racial bases of the nation he intends to subdue" (p.357). These quotations are taken from the 12th Edition, published in Munich in 1933.

18. Before the Party Congress of September, 1935, Chancellor Hitler declared that the first of the three groups "who were guilty of the German collapse" was the Jewish Marxists and their kindred, "the Parliamentary Democrats. . . ." In another discourse he said: "Capitalistic Jewry has never had any art of its own. Even the Temple of Jerusalem had to be completed by foreign artists. We do not intend to let the degenerate artists loose on our people." (Reported in the *Manchester Guardian*, September 12th, 1935.)
19. The extent to which this viewpoint has pervaded the German legal system will be seen in the cases described below, pp.196–201.
20. As was shown above, p.211, note 3, these principles are not of Roman origin, as the Prussian Minister of Justice mistakenly supposes. They were, historically, a victory of modern civilization over arbitrary feudal law. For example, the liberal Austrian (but certainly "Aryan") Code of Joseph II in 1787 abolished condemnation by analogy (Part I, Sec. 1, Part II, Sec. 3), quoted in von Bar, *op. cit.*, p.252. Furthermore the Bavarian Criminal Code of May 16th, 1813, in its very first article forbade the resort to analogy for the purpose of imputing criminality to an act. "For it is upon this principle," ran the official annotation to the Code (I, p.66), "that the security of the state and every individual depends."
21. *Frankfurter Zeitung*, No. 339, July 6th, 1935; *Reichsgesetzblatt*, I (1934), p.839.
22. This law apparently was drafted by the Official Penal Law Committee of the Ministry of Justice. F. Gürtner, *Bericht über die Arbeiten der Amtlichen Strafrechtskommission*, Berlin (1934), p.132.
23. *Völkischer Beobachter*, July 5th, 1935. It is evidently on the strength of a similar innovation in legal procedure that the Law of July 14th, 1933 (*Reichsgesetzblatt* [1933], No. 81, p.479) for the confiscation of the property of Communists and elements hostile to the state has been applied to such organizations as the following: The *People's Society for a Catholic Germany* (*Reichsanzeiger*, March 7th, 1935, No. 56, p.1); *The German Catholic Peace Society, the League for the Protection of Mothers*, and the *Free School Association* (*Reichsanzeiger*, January 18th, 1935, p.2.)
24. Yet, even before the repeal of this Section of Germany's fundamental law, the National Socialist Party had violated the principle of non-retroactivity embodied therein by the passage of the *Gesetz über Verhängung und Vollzug der Todestrafe* on March 29th, 1933 (*Reichsgesetzblatt*, I, p.151). This law, popularly called the "Lex van der Lubbe" with reference to the special case for which it was designed, imposed a retroactive punishment of death for certain acts committed between January 31st and February 28th, 1935, which at the time of their commission would have been more lightly punished.

Also, it should be noted that the abolition of the principle *nullum crimen nulla poena sine lege* fulfills the same desired purpose as the repeal of non-retroactivity by breaking down a plea based upon the non-existence of a certain prescribed punishment at the time of the commission of an act.

25. The *Denkschrift* of the Prussian Minister of Justice (p.124) heralds a new law which would punish "criminal intent" (*Gefährdungsrecht*). Under this rule, the intent to commit a misdeed is punished as severely as the crime committed. No objective proofs of intent, of course, can actually be adduced, so that only a simple "moral purpose" (*Seelischer Befund*) will be sufficient to impose criminal responsibility. For an expression of alarm at this subjective criminal law, written by a jurist in Germany, see Mezger, "Willenstrafrecht, Gefährdungsrecht und Erfolgstrafrecht," in *Deutsche Juristen Zeitung*. Mezger writes, "the vague principle of 'criminal intent' can only wipe out the distinction between a legal act and a crime. If an objective definition of crime is also abolished, the result will be the complete anarchy of criminal law and the loss of all existing guarantees."
26. For a discussion of the racial principle applied to the dissolution of marriages between "Aryans" and "non-Aryans," see the following:—von Jung, *Juristische Wochenschrift* (1933), pp.2367ff.; Schumacher, *Deutsche Juristen Zeitung* (1933), pp.1492ff.; Wohrmann, *Deutsche Justiz* (1933), pp.818ff.; Schneider, *J.W.* (1934), pp.868ff.; and, in addition to the cases cited below, see the arguments advanced by the *Reichsgericht J.W.* (1933), p.2041, and the *Oberlandesgericht* of Köln *Deutsche Justiz* (1933), pp.819ff.
27. March 2nd, 1934, reported in 22 *J.W.*, p.1371, and in the *Volkischer Beobachter* of March 8th, 1934, where the decision appeared under the headline: "A Landmark in the History of German Jurisprudence."
28. It is true that the German Supreme Court, upon appeal, refused to sustain the decision of the *Oberlandesgericht* (*J.W.* [1934] pp.2613–5). But it did not overrule the conclusion of law which the lower court expressed—namely, that race is the decisive personal "quality" of a spouse; and based its refusal to grant the divorce on the issue of fact involved, i.e., whether the Aryan clergyman was or was not aware of this personal "quality" of his wife at the time of marriage (p.2613). The Supreme Court believed that he was, since, as a clergyman at the time of marriage, he had not yet learned the laws of biology and the racial theory (p.2615).
29. *New York Times*, May 21st, 1934.
30. *Deutsche Justiz*, April 5th, 1935.
31. *Frankfurter Zeitung*, July 2nd, 1935.
32. The same decision has been handed down in numerous instances; see particularly, *Deutsche Justiz* (July 31st, 1933), p.1086.
33. The dialectic by which this totally unscientific result is obtained is explained above, p.151.
34. See decision of the Guardian Court of Hamburg, January 8th, 1935, quoted from the *Hanseatische Rechts und Gerichts-Zeitschrift* and reported in the *Frankfurter Zeitung*, April 14th, 1935.
35. *Deutsche Justiz* of May 24th, 1935.
36. *Juristische Wochenschrift* (1935), p.1410.
37. *Ibid.* (1934), p.443.
38. *Ibid.* (1934), p.1516.

39. A similar, but exceptional, case came before the Supreme Court of Bavaria (*Bayerisches Oberster Landes Gericht*) upon the petition of the official German Youth Department to remove an "Aryan" child from his "Aryan" father's care because the latter had, after the divorce granting him custody of the child, contracted a marriage with a Jewish woman. The Youth Department (Jugendamt) protested that the influence of the Jewish stepmother would lead to the mental degradation of the child; and that in contracting this second marriage the father had acted *contra bonos mores* and was therefore unfit as a parent. The Court, in its decision of October 3rd, 1934 (reported in *Juristische Wochenschrift*, 1935, p.136), while admitting that marriage of an "Aryan" to a Jewess was an act *contra bonos mores* and that children of a mixed marriage were an undesirable addition to the German population, believed that there was a possibility that the stepmother would give adequate care to the child. It decided, therefore, for the time being to await the results. This decision evoked a storm of protest, and was followed in the *Juristische Wochenschrift* by an editorial comment which pointed out that it violated the laws of life and common sense (*widerstreitet den Lebenserfahrungen und einfachen Denkgesetzen*).
40. *Frankfurter Zeitung*, No. 396, August 6th, 1935.
41. See above, p.155, for a full description of these laws.
42. *Juristische Wochenschrift* (1933), p.1794.
43. *Ibid.*, p.2788.
44. Reported in the *Frankfurter Zeitung*, July 24th, 1935.
45. *Juristische Wochenschrift* (1935), p.1509.
46. *Ibid.* (1935), p.35.
47. *Ibid.* (1934), p.442. The judge in question had already been removed from the Criminal Courts to a lower Civil Court of original jurisdiction, in accordance with the laws on the judiciary. The *Frankfurter Zeitung* of April 16th, 1934, commenting upon this decision, admitted that it demonstrated the difficulties faced by "non-Aryan" judges.
48. *Ibid.* (1934), p.1178.
49. *Ibid.* (1934), p.1684.
50. *Ibid.* (1934), p.1178.
51. *Ibid.* (1933), p.2406.
52. *Frankfurter Zeitung*, No. 356, July 20th, 1935.
53. *Reichsanzeiger*, No. 180, August 5th, 1933.
54. Prussian *Ministerialblatt*, I, p.1277.
55. For evidence of the connection of the Party with the boycott, see above, pp.182–5.
56. *Frankfurter Zeitung*, July 1st, 1935.
57. *Ibid.*, No. 370, July 23rd, 1935.
58. Reported in *Juristische Wochenschrift* (1935), pp.2763–4.
59. The Court thereby accepted *verbatim* the boycott definition of the National Socialist Party of March 30th, 1933, which was signed by Streicher. Article 5 of the Proclamation ran: "If the husband of a non-Jewish proprietress is Jewish, then the enterprise is considered Jewish."

60. *Jüdische Rundschau*, No. 42, May 24th, 1935.
61. *Juristische Wochenschrift*, 1934, pp.2160–1.
62. *Ibid.*, p.2161.
63. The decision of the *Reichsarbeitsgericht* on October 25th and October 28th, was reported in *Juristische Wochenschrift* (1933), p.122; that of the *Reichsgericht* on February 16th, 1934, *ibid.* (1934), p.1963. Neither of them, however, actually goes so far as to assert that contract rights of "non-Aryans" must be upheld. The *Arbeitsgericht* expressed the hope that, since each case should be decided on its merits, the Courts would be more reluctant to permit violations of labour contracts as a general rule. The *Reichsgericht* argued from a practical viewpoint that the "non-Aryan" legislation was not intended to have an immediate effect in the commercial sphere, or German business would be harmed.
64. *Frankfurter Zeitung*, March 12th, 1935.
65. *Juristische Wochenschrift* (1933), p.2919.
66. *Deutsche Juristen Zeitung* of May 1st, 1935; also 6 *Deutsche Justiz* of June 29th, 1935, p.403.
67. *Juristische Wochenschrift* (1935), p.814.
68. *Ibid.* (1934), p.379.
69. For examples of governmental invitation to emigrate, see below, pp.222–3.

Chapter IV

"Unwelcome Guests"

The programme of the German Government which is designed to reduce "non-Aryans" to a condition of impoverished unemployment and to take away from them the most elementary civil and political rights does not stop at defining their position as that of "unwelcome guests" of the German people [1] and rendering their continued existence in Germany unbearable.[2] It requires that these "unwelcome guests" should be forced to leave their homes in Germany. That this is the ultimate purpose of the National Socialist Government is evidenced both by the legislation which has already been put into effect and by the official statements of its leaders. This intent has been reflected particularly in the denationalization imposed upon "non-Aryans" and others who have not found favour with the Government, in the imprisonment of returning refugees, and in the refusal to sanction any measures of re-training or re-habilitation of "non-Aryans" except those which would lead to their mass emigration.

Deprivation of Citizenship and Denationalization

"Non-Aryans," and those to whom the National Socialist State is opposed have, because of their origin or political views, been deprived of their German citizenship; and have, as refugees, been left virtually stateless and without the protection of the German Government. In addition, the denationalization of particular individuals (that is, the annulment of their German nationality) has been carried out on a large scale, and has taken two principal forms: the revocation of naturalization on racial grounds; and the withdrawal of nationality on political grounds.

Both deprivation of citizenship and denationalization are,

for those within Germany, invitations to emigrate. The Law of September 15th, 1935, makes membership of the State contingent upon "German blood." Therefore, those of alien blood, particularly Jews, may not be members of the German community. Placed in a status approximating that of aliens, regarded as foreign to the German State, "non-Aryans" have been made to feel that because of their origin they have no place in Germany.[3] Furthermore, the denationalization of particular individuals leaves no doubt that the victims are henceforth to be regarded as aliens and therefore not even entitled to the diplomatic protection of the German State. A Law of July 14th, 1933, provides for the Withdrawal of Naturalization and the Loss of German Nationality in the following cases:[4]

(1) Where a person has been naturalized during the period between November 9th, 1918, and January 30th, 1933, and where his naturalization is now regarded as "undesirable" (Article 1);
(2) Where a German national, residing abroad, has "prejudiced German interests by an attitude contrary to his duty of loyalty" towards the Reich; or has refused to return when ordered to do so by the Minister of the Interior (Article 2).

The manner in which the decisive question of Article 1 is to be decided, namely, whether the naturalization of a person is regarded as "desirable," has also been set forth by law. The Acting Reich Minister of the Interior, Pfundtner, issued a decree on July 26th, 1933,[5] which declared that it should be determined according to "national racial" principles, and that in this connection the following were especially undesirable as German nationals:

(1) Jews from East European countries (Austria, Poland, Czechoslovakia, etc.), and
(2) Criminals, or those who have acted detrimentally to the welfare of the Reich or nation.[6]

The law also provides that denationalization shall likewise cancel the national status of members of the victim's family. In case of revocation of naturalization, the persons who would not have acquired nationality but for the act of the naturalized individual automatically lose their nationality together with him. For those whose nationality is withdrawn because of their alleged hostility abroad towards the National Socialist Government, it is to be decided in each case to what an extent this denationalization will apply to the spouse and legitimate or adopted children. Furthermore, their goods and property in Germany may be confiscated.

It should be remembered also, that the reasons for the withdrawal of nationality are not given to the party in question, and that recourse to law or to administrative tribunals to protest against a denial of right or an abuse of power is specifically prohibited.[7]

The number of individuals whose nationality is placed in jeopardy by this legislation, and who therefore face statelessness, is considerable. During the years 1919 to 1930, a total of 107,599 naturalizations took place. All of these individuals are thus within the purview of the law and in danger of losing nationality because their naturalization is now considered "undesirable." From 1919 to 1933, 10,300 individuals of Jewish descent and coming from East European countries were naturalized; the withdrawal of their nationality as a group is deemed especially desirable. Furthermore, the Law of July 14th, Article 2, places in jeopardy the nationality of all the 90,000 persons who have left Germany as refugees since June, 1933, if they express opposition to the policies which caused them to flee from their homes.

Such denationalization, particularly for the East European Jewish class, inevitably results in statelessness. For, the nationality laws of practically every state in the world provide that after naturalization the loss of former nationality results and that no automatic resumption is possible.[8] This dire penalty has been imposed upon those naturalized Jews of East European origin both retroactively and solely by reason of their descent. No fraudulent intent, no subsequent act of crime or of bad faith, no deed of commission or omission need be adduced to justify the denationalization. The extreme vagueness of the law, permitting the withdrawal of "undesirable" naturalizations, is sufficient to cover all cases. This arbitrary, retroactive denationalization applies, furthermore, to individuals who in order to become naturalized had to pass severe tests of character and morality. The German Law on Nationality[9] required that the applicant for naturalization show that he "has led a blameless life" and that he is "able . . . to support himself and his family." In addition, this retroactive penalty is being imposed upon individuals who migrated to Germany following the war upon the strength of a solemn promise made by the Imperial Government of the German State. General Ludendorf in 1915 issued a proclamation to the Jews of Eastern Europe which induced many of them to take up their residence in Germany and to become naturalized. His statement "to the Jews of Poland" read, in part:

> "We come to you as friends; the barbarian foreign *régime* has ended. The equal rights of the Jews will be built upon a firm foundation. It is now your sacred duty to muster all your strength to help in the liberation."

Until September 1st, 1935, a total of 4,137 withdrawals of nationality had been announced and officially published in the *Deutsche Reichsanzeiger*, the official gazette. Of this number, 4,001 were revocations of naturalizations (particularly of Jews of East European origin and their families) on the basis of Article 1 of the Law of July 14th; and 136 were withdrawals of nationality from those who as refugees had written or spoken in opposition to the National Socialist Government. The following table illustrates the persistency with which this process is being carried out:

PERIOD	ARTICLE 1		ARTICLE 2	TOTAL
	Total individuals	*Wives and children*		
1933				
August 25th	—	—	33	33
1934				
January–March	199	93	36	235
April–June.........	292	111	—	292
July–September	233	82	—	233
October–December..	283	110	28	311
1935				
January–March.....	1,322	659	—	1,322
April–June.........	831	275	39	870
July–September....	841	257	—	841
Totals	4,001	1,587	136	4,137

These denationalizations have averaged 172 per month; and in some months the figures have been as high as 797 (July, 1935), 425 (January, 1935), 445 (February, 1935), and 436 (March, 1935). The tendency during the past year has been for the number of denationalizations to increase. During the first nine months of 1935, for example, 2,944 denationalizations of individuals, principally East European Jews, took place; as compared with one-fourth of that number, viz. 742, during the same period of 1934. In fact, the average number of denationalizations per month in 1935 (first nine months) has been 335 whereas the average for 1934 (first nine months) was 87. It should be mentioned also, that in a great number of the cases of revocation of naturalization the victims were not born in countries of East Europe, nor had they been convicted of any crime.[10] Although born and raised in Germany, their nationality was withdrawn because their parents were East European Jews. The 136 withdrawals of nationality from those alleged to have carried on activity outside of Germany hostile to the National Socialist Party have resulted also in the confiscation of the property (including libraries) of the victims.

The Intent of the Government

The fact that the discrimination imposed upon "non-Aryans" is merely an invitation to leave Germany and not a pattern for their existence there was made clear by the official National Socialist newspaper, the *West German Beobachter*, on August 21st, 1935. It wished it "emphasized that by conceding Jewish activities within a Jewish community in various fields [i.e. in permitting "non-Aryans" to organize their own theatres and cultural life] Germany does not want to indicate that Jews may live in a specified manner within the state. There is another way recommended by every German and available to every Jew. It is 'Emigrate! Emigrate!' "

This intent of the National Socialist Government has received ample confirmation from official quarters. Thus, for example, the Reich Minister of Economics, Dr. Hjalmer Schacht, issued a decree in March, 1935, in consultation with the Reich Minister of Interior Frick, which declared that "any measure which promotes the emigration of Jews must be welcome." [11] Furthermore, as early as July 26th, 1933, the Reich Minister of Finance had published an order which stated that: "The emigration of persons of Jewish origin is desirable and must not, therefore, be prevented."

These unqualified expressions of official policy leave no doubt; they have been applied in the field of manual work to allow "non-Aryans" to carry on re-training only for the purpose of emigrating from Germany. As for students, the *Reichdevisenstelle*, in May, 1934, issued a circular permitting temporary emigration with a sum of money higher than that allowed by the exchange law where such a stay abroad would be highly desirable; this was particularly the case, the order ran, for "non-Aryan students whose studies in foreign countries may generally be considered as a desirable preparation for future emigration." [12]

Likewise, Reich Minister Rust has ordered that "non-Aryan" students may be granted permission to take examinations in the universities only if they are able to prove that they contemplate emigration.[13]

The aim of the Government to drive "non-Aryans" from Germany has also been less directly indicated by the confinement of refugees who return to Germany in what are called "re-education camps." The official *Völkischer Beobachter* has confessed that the purpose of this incarceration is to prevent "non-Aryans" and other refugees from returning to Germany.[14]

The Refugee Problem [15]

Thus, having left no field of activity open to "non-Aryans," having taken from them their civil as well as political rights, forcing them to the desperate conclusion that the land to which they had given their life's energies and their wholehearted allegiance regarded them as outcasts and aliens, the National Socialist Government allows only one escape from the trap it has set: emigration. But even emigration is a desperate way out. For, it is only as penniless and virtually stateless that most "non-Aryans" may leave Germany to seek asylum elsewhere. If, on the one hand, their intolerable position forces them to seek escape at any cost, and if they are made to realize that their presence in Germany is no longer wanted, many are faced on the other hand with a no less terrible fate—the poverty and insecurity which awaits them as homeless refugees. Yet, despite these conditions, over 80,000 individuals have emigrated.

Approximately 20 per cent. of the refugees up to the present time have been professional workers: lawyers, doctors, teachers, scientists. Among the number of refugees, also, are 700 professors, scholars, and scientists, leaders in the academic life of Germany, including two Nobel Prize winners in science. 15 to 20 per cent. are non-Jewish by confession and forced to leave Germany either because of their ideas (as pacifists, members of political parties in the German Republic which have been proscribed by the National Socialist *régime*, Protestants and Catholics who have protested against certain pagan tendencies which their consciences forbade them to accept, trade union leaders and intellectuals who are regarded as unassimilable in the totalitarian state) or because they have been defined as "non-Aryans" according to the racial formula, though they may be Christians (that is, because they have a strain of Jewish ancestry or have married "non-Aryans").[16] The majority are small merchants, craftsmen, commercial agents and clerks. Thousands are students who have been unable to continue their studies.

The majority originally took refuge in the countries of Europe immediately bordering upon Germany. France was at one time host to 30,000, and it is estimated that 20,000 of them have been sent on from there to other countries. In The Netherlands, 5,263 refugees were registered. Czechoslovakia also has given asylum for over 5,000 individuals. No less than 36,800 refugees had, by June 15th, 1935, gone overseas—to Palestine, the United States, South America and South Africa.

Perhaps at no time in history have conditions been less favourable to the settlement of such a difficult international problem. The severe and lingering economic depression has made recovery by the creation of new employment opportunities the chief preoccupation of Governments. The lands of immigration which once needed and encouraged the influx of foreign workers are closed. Commerce and the professions, the two main occupations of the refugees from Germany, find themselves especially in a state of contraction rather than of expansion.

The economic condition of the refugees from Germany is made doubly worse by the requirements relative to emigration imposed by the National Socialist Government. The German currency laws render it impossible for emigrants to take their property with them, and result in practical confiscation of the property by the Government. The *Reichdevisenstelle* demands from refugees a sum amounting to 25 per cent. of their property in Germany as a *Reichsfluchsteuer* (emigration tax).[17] But, even the 75 per cent. remaining has to be left in Germany as so-called *Sperrmarks* which in foreign countries are worth even less than 30 per cent. of their face value.[18] Thus, at most, only one-fifth of a refugee's property and savings in Germany is allowed him; four-fifths of it is taken directly or indirectly by the National Socialist Government. In actual fact, moreover, even this one-fifth is not realized. For, the value of the property owned by "non-

Aryans" and other potential emigrants within Germany has been brought down by the boycott and the forced liquidation of "non-Aryan" business which is encouraged by the Government. Thus, prospective emigrants are induced to sell their property at a figure far below its real value, and are only able to retain one-fifth of the already reduced sum. This process of governmental expropriation has rendered the economic condition of thousands of refugees one of dependency and forces them to seek charity and assistance. Eventually, and after they have exhausted their slim resources, they will increasingly be forced to become dependent upon relief.

But, their legal position is even more precarious. Over 4,000 individuals have had their nationality withdrawn by the German Government since January, 1934,[19] and most of them are residing as stateless refugees, subject to constant insecurity and even expulsion in countries outside of Germany. Thousands more are stateless without denationalization. Still thousands more are without German passports, though they be German nationals. And even those who still retain valid German passports and possess German nationality are virtually stateless because of the refusal of the German consular and diplomatic authorities to grant them the necessary papers or protect them as Germans. In numerous instances, moreover, their passports have been confiscated by the German consular authorities. As a result, a large proportion of the refugees from Germany are deprived of the most elementary rights of security, and are subject to the fear and danger of expulsion at any time. Many are considered to be illegally within their countries of refuge, and at the same time it is impossible for them to leave for another without violating the law. If a notice of expulsion is issued, they face either the prospect of returning to Germany, from whose intolerable persecution they have fled, and where they will be placed in concentration camps, or being cast into prison upon their expulsion for illegal entry into a country other than Germany, or evading the expulsion order and thereby becoming subject to imprisonment as criminals.

The psychological and spiritual effects of these conditions can hardly be over-stated. The number of suicides, the distortion of minds and the breaking down of bodies, the deaths of children through malnutrition—are tragic witness to these consequences.

NOTES

1. See p.144.
2. See Chapter II.
3. Court decisions have emphasized that Jews are, according to German public law, only "guests" of the National Socialist State. See above, p.206, for a decision of the Hamburg *Amtsgericht* on June 29th, 1935.
4. *Reichsgesetzblatt*, No. 81, 1933, I, p.480.
5. *Ibid.*, No. 87, 1933.
6. I.e. those who oppose the National Socialist *régime*.
7. Article 3 of the Law of July 14th.
8. The Polish Law of Nationality of January 20th, 1920, declares that "Polish citizenship shall be lost by acquiring foreign citizenship" (Article 11). The Austrian Law of July 30th, 1925, as well as the Nationality Laws of the other East European States, contain the same provision. See Flournoy,R. and Hudson,M. *A Collection of Nationality Laws*, pp.18–9.
9. The German Law of July 22nd, 1913, may be found in Flournoy and Hudson, *op. cit.*, p.307.
10. The figures given above do not include those who were denationalized because they were alleged to have attempted to take their property out of Germany as refugees.
11. *New York Times*, March 13th, 1935, p.13.
12. But, although emigration be encouraged, the Government does not want to lose a lucrative source of revenue in the tax placed upon emigration. As a result, even though the law requiring this emigrants' tax exempts from payment those whose emigration is in the interests of Germany, the Ministry of Finance refused to be bound by its previous encouragement of emigration of Jews as desirable. The tax must, it held, be paid. See above, p.209.
13. *Frankfurter Zeitung*, May 17th, 1934.
14. Issue of March 9th, 1935.

15. See, for more detailed information, the study by Prof. Norman Bentwich: *The Refugees from Germany*, 1933–35 (London, 1936).
16. See p. 149.
17. See p. 209, where the decision of the German Supreme Court of Finance requiring this tax, although the emigration of Jews was regarded as in the interest of Germany, is described.
18. Special arrangements permit the transfer of a higher amount for refugees going to Palestine or Italy.
19. See p. 221.

APPENDIX II

PETITION IN SUPPORT OF THE LETTER OF RESIGNATION OF JAMES G. McDONALD

Former High Commissioner for Refugees (Jewish and Other) Coming from Germany

ADDRESSED TO THE XVIITH PLENARY ASSEMBLY OF THE LEAGUE OF NATIONS

On September 30th, 1936, President Lamas of the League Assembly received a delegation of the signatories which transmitted the Petition to him. The substance of this Book was submitted as an Annex in support of the Petition.

TO THE XVIITH PLENARY ASSEMBLY OF THE LEAGUE OF NATIONS:

1. The discriminations against and persecutions of Jews, "non-Aryan" Christians, of Catholics, Protestants and others, which have been made a matter of national policy by the German National Socialist Government, and the relentless increase of this oppression, have because of their far-reaching effects in many other countries where the oppressed are forced to seek refuge become issues of international concern, meriting consideration and intercession by the League of Nations.

2. In his Letter of Resignation from the office of High Commissioner for Refugees (Jewish and Other) Coming from Germany, Mr. James G. McDonald submitted to the Council of the League of Nations an analysis of the "intensified perse-

cution in Germany" which, he stated, "threatens the pauperization or exile of hundreds of thousands of Germans." Such mass emigration places a heavy and increasing burden upon the states to which these refugees are forced to flee.

3. Mr. McDonald pointed out that by virtue of the numerous German laws, administrative decrees, judicial decisions and Party pronouncements and practices which he cited, not only Jews but also tens of thousands of Christian "non-Aryans" are deprived of citizenship, and excluded from public offices and the exercise of the liberal professions; he also made explicit reference to the persecutions of "Protestants and Catholics who in obedience to their faith and conscience dare to resist the absolute will of the National Socialist state." By making it impossible for all these many thousands to sustain life within Germany, they are forced to emigrate as refugees, in most cases penniless because of the German Government's prohibitions against the export of capital.

4. Therefore, the High Commissioner came to the conclusion that:

> "The efforts of the private organizations and of any League organization for refugees can only mitigate a problem of growing gravity and complexity. In the present economic conditions of the world, the European States, and even those overseas, have only a limited power of absorption of refugees. The problem must be tackled at its source if disaster is to be avoided.
>
> This is the function of the League, which is essentially an association of states for the consideration of matters of common concern. The Covenant empowers the Council and the Assembly to deal with any matter within the sphere of activity of the League or affecting the peace of the world. The effort of the League to ensure respect for

human personality, when not grounded on express provisions of the Covenant or international treaties, has a sure foundation in the fact that the protection of the individual from racial and religious intolerance is a vital condition of international peace and security."

5. For these reasons, the High Commissioner asked that the "moral authority of the League of Nations and the States Members of the League . . . be directed toward a determined appeal to the German government in the name of humanity and of the principles of the public law of Europe," demanding "a modification of policies which constitute a source of unrest and perplexity in the world, a challenge to the conscience of mankind, and a menace to the legitimate interests of the states affected by the immigration of German refugees."

6. The German National Socialist Government cannot by a defense of "domestic jurisdiction" or sovereignty prevent the legitimate concern of the international community over these discriminations and persecutions. It is within the province and competence of the League of Nations to treat this problem at its source not only on humanitarian grounds, but also because the actions and policies of the German National Socialist Government, having their immediate effects and working direct injury in the territory of other states, constitute a series of violations of the rights of these states, as well as a breach of solemn international undertakings and obligations.

7. In support of this Petition we append a Memorandum which reviews the precedents for international intercession in defense of the human rights now denied by the German Government and fully sustains the jurisdiction of the League of Nations over this defiance of the rights of states.

The German National Socialist Government has, by a system of discrimination and persecution against persons termed by it to be "non-Aryans," violated the express terms of a solemn pledge given to the Principal Allied and Associated Powers at the Peace Conference in June, 1919. This undertaking, according to the recognized principles of international law, is a valid and binding one. It gives the Allied Powers the right and the duty to take note of its non-observance and to intercede so that such violation may cease. Furthermore, the German National Socialist Government is deliberately imposing upon neighboring and other states the burden of a refugee problem which steadily has become and increasingly is a matter of international concern. It has by withdrawing the nationality of thousands of individuals after they have entered and while they remain in the territories of neighboring states, increased the weight of this burden. It threatens even more vigorous action. Furthermore, the existence of a system of espionage and terrorism directed against refugees from Germany, and entailing the direct responsibility of the German Government, has seriously disturbed international peace and security, and has violated the rights of neighboring states to grant asylum to those fleeing from persecution.

The right of a state to legislate as it pleases with regard to those within its jurisdiction is not an unlimited one. The abuse of that right to the detriment of other states, as well as in violation of a solemn international agreement, is a matter of grave international concern. Monsieur René Massigli, the representative of the French Government, pointed out before the Sixth Meeting of the League Council on January 24th, 1935 that the prevention of such an aggravation of the refugee problem is "too important a matter to pass over in silence." With regard to the withdrawal of nationality by

Germany, as he pointed out, there is "the right and the abuse of right"—an abuse which "through its repercussions and its generalizations . . . does come within the sphere of the League of Nations."

8. The League of Nations was constituted "to achieve international peace and security . . . by the firm establishment of the understandings of international law as the actual rule of conduct among governments." The Preamble of the Covenant of the League expressly set forth these purposes. The resolutions of the Council in 1922 and of the Assembly in 1934 urged States not bound by legal obligations to the League with respect to minorities to observe in the treatment of their own minorities the same standard of justice as is required by the treaties and by the League. It therefore has the right and is also entrusted with the duty of interceding with the German Government to uphold these principles of respect for international law and for the equality of all men irrespective of race, religion or nationality.

Wherefore, the undersigned organizations, representing many religious faiths, political views and nationalities, call upon the League of Nations to take action in defense of those elementary human rights which are the very foundation-stones of civilization and which constitute a primary condition of continued international peace and good-will.

The American Jewish Committee, New York City, U.S.A. President: Dr. Cyrus Adler.

The American Christian Committee for German Refugees, New York City, U.S.A. Secretary: Dr. Henry Smith Leiper.

The International Federation of Trade Unions, Paris, France. President: Sir Walter Citrine (Great Britain).

The Women's International League for Peace and Freedom, New York City, U.S.A. President: Mrs. Hannah Clothier Hull

The B'nai Brith, Cincinnati, Ohio, U.S.A. President: Alfred M.Cohen.

La Ligue des Droits de l'Homme et du Citoyen, Paris, France. President: Prof. Victor Basch.

Le Comité National de Secours aux Refugies Allemands, Paris, France. Chairman: Senator Henri Bérenger.

Le Comité Central d'Assistance aux Emigrants Juifs, Paris, France. Chairman: Prof. W.Oualid.

Le Comité pour la Défense des Droits des Israélites en Europe Centrale et Orientale, Paris, France. President: Senator Justin Godart.

Comité Voor Bijzondere Joodsche Belangen, Amsterdam, Holland. President: A.Asscher.

Individuals Endorsing the Petition to the Assembly of the League

Walter D.Agnew, President, Huntingdon College, Montgomery, Ala.
George W.Alger, lawyer
George Gordon Battle, lawyer
Prof. E.A.Beller, Princeton University, Princeton, N.J.
Prof. Clarence A.Berdahl, University of Illinois
Frederick S.Bigelow, editor and publicist
Prof. Franz Boas, anthropologist, Columbia University, N.Y.
Miss Lillian Broadwin, social worker
Dr. Dan B.Brummit, editor, *The Christian Advocate*, Kansas City, Mo.

Dean Charles Burdick, Cornell University Law School

Mrs. Carrie Chapman Catt, peace advocate

Rev. Samuel McCrea Cavert, Federal Council of Churches of Christ

Prof. Isaac Cox, chairman, Dept. of History, Northwestern University, Evanston, Ill.

James M.Curley, former Governor of Massachusetts

Dean Raimundo DeOvies, Cathedral of St. Phillip, Atlanta, Ga.

Miss Dorothy Detzer, Women's International League for Peace and Freedom

Gen. George B.Duncan, U.S.Army, retired

Prof. L.C.Dunn, Columbia University, N.Y.

David M.Edwards, President, Friends University, Wichita, Kansas

J.D.Eggleston, President, Hampden-Sydney College, Hampden-Sydney, Va.

Dr. Harry Emerson Fosdick, clergyman

Rev. Bradford E.Gale

Dr. Frank D.Gamewell, Board of Foreign Missions of Methodist Church

William E.Gilroy, editor of *The Advance*

Frank P.Graham, President, University of North Carolina, Chapel Hill, N.C.

Martha Gruening, author

Dr. S.Ralph Harlow, professor at Smith College and President of the National Association of Biblical Instructors.

Prof. W.Stull Holt, Dept. of History, Johns Hopkins University, Baltimore, Md.

W.T.Hornaday, zoologist

Rev. Walter M.Howlett, secretary, The Greater New York Federation of Churches

Dr. Alvin S.Johnson, New School for Social Research

R.A.Kent, President, University of Louisville, Louisville, Ky.
Robert E.Laramy, Superintendent of Schools, Altoona, Pa.
Dr. Charles S.MacFarland, General Secretary Emeritus, Federal Council of Churches of Christ in America
John D.Mackay, State Senator of Massachusetts
Warren H.Manning, landscape designer, Cambridge, Mass.
Vito Marcantonio, former Congressman, New York
A.Markle, Jr., banker, Hazleton, Pa.
Prof. Arthur J.May, University of Rochester, Rochester, N.Y.
Hill McAlister, Governor of Tennessee
Prof. James A.Montgomery, University of Pennsylvania, Philadelphia, Pa.
J.F.Owens, President, Oklahoma Gas and Electric Co., Oklahoma City, Okla.
Bishop Edward L.Parsons, Episcopal Church
George C.Peery, Governor of Virginia
Prof. Lawrence Preuss, Dept. of Political Science, University of Michigan
Miss Anna V.Rice, American Christian Committee for German Refugees
Rev. W.Glenn Roberts, minister, Brooklyn Friends Meeting
Miss Josephine Schain, chairman, National Committee on the Cause and Cure of War
Prof. Nathaniel Schmidt, Cornell University, Ithaca, N.Y.
Senator Morris Sheppard, Texas
Dean Wilbur H.Siebert, Acting Dean of College of Arts and Sciences, Ohio State University, Columbus, Ohio
Prof. Preston W.Slosson, University of Michigan
Alfred E.Smith, former Governor of New York State
Robert E.Speer, secretary, The Board of Foreign Missions of the Presbyterian Church, New York City
John Spargo, author

Lorado Taft, sculptor

Booth Tarkington, author

Wesley Foster Taylor, Jacksonville, Fla.

Rev. Albert C.Thomas, First Baptist Church, Fall River, Mass.

Norman Thomas, socialist leader

Oswald Garrison Villard, Editor of *The Nation*

Miss Lillian Wald, former director of Henry Street Settlement

Prof. A.S.White, University of New Mexico

Prof. W.F.Willcox, Cornell University, Ithaca, N.Y.

Prof. E.T.Williams, Professor Emeritus of Oriental Languages and Literature, University of California

Robert G.Woolbert, member of staff of *Foreign Affairs*

APPENDIX III

THE PERSECUTION OF "NON-ARYANS" IN GERMANY

A SELECTION OF EXPRESSIONS OF OPINION

(The expressions of disapproval of the persecution of Jews and "non-Aryans" in Germany have been so numerous that no more than a selection can be attempted here.)

1. *Statements on the Treatment of "Non-Aryan" and Other Minorities*
   - A. Statesmen and Professional Leaders (p.238)
   - B. Churchmen and Religious Bodies (p.244)
   - C. Organizations for International Peace and Brotherhood (p.248)
   - D. A Selection of Newspaper Editorials on the McDonald Letter of Resignation (p.249)
2. *The American Tradition* (p.251)

1. STATEMENTS ON THE TREATMENT OF "NON-ARYAN" AND OTHER MINORITIES

A. Statesmen and Professional Leaders

President Franklin D.Roosevelt in an address broadcast to the nation on January 30th, 1936:

> "We have sought by every legitimate means to exert our moral influence against repression, against intolerance, and against autocracy, and in favor of freedom of expression, equality before the law, religious tolerance and popular rule."

* * *

The General Assembly of Massachusetts, on August 12th, 1936, adopted a resolution expressing "alarm that certain inhabitants of Germany are being persecuted on account of their religious faith and nationality" and their "conviction and belief that freedom and equality of mankind, regardless of race, creed or color, is indispensable to the maintenance of modern civilization."

* * *

Senator Jesse H. Metcalf of Rhode Island in an address before the United States Senate on June 10th, 1933:

> "The United States should view with grave concern the racial persecutions apparent in Germany and should raise its voice in protest. Only with universal tolerance and understanding . . . can civilization hope to establish and perpetuate a universal community of peace and goodwill."

(Similar sentiments were expressed on the same day by Senator Joseph T. Robinson of Arkansas, Senator David I. Walsh of Massachusetts, Senator Royal S. Copeland of New York, Senator Henry D. Hatfield of West Virginia, Senator Robert F. Wagner of New York and Senator Millard E. Tydings of Maryland.)

* * *

Sir Austen Chamberlain in an address before the House of Commons on April 13th, 1933, said that for fifteen years he had been "the best friend that Germany ever had" but that now

> "Europe is menaced and Germany is afflicted by this narrow, exclusive, aggressive spirit, by which it is a crime to be in favor of peace and a crime to be a Jew. That is not a Germany to which we can afford to make concessions. Before you can afford to decide, or to urge others to decide, you must see a Germany whose mind is turned to

peace, who will use her equality of status to secure her own safety, but not to menace the safety of others; a Germany which has learned not only how to live herself, but how to let others live inside her and beside her."

* * *

Sir John Simon, then Minister for Foreign Affairs of the British Government, said before the House of Commons on April 13th, 1933, that Germany had

> "Gravely menaced . . . that civil liberty upon which the progress not only of great nations but of neighborly relations so often depends."

* * *

Viscount Cecil of Chelwood, speaking before the House of Lords on March 30th, 1933:

> "I have heard at Geneva . . . the representatives of the German Government pressing very strongly for the strict administration of those treaties [for the protection of minorities] and, indeed, urging that they ought to be made more stringent, and that the machinery of the League should be made more drastic in dealing with them.
>
> "Certainly it is a little astonishing that a country that has taken that line should regard it as legitimate to treat a certain section of its population in quite a different way from the manner in which it treats the majority. To put the thing quite simply it seems difficult to contend that anti-Semitism in Germany is perfectly legitimate but anti-Germanism in Poland is an act of tyranny."

* * *

Associating themselves with the statements of Sir John Simon, the members of the Federal Bar Association of New York, Connecticut and New Jersey adopted on April 17th, 1933, a resolution calling upon:

"all believers in human justice throughout the world to publicly condemn the indefensable course that has so far been taken toward those members of our profession, and other professions, by the present administration of the government of Germany."

* * *

Fifty-one leading members of the New York Bar in May, 1933, addressed the following protest to Secretary of State Cordell Hull with the request that it be transmitted to the German Government:

"As members of the New York Bar, we have been shocked by the reports of the action of the German Government toward the bench and bar of Germany in depriving judges duly appointed for life or during good behavior of their seats on the bench, and prohibiting lawyers from practicing their profession, because of their race or religion. . . . We respectfully direct your attention to the fact that at the Paris Peace Conference in 1919, Germany made express pledges to the United States and the Allies, guaranteeing protection of her own religious and racial minorities equal to that established for Poland's minorities by express treaty."

List of Signers

John W. Davis
Charles C. Burlingham
Samuel Seabury
James Byrne
Bainbridge Colby
G. W. Wickersham
Henry W. Taft
Wilson M. Powell
Charles H. Strong
Lewis L. Delafield
Joseph H. Choate, Jr.
Ogden L. Mills
Elihu Root
Albert Rathbone
Eldon Bisbee
Frank L. Polk
Walter E. Hope
Albert G. Milbank

Kenneth M.Spence
John Godfrey Saxe
Victor J.Dowling
Amos J.Peaslee
George W.Alger
Otto C.Wierum
Morgan J.O'Brien
Henry de F.Baldwin
William J.Donovan
James A.O'Gorman
C.E.Hughes, Jr.
W.A.W.Stewart
Walker D.Hines
Samuel H.Ordway
John A.Garver
James W.Gerard
J.G.Schurman, Jr.
Edwin de T.Bechtel
Raymond B.Fosdick
Paul D.Cravath
Carl Taulor
Bronson Winthrop
Charles S.Whitman
Nathan L.Miller
Robert T.Swaine
Boykin Wright
George S.Franklin
Grenville Clark
William T.Jerome
George G.Battle
Roscoe H.Hupper
Charles R.Hickox
T.Catesby Jones

* * *

On May 23rd, 1933, the American Association of University Professors passed a resolution which read in part:

> ". . . science and scholarship have long since become international, and the conditions of intellectual life in every important country are a matter of legitimate concern to every other. It is therefore resolved that this expression of the conviction of the Council and of its profound sympathy for members of the profession who have been subjected to intolerant treatment in these difficult times be . . . communicated to the Committee on Intellectual Cooperation of the League of Nations."

* * *

The National Liberal Federation of England unanimously adopted on May 4th, 1933, the following resolution:

"That this Executive regards with abhorence the persecution of men and women of the Jewish race in Germany and trusts that the German nation will quickly obtain a reversal of this regrettable policy."

* * *

Senator Robert F. Wagner of New York before the United States Senate on June 10th, 1933:

"The emergence of this destructive spirit is of concern not only to the Jewish people; it is a menace not only to the German people but it threatens to blot out every hope of mankind, for the disrupting force of prejudice spreads on the wings of the wind and blights every spot of ground over which it sweeps. If not checked at an early stage, its consequences are too horrible for contemplation. . . . My primary appeal is to the German people. I do not mean the German people who are proud of their cultural heritage, proud of Kant and Hegel, of Beethoven and Mendelssohn, of Goethe and Heine. How the souls of these great masters must be agonized in the face of the insidious discord which is drowning out the universal harmony to which they aspired! I appeal to the descendants of the forty-eighters who fought for German liberty and unity, who would have rebelled against cowardly attacks against innocent and defenseless people. I appeal, in good faith, to the millions of patriotic men and women of Germany who will unite with us in condemning and preventing the actions which are threatening the bases of civilization.

"I am not defending a creed or a race. Neither Judaism nor Germanism is the issue; the sacredness of human life and ideals is the issue. The peace of the world is at stake.

"The world cannot recover so long as discord and hatred are poisoning the springs of human activity. Our only hope lies in cementing bonds of friendship, and in building the progress of mankind upon the nobility of man, regardless of race or creed."

B. Churchmen and Religious Bodies

Twelve hundred clergymen in 406 cities in 41 of the United States and Canada signed a resolution in May, 1933, which contained the following protest against the persecutions of Jews in Germany:

"It is our considered judgment that the endeavor of the German Nazis to humiliate a whole section of the human family threatens the civilized world with the return of medieval barbarity. We deplore the consequences that must fall upon the Jews, upon Christendom, which permits this ruthless persecution, and in particular upon Germany itself. For, protesting thus against Herr Hitler's anti-Semitism, we conceive ourselves to be speaking as the sincere friends of Germany."

* * *

The Bishop of Durham (England) in an address before the West London Synagogue Association on February 6, 1936, said:

"Mr. James G.McDonald's Letter of Resignation as High Commissioner for Jewish and other Refugees from Germany, is one of the most amazing documents that ever issued from the press. It is a letter which ought to be in the hands of all, of whatever nation or creed, who believe in the unity of civilisation and who acknowledge in human intercourse the obligations of the moral law. It is a terrible indictment of Hitler's Government, and we do Germany an ill service if we refrain from speaking from the housetops with the utmost strength at our command, of the horror with which what we witness is inspiring us."

* * *

The following resolution was passed by the General Purposes Committee of the Methodist Church of England at its meeting in May, 1933:

"This Committee, representing the Methodist Church, expresses its indignation at the persecution of the Jews that is at present taking place in Germany. It deplores the revival of racial antagonism, with its attendant injustice and cruelty. It records its high sense of the eminent services to civilisation that have been made by the Jewish race, and appeals to the German rulers and people to make a complete and speedy end of a policy which effectually alienates the sympathy with the German people which was coming to prevail throughout the world.

* * *

Resolution of the Presbyterian Church of England, May 11th, 1933:

"The Assembly is gravely concerned, in common with Christian people everywhere, at the recent discrimination against Jewish people in Germany, and at the anti-Semitic views expressed by certain German Christians in positions of influence."

* * *

Resolution adopted at Annual Meeting of General Assembly of Unitarian and Free Churches, London, England, May 2nd, 1933:

"That this Annual Meeting of the General Assembly of Unitarian and Free Christian Churches deplores the continued failure on the part of the Governments of several countries to respect and ensure the rights of minorities in their respective territories, to which they pledged themselves under the Peace Treaties; and especially protests against the treatment of the Jews by the present Government of Germany and its agents, as an offence against common human nature for which no difference of race or religion affords any justification or excuse."

* * *

Pope Pius XI, on the occasion of the canonization of three new saints, said on February 24th, 1934:

> "The lives of these men were a shining example of Christian charity, a warning against a movement which wished to return to a paganism whose horrors had been seen in ancient times. The great and noble German people is at a tragic moment in its history. We say tragic because the menace of great evils is always terrible. It is a moment of exaltation of thoughts, ideas and practices neither Christian nor human, and of pride of race which cannot but produce pride of life as far as possible removed from the spirit of Christianity, or even of humanity."

* * *

The Archbishop of Paris, Monseigneur Verdier, "in the name of Christian charity and of the solidarity which must bind all the children of the same Father," on April 6th, 1933 urged the clergy and laity of his diocese to offer prayers as a "truly Christian protest" against the "inhuman program" of Nazi Germany, "so opposed to true civilization." [1]

* * *

The Archbishop of Canterbury, speaking at Queen's Hall in London on June 27th, 1933 said:

> "Injustice is abroad violating these elementary instincts of our common humanity" and "it is impossible either here or, I should have thought, in any part of the civilized world, for those citizens to whom these things are part of the heritage which they most constantly prize, to remain silent. They are bound to speak out if only for the relief of their own conscience." [2]

* * *

The Autumn Assembly of the Church of England on December 20th, 1935, passed the following resolution which was presented by the Bishop of Chichester:

> "That this Assembly desires to express its sympathy with the Jewish people and those of Jewish origin in the sufferings which are being endured by many of their number in Germany, and trusts that Christian people in this and other countries will exert their influence to make it plain to the rulers of Germany that the continuance of their present policy will arouse widespread indignation and prove a grave obstacle to the promotion of confidence and good will between Germany and other nations."

At the same Assembly, the Archbishop of Canterbury said:

> "The continuance of the present modes of persecution must seriously affect the good will with which the people of Britain desire to regard the German nation."

The Bishop of Durham at this meeting said, speaking in favor of the above resolution, that:

> "It is not possible for any constituent member of the civilized world to ignore certain fundamental obligations which are involved in its membership of this civilization. . . . We, as co-inheritors with the Germans of the great heritage of civilization desire to bring home to them that in the fervors and frenzies of their revolution they have been carried into a position which they can only maintain at the final price of excluding themselves from the fellowship of civilized people."

* * *

In 1936, there was organized an American Committee for Christian German Refugees, including as members former President Herbert Hoover, Dr. E.Graham Wilson (chairman), Bishop Manning, and Chancellor Harry W. Chase. Speaking in a motion picture on behalf of this Committee, Dr. Harry Emerson Fosdick said:

". . . remember that in Germany under the surface is going on the most cruel persecution a supposedly civilized country has been guilty of since the barbarous days of the Middle Ages, not against Jews only, but against all with whose opinions the Nazi Government disagrees.

"Einstein, the world's foremost living scientist, is an exile from Germany. He is a Jew. The statue of Mendelssohn, in the public square of Leipzig was recently torn down by Nazi order. Mendelssohn was a baptized Christian, although a Jew by race. But his music cannot be played in German schools today, nor his statue stand in Leipzig. The Nobel Peace Prize for 1935 was just awarded to Carl von Ossietsky. He is a peace lover whose health has been ruined by three years under the cruel barbarities of a German Concentration Camp, where he was sent for his pacifism. There you have the picture presented in incarnate form—Einstein, Mendelssohn, Ossietsky. Jew, Christian, Liberal—they all are under the ban. This is not a Jewish problem only."

C. Organizations for International Peace and Brotherhood

The International Federation of League of Nations Societies, in its 17th Plenary Congress, held at Montreux, Switzerland, from June 3–6, 1933, unanimously adopted a resolution expressing its deep concern over the policies undertaken by Germany, recalled Germany's past policy on the protection of minorities and pointed out to the German delegation that the principles of the League itself as well of the Federation required the "restoration of civil and political equality" to the Jews of Germany. Lord Cecil, as President of the Federation, wrote to the leader of the German delegation, Dr. Schnee, pointing out that "the events in question have caused a real and very serious disquiet in many parts of the world, principally in Europe and the United States." He also indicated that Germany's action gave the League jurisdiction because it violated Article 11 of the Covenant and had "disturbed the good understanding between nations."

* * *

The Council of the World Evangelical Alliance in a resolution passed in May, 1933 "deplored the persecution and wrong which the Jewish people in Germany are suffering at the hands of those who profess to represent the Christian faith, and who are guilty of acts utterly alien to all Christian spirit and teaching."

* * *

The Chest for the Liberation of Workers of Europe, representing the three million members of the American Federation of Labor, on January 15th, 1936 supported the demand of James G.McDonald, former High Commissioner for German Refugees, that "the nations of the world use all the influence and all the legal means they possess to stop the complete annihiliation of the Jewish race in the Third Reich and the brutal suppression of civic and religious freedom."

D. A Selection of Newspaper Editorials on the McDonald Letter of Resignation

The Nation, New York City, January, 1936:

"The value of Mr. McDonald's dramatic resignation lies not in its probable immediate results but in the challenge it presents to the conscience of the world. It thrusts under the noses of the nations detailed facts they might prefer to overlook. It gives official standing to authenticated charges of ruthlessness. It cannot be denied or ignored. It will stand with the Lytton report on the Japanese invasion of Manchuria as an unforgettable indictment of a nation which had abandoned even the pretense of civilized usages."

San Francisco Chronicle, January 8th, 1936

"Perhaps it is nobody's legal business. It is certainly nobody's military business. But when a nation which once stood among the leaders of the world's civilization descends to this uncivilized course, is it not the moral business of civilization?

"Commissioner McDonald has spoken the voice of civilization, on the front page of every newspaper in the world except those of Germany, which are not permitted to print it."

Washington (D.C.) *Post*, January 4th, 1936:

". . . The Nazi policies which have already driven more than 80,000 persons into exile and which threaten to make life in Germany intolerable for many more thousands of former citizens cannot be regarded as a matter of domestic concern by the rest of the world."

Dallas (Texas) *News*, January 4th, 1936:

"If the League that Wilson dreamed is to become a reality at all, it must assume authority and demonstrate its interest and, it is to be hoped, its power in protecting humanity of whatever race or creed regardless of national boundaries. Some of those boundaries cannot exist legally under the treaties which fashioned them so long as peoples within them are unjustly oppressed."

Burlington (Iowa) *Gazette*, January 4th, 1936:

"It is not pleasant to interfere in the domestic problems of any nation. But this is more than a domestic problem. If ignored, it may set a precedent from which other minority races will suffer and one of the avowed purposes of the League is to help oppressed minorities."

The Manchester Guardian (England) January 4th, 1936:

"Hitler and his Government declare that this is a 'domestic problem.' Not for many years now in Europe has the right of the Jews to full equality been regarded as a political problem or as a subject 'domestic' to any country; Bismarck himself, half a century ago, might be cited as a witness. Germany, in degrading the Jews, chooses an inferior status for herself. That is as she likes; but the injury which she does to these unhappy people and to the principles of our common civilisation is everyone's affair."

2. The American Tradition

The Declaration of Independence:

"We hold these truths to be self-evident—that all men are created equal; that they are endowed by their Creator with certain inalienable rights; that among these are life, liberty and the pursuit of happiness."

* * *

George Washington in a letter to the Jewish Congregation of Newport, R.I. in 1790:

"The citizens of the United States of America have a right to applaud themselves for having given to mankind examples of an enlarged and liberal policy—a policy worthy of imitation. All possess alike liberty of conscience and immunities of citizenship."

* * *

John Adams in his *Letters of Publicola* in 1791 wrote:

"This principle that a whole nation has a right to do whatever it pleases cannot in any sense whatever be admitted as true. The eternal and immutable laws of justice and of morality are paramount to all human legislation."

* * *

John Forsyth, Secretary of State, in a letter to David Porter, United States Minister to Turkey, August 17th, 1840:

"In common with the people of the United States, the President has learned with profound feeling of surprise and pain, the atrocious cruelties which have been practiced upon the Jews of Damascus and Rhodes. . . . As the scenes of these barbarities are in the Mahommedan dominions, . . . the President has directed me to instruct you to do everything in your power with the government of his Imperial Highness, the Sultan, to whom you are accredited, consistent with discretion and your diplomatic character, to prevent or mitigate these horrors—the bare recital of which has caused a shudder throughout the civilized world. . . . The President is of the opinion that from no one can such generous endeavors proceed with so much propriety and effect, as from the representative of a friendly power, whose institutions, political and civil, place upon the same footing, the worshippers of God, of every faith and form, acknowledging no distinction between the Mahommedan, the Jew, and the Christian. Should you, in carrying out these instructions, find it necessary or proper to address yourself to any of the Turkish authorities, you will refer to this distinctive characteristic of our government, as investing with a peculiar propriety and right, the interposition of your good offices in behalf of an oppressed and persecuted race, among whose kindred are found some of the most worthy and patriotic of our citizens. . . .

* * *

Daniel Webster, Secretary of State, in a letter to the Austrian Chargé d'Affaires in Washington on December 21, 1850:

"While performing with strict and exact fidelity, all their neutral duties, nothing will deter either the government or the people of the United States from exercising at their own discretion, the rights belonging to them as an independent nation, and of forming and expressing their own opinion, freely and at all times, upon the great political events which may transpire among the civilized nations of the earth. Their own institutions stand upon the broadest principles of civil liberty and believing those principles and the fundamental laws in which they are embodied to be eminently favorable to the prosperity of states, to be, in fact, the only principles of government, which meet the demands of the present enlightened age, the President has perceived with great satisfaction, that in the constitution recently introduced into the Austrian empire, many of these principles are recognized and applied."

* * *

President Ulysses S. Grant, in a letter appointing Benjamin F.Peixotto as United States Consul to Bucharest, Roumania, wrote on December 8th, 1870:

> "The United States, knowing no distinction of her own citizens on account of religion or nativity, naturally believes in a civilization the world over which will secure the same universal views."

William Ellery Channing, the American Unitarian Minister and scholar, in a letter to Jonathan Phillips, in 1839, wrote:

> "I maintain that there is a moral interference with our fellow-creatures at home and abroad, not only to be asserted as a right, but binding as a duty. . . . Does sympathy stop at a frontier? Does the heart shrink and harden as it approximates an imaginary line on the earth's surface? Is moral indignation moved only by crimes perpetrated under our own eyes? Has duty no work to do

beyond our native land? Does a man cease to be a brother by living in another state? Is liberty nothing to us, if cloven down at a little distance? . . . But when a community openly, by statutes, by arms, adopts and upholds an enormous wrong, then good men, through the earth, are bound to unite against it in stern, solemn remonstrance. The greater the force combined to support an evil, the greater the force needed for its subversion. Crime is comparatively weak until it embodies and 'sanctifies' itself in institutions."

* * *

Carl Schurz, at a protest meeting in New York City on May 27, 1903, said:

"May this event [the Kishineff massacre] serve to put in clearer light the fact that the history of the world exhibits no more monumental record of monstrous injustice than the persecutions inflicted upon the Jews during so many centuries."

* * *

Former President Grover Cleveland at the same meeting said:

"This demonstration furnishes cheering and reassuring evidence that our American sympathy for the oppressed and abused, wherever they may be, our American love of humanity, and our attachment to justice and right, are still active and unimpaired. There is another American trait inwoven with the warp and woof of our national character, which is here exhibited in most gratifying freshness and strength. Our people, when their sympathies are touched, when their humane instincts are challenged, and when their hatred of oppression is aroused, are not afraid to speak; and in such circumstances it is not their habit to smother or cautiously soften their words. . . . In the meantime, let the people of the United States, gathered together in such assemblages as this, in every part of the land, fearlessly speak to the civilized world, protesting against every pretense of civilization that permits medieval persecution, against every bigoted creed that forbids religious toleration and freedom of conscience, against all false enlightenment that excuses hatred and cruelty towards any race of men, and against all spurious forms of government protection that withhold from any human being the right to live in safety and toil in peace."

* * *

President Theodore Roosevelt in addressing a delegation which presented a petition to him on the Kishineff massacre:

"It is natural that while the whole civilized world should express such a feeling, it should yet be most intense and most widespread in the United States; for of all the great Powers I think I may say that the United States is that country in which from the beginning of its national career most has been done in the way of acknowledging the debt due to the Jewish race and of endeavoring to do justice to those American citizens who are of Jewish ancestry and faith. . . . Exactly as I should claim the same sympathy from any one of you for any tragedy that happened to any Christian people, so I should hold myself unworthy of my present position if I failed to feel just as deep sympathy and just as deep sorrow and just as deep horror over an outrage like this, done to the Jewish people in any part of the earth. I am confident that much good has already been done by the manifestations throughout the country, without any regard to creed whatsoever, of horror and sympathy over what has occurred. . . . In any proper way by which beneficial action may be taken, it will be taken, to show the sincerity of the historic American position of treating each man on his merits without the least reference to his creed, his race or his birthplace."

Letter of Dr. Charles S.MacFarland, General Secretary Emeritus of the Federal Council of Churches of Christ in America, to Adolf Hitler, the German Chancellor, June 2, 1937:

". . . You are isolating Germany from the rest of humanity, while, by persecution and exile, you are contributing to other peoples many of Germany's finest minds and spirits. Your associates assail American Christians for using a film to portray the flight of Christian refugees, in order to secure support of them, forgetting that they themselves are responsible for this humiliation of Germany.

In the four years you asked, whatever you may have done for the economic life of Germany, you have wrecked its Christian ideals. As the conclusion of my study, I can only say that you have, by consenting or approving, permitted the desecration of ideals of honor, integrity, truth and humanity associated with the Germany of my student days; that you are forfeiting the respect of the civilized world and that you are leading your adopted nation to an abyss, for you cannot build an enduring nation upon force and hate . . ."

* * *

Resolution adopted in June, 1937, by the Executive Committee of the Federal Council of Churches of Christ in America:

"Definite word having just reached the executive committee of the Federal Council of Churches of Christ in America that the German Government will not permit the delegates or appointees of the Evangelical Churches to attend the World Conference of the Churches on Church, State and Society in Oxford, England, July 12 to 26, and other events in Germany having left no possible ground for doubt as to the hostility of the present government to the life, the teaching and the influence of the Christian Church, in direct violation of those promises of protection for positive Christianity which led so many loyal Germans to accept a régime which claimed to have conquered atheism.

"Therefore, it is the painful duty of the council to call to the prayerful consideration of all Christian people everywhere the tragic plight of our fellow-Christians in Germany, and to stress the fundamental character of the struggle which has been taking more and more serious form in the four years of the present régime, again in contravention of the clearly expressed promises of the present head of the German State.

"It is necessary to recognize, as leaders of the churches in Germany have emphasized, that what is happening in Germany is not merely of local significance but of importance to the life of Christians the world over, and is perhaps only the visible and dramatic outbreak of flames which are still merely smoldering elsewhere . . . "

* * *

NOTES

1. Other statements of the same tenor on the part of Catholic leaders came from: *France*—Cardinal Morin, Archbishop of Lyon; the Bishop of Nice; Cardinal Lienart, Bishop of Lille; *Great Britain*—The Bishop of Nottingham; the Bishop of Oxford; the Bishop of Birmingham; the Bishop of Liverpool; *Roumania*—Monsignor Robu.
2. Other protests on behalf of *English Protestantism* came from: The Bishop of Bradford; the Bishop of Down; the Bishop of Glasgow; the Bishop of Southwell; the Bishop of Winchester; the Dean of St. Paul; the Bishop of Leicester; the Bishop of Fulham; the Bishop of Llandoff; the Bishop of Manchester; the Rev. K.L.Parry, President of the Free Church of Manchester; the Bishop of Nottingham; The Baptist Church of Scotland. *French Protestantism*—The Council of the French Protestant Federation; Wilfred Monod, for the Occumenical Council of Practical Christianity. *Swiss Protestantism*—The Free Evangelical Church of the Canton of Vaud; The Churches of Geneva.

POSTSCRIPT

By Josiah C. Wedgwood, M.P.

WHEN persecution of minorities becomes a matter of declared national policy an international issue is raised. The world's moral judgment is required. During the past two centuries there has been a steadily increasing recognition of this principle. The minority treaties after the world war, and the covenant of the League of Nations both gave express recognition to the international aspect of persecution of minorities whenever such persecution becomes a matter of national policy. During many decades leading statesmen of the world have given voice to such views. This book makes a powerful case in support of these principles. The refugee problems created by persecutions and even eliminations, which are matters of national policy, cannot be solved by philanthropic action. They must be faced and grappled with at the source. Civilization, enlightened world opinion, the conscience of mankind, and sound and strongly supported principles of international law call for intercession and for a moral judgment against those nations which violate the ultimate principles of morality upon which rest the very foundation stones of civilization. This book, in marshaling the opinion and conduct of civilized mankind in respect to these matters, is of importance and of value.

The principles for which this book argues have long been supported by liberal statesmen and enlightened governments. The failure to support such principles would be a tragic acknowledgment of moral bankruptcy by what we are pleased to call the civilized world. There can be no amity in the family of nations if members of that family are permitted without protest to make persecution a cornerstone of their national policy.

JOSIAH C. WEDGWOOD, M.P.

INDEX

Abuse of power in international law, 47–48, 57, 67, 68; by Nazi Germany, 49–60
Aix-la-Chapelle, Congress of (1818), 11
Åland Islands, 46, 126, 127
Albania, 30, 126–27
Algeciras Conference (1906), 20
Aliens, position of, in Nazi Germany, 87–93. *See also* Aryan laws.
Ambassadors, Conference of, 33
American Revolution, effect of the, 9
Anders, Fritz, 41
Andrassy, Julius, count, 15
Anzilotti, Dionisio, quoted, 100–01
Armenians, 56, 57–59
Aryan laws, 60–64, 72–78, 146–70 *passim*; applied by the courts, 191–216
Asylum, right of, 55, 71, 78–79, 84; Nazi Germany and, 94
Aufklärung, effect of the, 9
Augsburg, Peace of, 6
Austria, 28, 62, 63n., 67n., 75n., 77
Austria-Hungary, 12n., 15, 62; intervention in, 8–9

Balkan States, intervention in, 11–12, 15–19, 42. *See also* names of states.
Bar, K.L.von, quoted, 53n.
Bayard, T.F., quoted, 92–93
Beaconsfield, Benjamin Disrael, earl of, 15
Belgium, 9, 67n., 70
Beneš, Eduard, quoted, 119
Bérenger, Henri, quoted, 108, 117–18
Berlin: Congress of (1878), 14–16, 21, 42; Treaty of (1878), 4, 18, 26, 35, 56, 77n., 102; quoted, 15–16, 21
Bernheim (Franz) Petition, 104, 107–08, 110–18
Bismarck, Prince O.E.L.von, 15, 43; quoted, 42
Blaine, J.G., quoted, 23–25, 57
Bluntschli, J.K., quoted, 5
Boeck, C.de, quoted, 53
Boffolo case, 53
Borchard, E.M., quoted, 4n.
Bourgeois, Léon, quoted, 128
Bourquin, M., 104, 115
Boycott of Jews, 121, 181–87
Bucharest: Conference of (1913), 18; Treaty of (1918), quoted, 43
Bulgaria, 15, 28
Bülow, B.W.von, 40n.

Caclamanos, Demetrius, quoted, 126–27
Catholicism, Roman, in Germany, 6–7
Cecil, Lord Robert, 29–30
Child, R.W., quoted, 58
Children, Nazi laws concerning, 199–201
Christensen, Peter, 81
Christians, rights of: safeguarded, 8–9, 21
Citizenship, deprivation of. *See* Denationalization.
Civil and political equality. *See* Equality, civil, and political.
Cleveland, Grover, quoted, 93
Conference of. *See* name of conference.
Confiscation of property, German, 62
Constantinople, Conference of (1856), quoted, 12
Criminal jurisdiction in Nazi Germany, 49, 62, 76–77
Cromwell, Oliver, 7
Curtius, Julius, quoted, 38, 39, 123–24
Cutting case, 92–93
Czechoslovakia, 28, 62, 67n., 119; refugees in, 51, 78–81

De Graeff, A.C., quoted, 51
De Leon Report, quoted, 127
Denationalization, 76–77; by Nazi Germany, 49, 60–78, 125, 217–22; (numbers), 62–63, 221
Denmark, 81, 99–102
Deportation. *See* Emigration, forced.
Diplomatic notes, 2–3, 97–98, 103
Divorce, Nazi law of, 196–99
Droysen, J., 41
Druses, 20–21

Eagleton, Clyde, quoted, 82n.
East, the. *See* Orient, the.
Educational rights: in pre-Nazi Germany, 34–35; in Nazi Germany, 50n., 158–61, 175–77; of German minorities, 34
Emigration, forced, 53–54, 71; Nazi, 49–71 *passim*, 109, 122–25
England. *See* Great Britain.
Enlightenment, effect of the, 9
Equality, civil and political, 2, 26–40 *passim*; in Belgium and Holland, 9; in Nazi Germany, 32–40 *passim*; in Poland, 35; in Turkey, 35
Equality, racial. *See* Racial discrimination.
Equality, religious, 2, 9–10, 26–27; in the Balkans, 11–12, 15–16, 19; in Belgium and Holland, 9; in Damascus, 19; in the Germanic Confederation, 10–11; in pre-Nazi Germany, 6–7, 32–40; in Nazi Germany, 1–3, 40–43 and *passim*; in Greece, 11–12; in Moldavia and Wallachia, 12–18; in Morocco, 19–20; in Persia, 19; in Tsarist Russia, 22–27; in Turkey, 20–21; in the U.S., 9n.
Espionage, Nazi, 78–94 *passim*, 109
Estonia, 30
Expatriation, voluntary, 76
Extra territorium jus . . . , 91

Fauchille, Paul, quoted, 4
Finland, 46, 67n., 103, 126
Finlay, Lord R.B., quoted, 90–91
Fish, Hamilton, quoted, 13–14
Formys, Rudolf, 79
Forsyth, John, 19
Foster, J.W., quoted, 22, 98
France, 12n., 54, 59, 64–66, 67n., 70, 90–93, 108, 119; guarantees religious equality, 9n.; intervention by, 11–12, 21; intervention in, 7; Jews in, 119; refugees in, 51
Frederick III, emperor of Germany, 41
Freedom of speech and press, in Nazi Germany, 89n., 90
Frelinghuysen, F.T., quoted, 24
French Revolution, effect of the, 9, 10
Frick, Wilhelm, 49–50n.

Geneva Convention, 108, 112, 113, 115, 117
German Secret State Police, 79–94 *passim*
Germanic Confederation, religious equality in, 10–11
Germany, Nazi: international obligations of, 94–109; international legal aspects of policies of, 44–109; Jews in, 1–3, 17, 40–256 *passim*; exceptions in discriminations against, 161–62; in educational and cultural fields, 158–61, 175–77; in government service, 146–54; in industry, agriculture and commerce, 163–68, 177–81, 204–10; in the professions, 155–58, 172–77; opinions on treatment of, 238–56
Germany, pre-Nazi, 14n., 15, 28, 32–39, 44, 54, 75n.; promises to protect minorities, 34–36, 37, 94–97, 101–10
Gestapo. *See* German Secret State Police.
Giletti case, 55n.
Goebbels, P.J., 116
Goering, Wilhelm, 87
Gortschakoff, Prince A.M., 15

Great Britain, 12n., 24, 59, 65, 67, 98n., 108, 126–27; intervention by, 8–9, 11–16, 18, 19–20; Jews in, 23–24, 119; refugees in, 51
Greco-Turkish Mixed Arbitral Tribunal (1928), 73
Greece, 12n., 28, 59, 73, 126; intervention in, 11–12
Greenland, 99–102
Grotius, Hugo, quoted, 3
Gutzeit, Herr, 79

Hague Codification Conference (1930), 69–70; quoted, 6, 72–75
Hall, W.E., quoted, 92n., 98n.
Hardenberg, Prince Carl von, 41, 43
Harrington, Lord William, quoted, 8–9
Harrison, Benjamin, quoted, 25, 52
Hatti-Humayoun (1856), 20
Hay, John, quoted, 16–18, 24–25, 56–57
Heffter, A.W., quoted, 5
Hering, Hermann, quoted, 72
Hindenburg, Paul von, 37
Hitler, Adolf, 83n., 88, 89, 106
Holland, 9, 67n., 69–70; intervention by, 7, 8; refugees in, 51, 78, 79–80
House, E.M., and Seymour, C., quoted, 97n.
Huber, Max, 104, 115
Humboldt, William von, quoted, 41–42
Hungary, 28, 57n., 75n. *See also* Austria-Hungary.

Ihlen, 99–100
India, 67n.
Institut de Droit International. *See* Institute of International Law.
Institute of International Law, quoted, 47–48, 54n., 66n., 70n.
Intercession, international: practice of, 6–27; right of, 2–6, (recognized by Germany) 3. *See also* International action.
International action to safeguard human rights, precedents for, 1–43 *passim*
International Labour Conference (1933), quoted, 50
International law: governs questions of nationality and denationalization, 64–78 *passim*; limits rights of a state, 44–47, 52; Nazi policies and, 44–109 *passim*; on territorial sovereignty, 81–94 *passim*; recognizes right to give asylum, 55n., 71
Intervention, meaning of, 5. *See also* International action.
Ionian Islands, 12n.
Irredentism, 124
Italy, 28, 55, 59, 77, 108

Jacob. *See* Salomon, B.J.
Japan, 67n., 99n., 103n., 108
Jews in: the Balkans, 12–18, 27, 55, 56, 77n.; Bohemia, 8–9; Czechoslovakia, 119; Damascus, 19; France, 119; Germany: pre-Nazi, 11, 32–39, 41–42; Nazi, 1–2, 17, 40–256 *passim*; Great Britain, 23–24, 119; in Moldavia and Wallachia, 12–17; in Morocco, 19–20; in Persia, 19; in Poland, 35, 119; in Prussia, 27; in Roumania, 16–18, 27, 43, 55, 56, 77n.; in Tsarist Russia, 22–27, 42, 52, 55–56, 57; in Serbia, 15; in Teheran, 19; in the U.S., 23–25, 119
Judiciary, Nazi, 172–74, 193–96, 201–10
Jugoslavia, 28

Keller, A.F.W.von, 45n., 118n., quoted, 37n., 108, 113, 117, 119
Kidnapping by Nazis, 79–94 *passim*, 109, 125
Kirchhoff, G.R., 41
Koch-Weser, Erich, 38

Kurtzke, Herr, 80
Kutchuk-Kainardji, Treaty of (1774), quoted, 8

Lampersberger, Joseph, 80
Lange, C.L., quoted, 114–15
Language as ground of discrimination, 27–31 *passim*
Lansing-Ishii agreement, 99n.
Launay, Count E.H.L.A.de, 15
Lausanne Conference, 57–59, 126
Lawyers in Nazi Germany, 155–56, 172–74, 201–10
League of Nations (often quoted), 29–34, 37–40, 46, 49, 50–51, 70–71, 73–74, 95, 103–04, 105, 108, 110–29; aims of the, 31n.; letter of McDonald to the, 131–45; petition to the, in support of McDonald's letter, 229–37
Lessing, Theodore, 79
Lester, Sean, 115
Liechtenstein, 80
Loder, B.C.J., quoted, 91
London: Conference of (1830), quoted, 11
Lotus, S.S., case, 90–93
Lowell, J.R., 23
Ludendorff (Erich von) Manifesto, 76
Lytton Commission, 103n.

McDonald, J.G., 17, 51; letter of resignation of, 131–45; petition in support of letter, 229–37
Madrid Conference (1880), 20
Maestrecht, 7
Manchuria, 103n.
Maria Theresa, empress of Austria, 8–9
Marriage, Nazi law of, 196–99
Martens, F., quoted, 4
Martos, Christino, 99n.
Massigli, René, 70
Mehemet Ali, 19n.
Mexico, 70, 92–93
Minorities, rights of, 27, 105, 122–24; in Nazi Germany, 94–97, 101–09, 127–28, *passim*; in pre-Nazi Germany, 3, 7, 32–40, 94–97, 101–10; in Poland, 96–97, 104–07, 111–12; in Turkey, 102
Minorities Treaties (1919), 3, 27–29, 32–33, 37, 75, 104, 107, 108, 110, 111, 114, 117, 119, 127
Moldavia, 12–18
Mommsen, Theodor, 41
Montagna, Raffaele, 59
Montefiore, Sir Moses, 19–20
Moore, J.B., 90; quoted, 82n., 92
Morocco, 64–66; intervention in, 19–20
Motta, Giuseppe, quoted, 31, 123, 124n.
Mowinckel, J.L., quoted, 116
Müller, Hermann, 38
Murder: by Nazis, 79, 80, 83; charge of ritual, 19, 186–87
Murray, Sir Gilbert, quoted, 30–31, 123n.

Nationality, international law and, 64–78
National Socialist Party, 83, 106, 171–216. *See also* Germany, Nazi.
Naturalization, 64–78 *passim*; in Nazi Germany, 61–78 *passim*, (by marriage), 76, (fraudulent), 76
Netherlands, the. *See* Holland.
Neurath, Baron Konstantin von, 38, 39–40; quoted, 113n.
Nisot, J., quoted, 73n.
Non-Aryans. *See* Racial origin.
Norway, 99–102
Nuremberg laws, 51, 106–07

Orient, the, religious equality in, 8–9
Ormsby-Gore, W.G.A., quoted, 118–19
Ottoman Empire. *See* Turkey.

Paderewski, Ignace, 32
Palestine, 51

Paris: Convention of (1858), 13; Peace Conference (1919), 27–28, 32–33, 34, 94, 109; Treaty of (1763), quoted, 7–8n.; Treaty of (1856), 20–21
Paul-Boncour, Joseph, quoted, 114
Pedroso, 104, 115
Peixotto, B.F., 13
Pellé, General Maurice, 59
People's Court, German, 88
Permanent Court of International Justice (often quoted), 29, 36, 44–45, 46, 48, 64–66, 90–93, 96n., 99–102, 103, 104, 107
Pfundtner, Hans, 62
Phillimore, Lord W.G.F., 48
Phillimore, Sir Robert, quoted, 5
Physicians and dentists in Nazi Germany, 156–58, 162, 174–75
Poland, 7, 28, 33, 39, 44, 62, 63n., 66n., 70, 75n.; minorities in, 35–36, 94–97, 104–07, 111–12, 119
Poles discriminated against, 27, 32–40
Politis, N.S., quoted, 105
Preuss, L., quoted, 71, 83
Protestantism: effect of rise of, 6; in Germany, 6–7
Prussia, 12n., 27, 36, 40, 41

Racial discrimination, 27–33 *passim*, 107; in Nazi Germany, 1–2, 35, 60–62, 77–78, 94, 107–223 *passim*
Raczynski, Count, quoted, 114
Ralston, J.H., quoted, 47, 53
Rau, Reinhold, 79
Refugees, 122; German, 1, 50–129 *passim*, 223–27; in U.S., 25, 55n., 56–57
Religious equality. *See* Equality, religious.
Ricci-Busatti, quoted, 48
Richter, Walter, 86
Rights, human, international action to safeguard, 1–43 *passim*
Rosenberg, Alfred von, 38
Rotter, Fritz and Alfred, 80
Roumania, 28, 60, 67n., 77n., 105–06; religious equality in, 12–18, 27, 43, 55, 56–57
Rumbold, Sir Horace, quoted, 59
Rush-Bagot agreement, 98n.
Russia, Tsarist, 8, 12n., 14n., 15, 55–56, 60; intervention by, 11–12; intervention in, 1, 22–27, 52, 57; Jews in, 42; treaty of (1832), with U.S., 25–26
Rust, Bernhard, 50n.
Rutgers Report, 125; quoted, 128–29

Salisbury, R.A.T. Gascoyne-Cecil, 3d marquess of, 15; quoted, 21
Salomon, B.J., 80, 84–87, 88–89
Sandler, R. I., quoted, 116
Sazonov, S.D., 26
Scelle, G., quoted, 65n.
Schacht, Hjalmar, quoted, 49–50n.
Schiele, Martin, quoted, 37
Schubert, Carl von, 38; quoted, 113, 128n.
Seipel, Ignaz, quoted, 123n.
Sherman, John, quoted, 19
Sickles, General D.E., 99n.
Siemens, Werner von, 41
Sovereignty. *See* Territorial sovereignty.
Spitzbergen, 100–01
Stresemann, Gustav, 41; quoted, 38
Sweden, 7, 46
Switzerland, 67n.; refugees in, 78, 80, 84–87, 88–89

Taft, W.H., 26
Territorial sovereignty, 44–129 *passim*
Terrorism, Nazi, 78–94 *passim*
Thielan, 14n.
Toleration, religious, 6–9, 26. *See also* Equality, religious.
Treason in Nazi Germany, 87–90 *passim*
Treaties, 3, 5, 6, 7, 9 (quoted), 12n., 25–26, 73–74, 85, 97–98, 103. *See also* names of treaties.

Triepel, Heinrich, quoted, 69, 76n.
Tunis, 64–66
Turkey, 28, 35, 56, 57–59, 60, 73, 90–93, 102, 126–27; promises religious equality, 8, 20–21

United States, 9, 58–59, 67, 74–75, 98–99, 108; guarantees religious equality, 9n.; intervention by the, 1, 13–14, 16–20, 22–27, 52, 57; Jews in the, 23–24, 25, 119
Upper Silesia, 33, 39, 104, 107–08, 111–18, 121

Van Buren, Martin, quoted, 19
Venizelos, Eleutherios, 59
Versailles, Treaty of, 34–35, 36, 75, 95, 96, 103, 104–05, 114
Vienna, Congress and Treaty of (1815), quoted, 10–11
Virchow, Rudolf, 41
Vogt, P.B., quoted, 100–01
Volksgericht, 88

Waddington, W.H., quoted, 14
Waldenses, 7
Wallachia, 12–18
Weber, W.E., 41
Weimar Constitution, 36
Weiss, André, quoted, 91
Westlake, J., quoted, 97
Westphalia, Treaty of (1648), 7
White, Henry, 20
Williams, Sir J.F., 68–69 (quoted)
Wilson, Woodrow, quoted, 28, 122n., 128